The
JUNGLE
JOURNAL

D1214145

'Java, a most beautiful and enchanting island, witnessed unspeakable horrors against both man and beast during the Japanese military occupation, 1942–45.'

Ron Williams, 1946

The
JUNGLE
JOURNAL

Prisoners of the Japanese in Java 1942–1945

Frank & Ronald Williams

This book is dedicated to my mother, Margaret, now in her mid-nineties, who had to endure four years of early marriage (November 1941 to October 1945) without my father, Ronald. For nearly sixteen months, she did not know if he was dead or alive in the Far East. She was only fifty years of age when he died and never remarried. Margaret joined the Japanese Labour Camps Survivors' Association to help keep the plight of civilians and service members who had been in the Far East under Japanese rule in the media and political spotlight. Eventually, the British Government paid some reparations for the hardships suffered. Unfortunately, the Japanese remain in denial of war atrocities committed by their military, against many nationalities, from 1930 to 1945.

All royalties earned from the sale of this book are shared between Help for Heroes and the Java FEPOW Club 42.

First published 2013
by Spellmount, an imprint of

The History Press
The Mill, Brimscombe Port
Stroud, Gloucestershire, GL5 2QG
www.thehistorypress.co.uk

© Frank and Ronald Williams, 2013

The right of Frank and Ronald Williams to be identified as
the Authors of this work has been asserted in accordance with
the Copyrights, Designs and Patents Act 1988.

All rights reserved. No part of this book may be reprinted
or reproduced or utilised in any form or by any electronic,
mechanical or other means, now known or hereafter invented,
including photocopying and recording, or in any information
storage or retrieval system, without the permission in writing
from the Publishers.

British Library Cataloguing in Publication Data.
A catalogue record for this book is available from the British Library.

ISBN 978 0 7524 8721 2

Typesetting and origination by The History Press
Printed in Great Britain
Manufacturing managed by Jellyfish Solutions Ltd

Contents

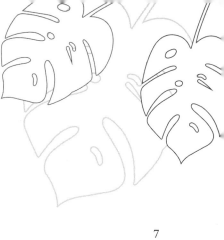

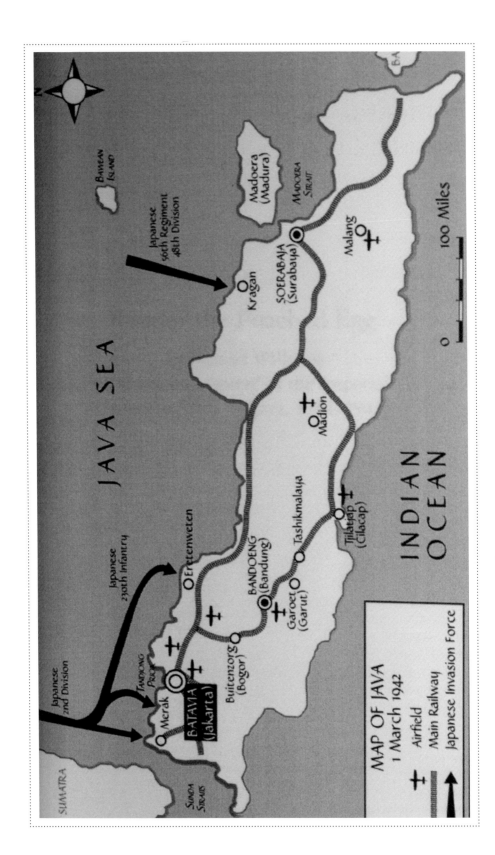

MAP OF JAVA
1 March 1942

✈ Airfield
▓▓▓ Main Railway
➔ Japanese Invasion Force

JAVA SEA

INDIAN OCEAN

SUMATRA

SUNDA STRAITS

Merak

Japanese 2nd Division

TANJOENG PRIOK

BATAVIA (Jakarta)

Buitenzorg (Bogor)

Japanese 230th Infantry

Eretenweten

BANDOENG (Bandung)

Garoet (Garut)

Tasikmalaya

Tjilatjap (Cilacap)

Madion

Kragan

Japanese 56th Regiment 48th Division

SOERABAJA (Surabaya)

Madoera (Madura)

MADOERA STRAIT

Malang

BAWEAN ISLAND

BAWEAN

0   100 Miles

Foreword by Major General Morgan Llewellyn

On 25 October 1945, Ronald Williams wrote that he was 'seriously considering publishing a book about his experiences in captivity'. Now, after more than half a century, his son Frank has brought this book to fruition. Frank has done this with great skill, weaving his father's own writings into a narrative that deserves to be widely read. Not only does Ronald write about a theatre of the Second World War that has, undeservedly, been neglected by historians, but he does so with great perception, sensitivity, and often with a hint of humour which could only survive in a man who possessed an honourable and courageous nature. This book tells his story from the moment he volunteered for service in the Royal Artillery Regiment of the Territorial Army until he was eventually released from military service in 1946.

The book takes the reader on the long journey to the Far East, where Ronald gives his own graphic account of the fierce attempt to defend the island of Java from the Japanese – against the odds – and gives us a unique insight into the humiliation of surrender and the horrors, depravation and cruelty of life in a Japanese prisoner-of-war camp. However, there are lighter moments with Ronald's involvement, as editor, in the production of a camp magazine, *The Jungle Journal*. His story ends with the defeat of the Japanese and his return home at the end of the war.

For me the story is particularly poignant as my father was chairman of a company that grew rubber and coffee in Java and Sumatra. Ten years after the end of the war I, too, went to serve in the Far East and was to return on one of the troopships, the *Dunera*, which formed part of the convoy in which Ronald sailed from the Clyde. For a short time, at the end of the Malayan emergency, I lived in the Selarang Barracks where, Ronald recounts, prisoners of war were forced to sign oaths of good behaviour by the Japanese.

All young people at school who are studying the Second World War as part of the National Curriculum should read this book. It tells of an important theatre of war and a human experience that should never be forgotten.

There is an immense amount to be learned from it. Aspects of this forgotten war will, no doubt, seem strange to young people today. However, some of Ronald Williams' experiences of action and fortitude will, no doubt, have been echoed in recent years, albeit in widely differing circumstances, by those fighting in Iraq and Afghanistan. This shows how the human spirit can transcend even the harshest and most demoralising of conditions and rise to acts of compassion and creativity.

Ronald Williams is self-effacing about the quality of his own poetry that is included in this book. I am no literary critic when it comes to poetry, but I find that his verses move me because they are an uninhibited expression of the ever-changing emotions of prison camp life. They show that even in degrading camp conditions there survives nobility which demands admiration. His poetry reflects the intensity of his friendships, his patriotism and his faith; qualities which are much needed in today's world.

His son, Frank, is to be congratulated on bringing his father's legacy into the public domain and the book is commended to all who share Ronald Williams' values.

Major General the Revd Morgan Llewellyn, CB, OBE, DL,
General Officer Commanding Wales, 1987–1990

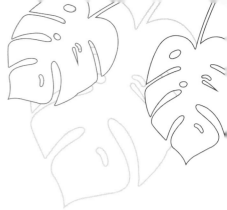

Acknowledgements

The publishers and I would like to thank Richard Reardon-Smith, Peter Williams, Karen Williams, Margaret Williams, Ann and Sandra Williams, Barrie and Jan Williams, the late Brynmor Davies, Richard, Roger and Liz Thomas especially; the Imperial War Museum (IWM), particularly Roderick Suddaby (FEPOW expert); The Java 42 Club with considerable help from Lesley Clarke, Margaret Martin and Bill Marshall; Kathleen Booth (daughter of Gunner Harry Hamer) for manuscript corrections and her invaluable assistance with personal details through her encyclopaedic knowledge of the 77th HAA Regiment; Mrs Adèle Barclay for permission to reproduce illustrations from *The Jungle Journal*; the National Archive, Kew; the Artillery Association, Woolwich; *Western Mail* newspapers; COFEPOW Association; *De Pen Gun* newspaper; and Raymonde 'Nikki' Sullivan.

My father also wished to thank the following for their help when he was writing his original manuscript:

I wish to extend my sincere appreciation to Charles Holdsworth, who collaborated with me in the production of magazines in prison camps and supplied the artistic illustrations for this book. I would also like to thank Jean Teerink for the information embodied in the article 'Life in a Women's Internment Camp on Java'. To the men, British, Commonwealth, Dutch and American, who supplied drawings and inspiration – you will always be in my thoughts, particularly those who did not make it back to freedom.

The Netherlands newspaper *De Pen Gun* provided material for the article 'When a Dark Night Descended on the Dutch East Indies'. For the chapter on the history of Java, I am indebted to a book entitled *Ons Zonneland* by A.J. Krafft, M.J. Overweel and M.J. Offringa, published by J.B. Wolters 'Uitgevers-Maatschappij', of Groningen and Batavia. This was a constant companion to me during my time in captivity which helped me to learn Dutch and discover the intriguing history of the Dutch East Indies. I found useful references from the *Encyclopaedia Britannica* and for the short historical sketch I consulted *The Lights of Singapore* by Roland Bradell, published by Metheun and Co. Ltd.

I express my sincere gratitude to all.

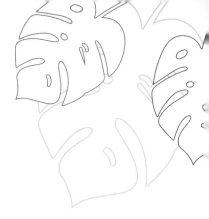

Introduction

It is over forty years since my father died, aged 58 years. He died from a heart attack, in part because of the effects of smoking (a habit he picked up during the war years), but it was also due to the long-term debility he suffered through privation, disease and malnutrition from over three and a half years' incarceration in Japanese prisoner-of-war camps in Java.

Premature death rates amongst ex-FEPOWs (Far East Prisoners of War) were four times greater than other Second World War Allied POWs, those held by the Germans and Italians, and war veterans.[1]

My father documents in his papers, passed on to me by my mother on the 60th anniversary of VJ (Victory against the Japanese) Day, that it would have been his intention to publish them on his retirement. He spoke very little of his own immediate prisoner of war experiences to family and friends, a common trait amongst ex-FEPOWs.

I remember, when I was young, a close friend and ex-POW colleague of my father, 'Mossie' Simon, would visit and they would engage in long conversation about old times behind closed doors. My father also kept in close contact with four fellow Australian POWs, part of 'Sparrow' Force captured on Timor and transported to Java: George Gunn, 'Scotchie' Morrison, Don Junor and Ray Vincent. They remained close friends until my father's premature death.

After my father's death, my mother wrote on a number of occasions to the Australians, seeking insight into what had happened on Java, but they said, 'Don't ask!' The Australians did state that Ronald was one of the most popular of the Allied junior officers because he placed other prisoners' welfare above his own. It seems probable that he would have been beaten up by camp guards for sticking up for his men. This would have been a humiliating experience for a former schoolboy boxing champion and a man who always believed in fair play but who could not retaliate on pain of death.

Fellow POW Arthur Holt (ex-RAF) wrote in a citation for my father:

> I have known in days of privation, and suffering, the strength of his [*Lieutenant Williams'*] steadying influence. All those 'other ranks' who, like myself, had the good fortune to know Mr Williams, and those were numerous, will testify to his unfailing efforts to make their lot a more comfortable one, to his remarkable sense of humour when it was most needed, and to his utter unselfishness which

commended him to all with whom he came into contact. A man's true character quickly came to the fore in those dark days.

My father mentioned to me that fellow internee Laurens van der Post, the well-known South African novelist, put the matter of dealing with the Japanese (Jap or Nip for short) and Koreans very succinctly: 'It is one of the hardest things in prison life: the strain caused by being continually in the power of people who are only half sane and live in a twilight of reason and humanity.'[2]

Ronald said that he did not suffer from the 'Rip Van Winkle' effect of waking up from a dream, which many ex-POWs were supposed to have experienced; his experiences remained vivid, although he chose to talk little about Java until a short time before he died. It has recently come to light that returning FEPOWs were told by RAPWI (Recovery of Allied Prisoners of War and Internees) officials that discussing their POW experiences with family and friends was inadvisable and there was general discouragement by the authorities to mention anything regarding the 'Japanese experience'. The reason given was that such discussions would be detrimental to the mental healing process. In my view, however, this was a deliberate attempt to avoid embarrassing the post-war Japanese Government and to suppress the apportioning of blame for the calamitous Allied Far East military campaign during 1941-42. Ronald felt that FEPOWs were an embarrassment to the Allied authorities due to the abject failure of the 1942 campaign in the Far East.

Ronald felt fortunate to have remained on Java throughout his captivity as many of his friends who were drafted to other South East Asian islands and the Japanese mainland had died on their transport ships (usually sunk by Allied planes and submarines because of the Japanese refusal to put any recognition marks on their boats indicating the presence of POWs and wounded). Others had to undertake inhuman work in places like Siam (now Thailand), Burma and Japan. Many died from this experience.

He survived a number of serious illnesses during captivity. He told my mother that during times of ill-health his men would drag him out on a work detail, prop him up in the shade with a hoe, and do his work for him (Allied junior officers were responsible for work details and increasingly forced to undertake manual work). They also gave him extra food. Without this help, he said, he would have perished either 'naturally' or through the thrust of a camp guard's bayonet.

On 7 December 1941, Ronald had left Gourock Docks, Glasgow, aboard the troop ship *Empress of Australia*, the very same day Pearl Harbor was bombed by the Japanese. He was expecting to be fighting the Germans in the Middle East, but ended up fighting the perpetrators of this notorious act.

After capture, he was not heard from again until news came through from New Zealand to Burnie, Tasmania and finally Pretoria, South Africa, in June 1943 that his name, family address and a simple message had been broadcast on Tokyo Radio on 23 April 1943.

He did not receive any mail from my mother until May 1944 (although he had received two notes from his father, Frank Sr, in 1943); then followed a deluge of mail, some three years old. Prisoner mail went on a circuitous route via Japan and was viewed by various Japanese censors. This process alone could take nine months to a year!

Following the Japanese surrender in 1945, the POWs were not 'out of the woods'. There was a risk that the POWs would be massacred by their former guards, or by the hostile Indonesian nationalists. This did happen in some camps but, fortunately, not in my father's camp, where some of the Japanese guards remained armed to protect their former charges.

There had been instructions from the Japanese High Command in Tokyo to eliminate all evidence of Allied Prisoners of War. The plan had been to poison the civilian prisoners and bayonet the POWs, then burn their bodies or bury them in mass graves. This was known as the 'Final Disposition' and did occur on some of the islands. This strategy was designed to allow Japanese soldiers to return immediately to Japan to repel any Allied invasion and remove all evidence of the countless atrocities that had been committed in the Far East. The atomic bombs dropped on Nagasaki and Hiroshima subverted these directives.

Ronald wrote a great deal of poetry whilst in captivity and two Dutch books, *En eeuwig zingen de Bosshen*, by Dr Annie Posthumus, with a distinct Javanese cover design, and *Ons Zonneland*, were my father's constant companions during captivity and contained much of his written work, drawings and pressed flowers. He also organised a camp journal, *The Jungle Journal* – although production was often interrupted by camp guards confiscating pens and paper. Some of this material, which has recently come to light in the Imperial War Museum, is included in this book, which is, partly, based on a combination of handwritten material and a typed manuscript my father was intending to publish. The remainder I have compiled from archival material, newspaper articles, family letters, other personal accounts, and archive material from the Imperial War Museum that covers the period from Ronald joining the Royal Artillery in 1939 to his homecoming in 1945.

My father returned home in late October 1945. My mother's description was of a barely recognisable, emaciated man with severely cropped hair, yellowish skin, sunken eyes and dreadful teeth (due to severe gum disease, Ronald lost his teeth in his early forties although he had good healthy teeth and gums prior to the Java POW experience). He weighed only a little over seven stones, just over half his normal body weight. Considering he had been well fed since release, his physical state was still appalling. Many released FEPOWs believed that their stomachs had shrunk, due to years of starvation, and they could not rapidly build up their body weight. My mother said that his appearance turned heads in public for several months and he never recovered the self-confidence and self-esteem he had prior to going to Java. For a number of years after the war he had nightmares and he became anxious if left on his own for more than a few minutes.

This book is a unique record of a forgotten part of the war, which helps paint a picture of what Japanese prison camps in west Java were like. No official Allied military records survived the Java campaign and personal records are sparse, although Lieutenant Colonel (Lt Col) H.R. Humphries, Commander of the 77th Artillery Regiment, did manage to keep some records of events on Java on six pieces of rice paper, which he kept in a wooden box (a transcript of which can be found in the

National Archives at Kew). The Japanese burnt all archives of POW camps and often silenced, permanently, any witnesses to their atrocities.

Unlike Ronald, who said he would be happy to shake a Japanese person's hand, many men who survived being Japanese POWs maintained a deep hatred of their former oppressors. However, Ronald would not purchase post-war Japanese merchandise as he felt this would be his best form of protest. He was deeply disappointed that many bad Japanese and Koreans were never brought to war crimes trials. He would have been dismayed that the Japanese royal family and government ministers continued to pay homage at the Yasukuni Shinto shrine, Tokyo, which subsequently contained the remains of many 'Class A' Japanese war criminals.

It has been alleged that, in 1949, the US Government deliberately curtailed Japanese war crimes investigations, as the trail was leading directly to Emperor Hirohito.[3] Thus, many cases of Japanese brutality, cannibalism, prisoner experimentation for bio-warfare, and mass sexual slavery have remained uninvestigated and unchallenged to this day. There has been no hunt for Japanese war criminals, which is in stark contrast to the clamour for finding Nazi war criminals by the Simon Wiesenthal Centre.

Frank Williams

---

3   In 1971 Hirohito was made a Knight of the Garter by the British Government, much to the consternation and protest of many ex-FEPOWs. I am relieved that my father was no longer alive to witness this extraordinary event.

Part I: 'Under the Poached Egg'

By Ronald Williams (Unwelcome 'Guest' of the Imperial Japanese Army on Java, 1942-1945)

The Japanese flag was often referred to, for obvious reasons, as a 'poached egg' and the POWs were the 'toast' for over three and a half years! Illustration by Charles Holdsworth

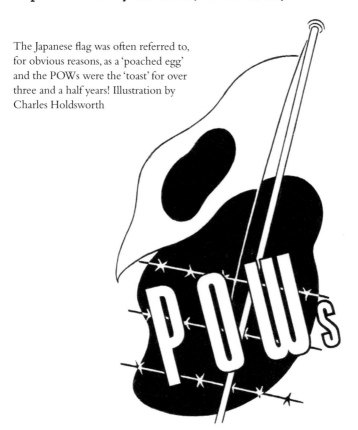

[*This was to be the original title of Ron Williams' book which he was planning to write on return from Java. He contacted many old friends after the war to help fund its publication, but this proved ultimately too difficult. His later ambition was to produce the book on his retirement but this was not to be, due to his premature death.*]

Dedication

This small volume is dedicated to those men and women, from all services and walks of life, and of all nationalities, who maintained their pride with great courage, while captives of the Japanese in the Far East, from 1941–1945.[4]

Please note that sections in italics, throughout the following text, are comments by Frank Williams.

4   For the Japanese the dates are 2602-05, according to their calendar.

1: Diary of the 77th's 'Hell on Paradise Island'

Beginnings

On 5 December 1941, I was on a train to Gourock Docks, on the Clyde, with my regiment and later that day, as my diary notes, 'took a ship's tender to a converted ocean-going liner, the *Empress of Australia*'. This was to be our troopship for the next couple of months. We were part of the Convoy WS (William Sail) 14, which included the *Warwick Castle* (a converted Union ship), the *Empress of Asia* (later sunk in Singapore harbour), and *Dunera*, all troopships, and *Pretoria* and *Troilus* (later a stalwart in Malta convoys) carrying heavy equipment. [*The 77th Artillery Regiment was 1,007 strong on departure.*]

We had been joined by Light Anti-Aircraft Regiments the 21st, 48th, and 79th and accompanied by a Royal Naval escort. After we were under way, news was coming

Royal Artillery cap badge. Illustration by Sgt J.D. Bligh of 239 Bty.

through that the Japanese had attacked the American Pacific Fleet at Pearl Harbor and also bombed Singapore and Hong Kong. We had no idea at this time that the Japanese would be our enemy in less than two months, as we were expecting to be joining General (Gen.) Auchinleck's forces in the Middle East. [*Sixteen warships were sunk or severely damaged in the bombing of Pearl Harbor, including four battleships, 188 aircraft were destroyed and 2,400 Americans were killed and 1,178 injured.*]

Empress of Australia was a very comfortable troop ship. [Empress of Australia *carried 239 and 241 Battery (Bty) and* Warwick Castle *carried 240 Battery. The Regimental HQ was split between the two ships.*] We had good meals and plenty of time and space for relaxation, but then, several days out to sea, we came under attack from German bombers. There were no direct hits but transporter *Pretoria*, while avoiding the bombing, began shifting cargo and started listing. We subsequently learned that a great deal of damage to vehicles and heavy equipment had occurred on board the *Pretoria* – 'bad luck for us, but lucky German bombers!' In fact, damage to some of our equipment did cause us significant problems later, on Java. [*Lt Col Humphries reported that he had complained about the handling and loading of fragile equipment at Gourock, by the Royal Engineers (RE). Heavy equipment had been placed on fragile equipment and colour markings for each gun unit had not been adhered to, either by the RE or ship's tender operators.*]

Vigilance was required out at sea as further bombing was anticipated. We underwent weapons training and operated guns on rotation. The ships practised anti-submarine manoeuvres from time to time and lookouts were posted for submarines and surface magnetic mines. I relaxed by writing, mainly poems and short stories, and by getting my men to provide cartoons and drawings.

Our original 'mystery' destination, we were informed, would be Basra, in the Persian Gulf, where we were to protect the docks and railhead. We had a brief stop in Freetown, Sierra Leone, to refuel and take on provisions (a very hot Christmas Day!), before a good break in Cape Town, South Africa between New Year's Eve and 4 January 1942.

I had to keep an eye on some of our boys who were being offered a 'king's ransom' to work in the gold mines. Many of the 77th were from mining areas, particularly the Rhondda valley. Spirits were very high at the time and we were just looking forward to giving 'Jerry' payback for their imperialistic menace in the Middle East and most of Europe.

On setting sail from South Africa things began to change – there were strong rumours that our convoy would be heading into the Indian Ocean as the Japanese had advanced through Malaya and the Philippines at an alarming rate, with the battleship *Prince of Wales* and consort vessel *Repulse* having been sunk (on 10 December 1941). The destination was to be somewhere in British South East Asia – this venture would be an interesting experience since we were all geared up for desert, rather than tropical, warfare!

We learned that our old chums of 242 Bty were to head for Basra, but the rest of us were to go to the Far East. The convoy split east of the Cape – we were likely to be heading for the 'Fortress City', Singapore. This was in fact the destination for part of 241 Bty. We learned subsequently that we were on our way to the Dutch East Indies 'Spice Islands' – Japanese here we come!

At that time, although Pearl Harbor and the rapid advance in the Philippines and Malaya were recognised, we were led to believe that the Japanese would run out of steam owing to lack of equipment, air support and the presence of a great many conscripted troops. Our morale remained high and we anticipated stopping the Japanese advance. Unfortunately, the Allies seriously underestimated the fighting ability of the enlisted Japanese soldier.

On 3 February we entered the Sunda Strait, west of Java and south of Sumatra, accompanied by HMS *Exeter* and the Dutch cruiser *Java*. We docked at Rotterdam wharf, Tandjong Priok, Batavia (later called Djakarta), west Java, part of the Dutch East Indies. A Japanese reconnaissance plane had already spotted our convoy and shortly afterwards we were subjected to a period of moderately heavy bombing from Japanese planes coming from Celebes and southern Borneo. The ship's anti-aircraft guns opened up on the bombers and, as we were concerned for the men and equipment, delayed disembarkation until the bombing ceased. [*Humphries' records indicate that 239 Bty disembarked at 1900 hrs on 3 February under Major (Maj.) Leslie Gibson and 240 and 241 Btys disembarked at 0600 hrs on the 4 February and entrained to Soerabaja .*]

Early next day, on 4 February, the men and some equipment moved off the ships. I was partly responsible for helping organise gun battery emplacements around the port of Batavia. 239 Bty was to stay in Batavia while the rest of the regiment was to travel east to the main Dutch naval base at Soerabaja (later called Surabaya). [*Humphries records that air raid alarms were frequent at the port, which disrupted the moving of equipment off the ships. It took seven days to completely unload and organise stores and equipment.*]

It was apparent that Soerabaja was suffering heavy bombing, with the eastern Allied airfields at Madion and Malang subject to intense daily bombing. Unfortunately, some of our equipment was either incomplete or damaged and in need of repair, particularly the gun springs, some of the range finders and gun transporters. This was the inevitable consequence of the convoy splitting in the Indian Ocean and the bombing.

We stayed at the Dutch KNIL (*Koninklijk Nederlansch Indish Leger*), Royal Dutch East Indies Army Cornelius barracks, Batavia. Brigadier (Brig.) Hervey Sitwell, an artilleryman, arrived to be our C-in-C. Arrangements were made for the transfer of 240 and 241 Btys and the Regimental HQ, including our own commanding officer, the monocled and gatered Lt Col H.R. Humphries (affectionately known as 'HRH' or 'Col Bob'), with his faithful shooting-stick, to Soerabaja on a fast troop train. Problems were encountered with the heavy gun transfer by train, owing to overhead obstructions.

5 February

The bulk of the officers and NCOs went on the train to Soerabaja, while the guns and heavy equipment went by road, a good 500 miles on not very good quality roads. Some units of other regiments have been transferred by ship to Sumatra, Bali and Timor to protect ports and airfields. Vehicles heading for Soerabaja required green netting to conceal the desert camouflage!

6 February

In the early hours of this morning (at about 0245 hrs) a major disaster struck. The train carrying the 77th officers and NCOs was in a head-on smash with a stationary train carrying munitions and fuel on a single line at Lahwang, near Malang. It was probably an accident due to brake failure, though some suspect sabotage as the stationary train's driver was missing and the area was known to be rife with Japanese collaborators. There are also likely to be Japanese agents on the island, as the Japanese had free access to Java up to the declaration of war.

It is reported that thirty men were killed (five officers and a large number of NCOs) and up to one hundred injured (forty-three seriously), including my best friend, Medical Officer Captain (Capt.) John W. Goronwy, (RAMC), who suffered a broken jaw and arm, and also Flight Liuetenant (Flt Lt) Dawson, another medic. A Section of 241 Bty suffered the highest number of casualties. Killed were Capt. H.M. MacMillan, and Lieutenants (Lt) J.K. Ainsley, W.L. Black, J.A. Boxall, J.H. Stoodley, and D.P. Cox (who died later from his wounds). Stoodley, Black, Boxall and Ainsley were all good friends and likely to have been together at the time of the accident. Gunner (Gnr) Harry Hamer commented about the rail crash:

> Amongst the debris lying around,
> T'was death and mutilation we found.
> The number of victims was very large;
> T'was a question of accident or sabotage?
> Through all sorts of storms in life I've been,
> And I have witnessed its seamier lights,
> But never again in all my life,
> Do I want to witness such ghastly sights.

[*There are no official records recording deaths and injuries from this accident although Humphries records that ten coaches were badly damaged, with the first four completely wrecked. Twenty-one died at the scene: five officers and sixteen ORs (other ranks). Forty-three were wounded: three officers and forty ORs with 241 Bty taking the brunt. Brig. R.J. Lewendon wrote in the* Journal of the Royal Artillery (1981) *that thirty men of the 77th RA died as the result of the accident and 100 were injured. Fifty gunners from the 6th HAA (Heavy Anti-Aircraft) were transferred to the 77th following the rail crash.*]

Unfortunately, my fellow Battery Sergeant Major (BSM), Ken (wyn) Street, was also killed. As a result of this tragedy, I've been commissioned to second lieutenant and set to be posted to Soerabaja to help replace killed and injured officers.

7 February

I continue to help organise the artillery defence of Tandjong Priok with the Dutch KNIL. Unfortunately, no proper replacement parts can be found for damaged and missing gun counter-balance springs so we've requested the REME (Royal Electrical and Mechanical Engineers) make suitable improvisations. We've heard that Soerabaja (Sidotapo) has been taking a real pounding. (It was later confirmed that fifty-one artillery men had been killed and fifty injured). [*The Regimental HQ was established at Tandjong Priok railway station.*]

9 February

The bombing has intensified. We blasted away with partial success, though I do not know how many aircraft we actually shot down.

10 February

I've received orders that I will finally be proceeding to Soerabaja to replace the lost and injured officers of 240 Bty. I am to be the OC (officer-in-command) of the convoy to take replacement artillerymen by road. We've been warned about saboteurs and to keep a close watch on vehicles at night. In addition, Japanese fighter planes are hitting road convoy vehicles. Although the jungle canopy has proved very helpful as extra camouflage, the Japanese do seem to be aware of the movement of our road convoy!

11 & 12 February

There's been a lull in the bombing (it was later confirmed that the Japanese were concentrating on the capture of Palembang in southern Sumatra, so air attacks decreased significantly on Java for the next four days). GHQ (General Head Quarters) confirmed the decision for me to transfer to Soerabaja. Many evacuees are arriving from Singapore and Sumatra to Tandjong Priok – these are mainly civilians and RAF personnel, but, unfortunately, with no useful equipment.

   I proceeded to Soerabaja, a journey of over two days by road, and arrived there late afternoon. Fortunately, we did not come under attack and there was no overheating of vehicles – another concern for lorry convoys. [*According to Humphries, at 0900 hrs on 12 February the main guns and heavy equipment left Batavia for Soerabaja under the command of Capt. J. Mellor (RAOC). Lt Col Humphries and his adjutant flew to Soerabaja after supervising the despatch. BSM Ronald Williams was promoted to 2/Lt and transferred to 240 Bty. Sgt [Sergeant] Cecil West and Sgt Adrian Davies were promoted to 2/Lts, 241 Bty; Lance Bombardier (L/Bdr) Frederick Fawcett promoted to 2/Lt, 240 Bty.*]

13 February

Capt. G. Smyth took the remainder of the convoy to Soerabaja (small fast vehicles).

15 February

More bad news – we've heard that Singapore has fallen and Palembang (southern Sumatra) has also been captured. This places Java in a precarious position. A fresh wave of bombing on Soerabaja has commenced; things are beginning to look ominous.

16 February

I was transferred, by motor launch, with a small party of artillery-men, to Kamal, near Bangkalan, Madoera Island, east of Soerobaja. The island contains KNIL batteries and a secret radio station. Japanese attacks are expected imminently on Bali and Timor. [*According to Humphries' records, Right Troop of 240 Bty was to occupy a site on Madoera*]

Island. Two 3.7-inch guns were transferred on 20 February and two further heavy guns on 21 February.]

[There is no further information about Ronald's activities till 28 February. However, he wrote a play, One Came Back Home, a small extract of which follows as Appendix 6 in Part II, which gives a flavour of what might have been happening on Madoera Island.

Madoera had a Dutch artillery battery (12 x 78mm guns), and a secret radio station. It was also a forward observation post for the detection of a likely Japanese invasion by sea from the east of Java.

Although the Japanese had used paratroopers for invading some of the East Indies islands, Java was considered to be unsuitable for a major paratrooper landing, with the exception of the airfields, due to dense jungle and volcanoes. Seaborne invasion was thought most likely, coming from the west, east and south. The north coast, ultimately a major invasion point, was considered less likely owing to poor roads and jungle obstacles – but this, in fact, proved to be no obstruction to the Japanese invasion.

17 February
The Japanese Naval Force was heading for Bali, through the Makassar Strait. Allied submarines should have been a major force in combating the Japanese invaders but were unfamiliar with local waters and, in fact, USS Sea Wolf ran aground. Torpedoes fired by Allied submarines largely missed their intended targets and Allied B-17 bombers scored few direct hits on Japanese naval vessels.

18 February
The Japanese invaded the island of Bali. Unfortunately, Dutch troops left the airfield intact and as a consequence there were increased enemy bombing sorties over Java. The ill-fated Battle of Badoeng Strait commenced. (This is well documented in naval warfare history.) The 77th Artillery in Soerabaja shot down five or six enemy aircraft on this day and escaping Allied artillerymen arrived from southern Sumatra, minus their guns!

19 February
Fresh and heavy bombing recommenced on Soerabaja, from southern Sumatra and Bali. There was dog fighting over Java, reminiscent of the Battle of Britain. The Allies lost seventy-five aeroplanes. Air defences were becoming very thin and ground defences were under severe pressure. Radio silence was maintained on Madoera for the Battle of Badoeng Strait.

Unfortunately, tactical errors by Rear Admiral Karel Doorman's ships led to severe setbacks. The use of close-range artillery was ineffective and Dutch destroyers, employing searchlights at night, lost any element of surprise.

Unlike the Allies, the Japanese had been well trained for night fighting. Ideally, some Allied warships should have been kept in reserve, and repaired, for the anticipated Battle of Java Sea, which may have tipped the balance back in the Allied fleets' favour. There were no aircraft carriers available and, therefore, deployment of aircraft proved difficult.

20 February
The Battle of Badoeng Strait was effectively lost by the Allies. All airfields supplying Java were now in enemy hands. There were Japanese landings on Timor.

21 February

An Allied naval force left Batavia to head for Soerabaja. The De Ruyter and Java (Dutch light cruisers) and Houston (US heavy cruiser) joined the Eastern Strike Force in Soerabaja.

22 February

Overall military command was handed over to the Dutch East Indies' Army chief, Gen. Hein ter Poorten. Churchill had communicated to Wavell to fight on – but no reinforcements would be forthcoming, as these would be sent to Burma and India. Churchill signals, 'I send you and all ranks of the British forces who have stayed behind in Java my best wishes for success and honour in the great fight that confronts you. Every day gained is precious and I know that you will do everything humanly possible to prolong the battle.' General ter Poorten stated that it was 'better to die standing than live on your knees.'

The records of Lt Col Humphries state that Brig. Hervey Sitwel, commanding the 16th AA Brigade, when inspected the gun sites in Soerabaja. 240 Bty, on Madoera Island, saw them shoot down two enemy aircraft.

23 February

ABDACOM (American, British, Dutch and Australian Command), formed at the Washington DC Conference in December 1941, was dissolved and Wavell headed for New Delhi on 1 January to set up command in Java at Lembang. Brig. Sitwell was promoted to major general and became general officer commanding (GOC) of all British forces.

24 February

A number of senior Allied officers left Java for India and Australia. A large Japanese naval force was reported to be heading through the strait of Makassar towards Java. West and east Java were reasonably well defended, but most of the north of the island was undefended. Gen. Sitwell felt that forces should be concentrated in the west, east and south to delay the enemy invasion as long as possible.

Unfortunately, there were a large number of military non-combatants, mainly RAF, on Java and time was considered much too short to train them for combat. The Dutch were being heavily relied upon for communications but these were becoming increasingly fragmented across Java.

A further concern was the use of a wide variety of ammunition calibre for light weapons (each nationality had different calibre ammunition), which produced considerable problems in re-supply. Gen. Sitwell moved some of the LAA (Light Anti-Aircraft) Btys from Soerabaja to defend the airfields of Malang and Madion.

240 and 241 Btys stayed in Soerabaja. Batavia received a heavy bombing raid with six Japanese raiders shot down.

25 February

Rear Admiral Doorman set sail from the Dutch Royal Naval base of Soerabaja, and Dutch Admiral C.E.L. Helfrich sent HMS Exeter, Perth (Australian Navy), Jupiter, Electra, and Encounter (British destroyers) from Batavia to join Doorman. A sweep of the sea area north of Java took place and a Japanese convoy was sighted near Bawean Island.

26 February

Admiral Doorman intercepted Japanese troop carriers with limited success, causing damage and slowing their progress. In addition, American bombers destroyed some troopships and a US submarine destroyed the Japanese radio station on Bawean.

Churchill wired Admiral Maltby (Senior British Naval Commander) to continue fighting for as long as possible: 'Every day gained in the defence of Java is precious.'

Humphries' records state that AA Brigade HQ ordered that 77th HAA Regimental HQ and 240 Bty proceed to defend Tjilatjap, in the south, leaving 241 Bty to defend Soerabaja under Dutch command. Most of 240 Bty left Soerabaja at 1130 hrs on the 26 February and arrived in Tjilatjap on 1 March.

27 February

This day was probably the turning point of the defence of Java, as the Battle of Java Sea commenced. (The Java Sea battle is reviewed in Part II, chapter 2.) There were major Allied losses. The Dutch cruisers, De Ruyter (Flagship), with Rear Admiral Doorman, Java and Kortenaer were sunk, as were the British destroyers Electra and Jupiter. Houston ('the galloping ghost of the Java coast') and Perth (Australian Navy) managed to return to Tandjong Priok and the battle cruiser Exeter was badly damaged.

Later there was heated debate as to why the battle had gone so badly wrong for the Allies — some of the main reasons identified were the following:

- The Japanese had mostly modern warships with accurate long lance oxygen-driven torpedoes, which they used to great effect.
- The Japanese were also a more efficient fighting force and outnumbered the Allies.
- The Allies had incompatible communication systems and were a disparate group of warships.
- Many of the Allied ships had previously been damaged and remained un-repaired.
- The Allied men were extremely weary.
- There was almost a total lack of air cover for the Allies by this time and poor air reconnaissance.
- The Allies had no aircraft carrier; USS Langley had been sunk earlier.
- There were increasing fuel shortages.

Despite all of this, it was felt the Japanese invasion had been delayed by two days as a result of this sea battle and some felt that the two weeks the Japanese took to overrun Java prevented intended Japanese landings on northern Australia.

28 February

I returned from Madoera to Soerabaja. There have been orders to move 240 Bty to Tjilatjap, south Java, to defend the main port and airfield. The Japanese commence landings in the west and north. However, before moving artillery from Soerabaja it accounted for at least sixteen enemy aircraft. The plan is to leave 241 Bty, 131st US Field Artillery (Texan National Guard) and the Australian Pioneer Corps to defend Soerabaja and the airfield at Malang. Right Troop has set off for Tjilatjap

[Humphries: there were problems moving equipment and heavy guns off Madoera Island. Maj. L. Street visited to try and sort it out but could not obtain suitable transport. Later Maj.

Gerald Gaskell and Capt. Fobber (Dutch Liaison Officer) managed to obtain two reasonable sized barges.]

Unfortunately, HMS *Exeter*, whilst escaping from Soerabaja, has been sunk. Destroyers, HMS *Encounter* and USS *Pope* suffered a similar fate. A strong Japanese force, with light tanks, landed at Ereten Wetan near Soebang, north Java, and make rapid headway inland.

1 March

RHQ, 240 Bty arrived at the port of Tjilatjap. The Japanese have landed at Kragan, on the north-west coast; there was still some air defence from Madioen, but unfortunately, Kalidjati airfield has been captured (with heavy losses for 48th LAA Regiment and 6th HAA Regiment, Royal Artillery). Also, on this inauspicious day, *Houston* and *Perth* were sunk by Japanese destroyers after entering the Sunda Strait and running into a major Japanese invasion force off Batavia.

2 March

Right Troop of 77th HAA arrived at Tjilatjap. We've learned that some of 241 Bty were cut off by the Japanese invasion of Soerabaja and have been captured. Roads to Tjilatjap are now seriously congested with fleeing colonials and other civilians. The convoy suffered some damage from air attacks. So far we have not met any opposition on land.

3 March

We rapidly set up defensive gun positions. Right Troop, 240 Bty deployed three 3.7-inch guns on a creek west of Tjilatjap (No. 3 gun-site). The gun-sites immediately came under attack from Japanese bombers and fighters. 239 Bty was moved from Batavia to defend the Bandoeng district. (The Japanese also attacked the Australian mainland at Broome, a north-west Australian port, destroying all Allied military aircraft and flying boats containing civilian escapees from Java.)

4 March

All hell has broken out! One main defensive position is a large football field north of the docks and here there was major action, with waves of attacks from Japanese dive-bombers with low-level bombing and Zero/Zeke fighters strafing the gun-sites with machine-gun fire. The port also came under fire from naval bombardment, with many ships being damaged or sunk. One of our gun emplacements (four guns) took a direct hit. An estimated ninety [*Humphries' report puts the figure at 150!*] Japanese medium and light bombers and fighters were attacking us. We shot down in excess of fifteen enemy aircraft and damaged others. The brave Bren gunners did a sterling job in keeping the Jap Zeroes at bay, a number of whom lost their lives and others were seriously injured in the process. The docks have also been heavily bombed.

5 March

We are all bloody exhausted! Further heavy aerial bombardment has continued from planes and ships, though we've again had reasonable success in shooting down aircraft, about the same numbers as yesterday. We've heard that Batavia has been over-run. There were three major invasion points on Java, west, north, and east of the island (at Merak, Ereten Wetan and Kragan), by the Japanese 16th Army under Gen. Imamura. All ships in Tjilatjap harbour have been sunk.

It appears that there was little resistance in the north, where the airfields were quickly over-run, although there was brave defence of Kalidjati airfield by British soldiers and RAF men, resulting in most of the airmen being killed in action.

[*Research by Brig. R.J. Lewendon, on behalf of the Royal Artillery Institution, indicates that during the period 3–5 March, twenty-six Japanese planes were definitely destroyed and thirteen probably destroyed by British artillery fire.*]

6 March

We are dog-tired. The Japanese continue to advance rapidly. There have been problems with the Dutch Army abandoning useful equipment and failing to destroy both guns and trucks, which then fell into Japanese hands, so we were ordered by Gen. Sitwell to destroy or disable all our heavy equipment. We successfully spiked (exploding and splitting gun barrels) all our big guns and smashed instruments – a sad sight! We are still fighting with Bren guns mounted on any tripod that could be constructed. It appears that we are heading for Tasikmalaja airfield, to fight on with light weapons. Things are looking ominous!

Lt Col H.R. Humphries had a major altercation with the local Dutch commander at Wangon crossroads (a small town between Tjilatjap and Purwokerto), where we ran into the Dutch force moving up from Tjilatjap. 'Col Bob' tried to persuade the Dutch commander (probably Maj. Gen. Pierre A. Cox) to join forces, but it was clear the Dutch were not keen to fight on, as they thought the situation had become hopeless. ('Col Bob' later wrote that his entire regiment was adequately armed with light automatics, Thompson machine guns, and rifles and could have rendered an excellent account of themselves should any opposition be encountered. However, despite repeated efforts, the Dutch commander could not be persuaded to join forces, saying he had 'no orders' to fight on). [*According to Humphries, the Wangon crossroads incident happened on 7 March. Despite their 'adequate' arms, Ronald said that the only time he actually used his service revolver during his time on Java was to put down a seriously injured horse! Although he and a number of his battery did take turns at firing 'pot-shots' at low-flying Jap aircraft with Bren guns to display continuing resistance.*]

7 March

We've learned that the Dutch are on the point of capitulation, as the Japs now occupy Tjilatjap and Lembang, thus blocking the final escape route from Java. (Dr Hubertus van Mook, the head of government on Java, and some of his cabinet, just managed to escape to Australia. Van Mook set up a government in exile in Adelaide. He complained bitterly about the lack of Allied help on Java.) It seems to be a case of just heading for the mountains, Tjakadjang, to continue fighting.

There was a radio broadcast from Gen. ter Poorten, stating all Allied resistance was to cease. Our top brass are not happy with this and Maltby is keen for continued guerrilla-style warfare. However, the options are not great for us, as we'd need to rely on the local Javanese for support. We are seen as part of the increasingly disliked Dutch colonial set-up and the Japanese already have a terrible reputation for killing civilians when they are known to be supportive of any sustained enemy resistance. There are also too many Allied military non-combatants (the RAF referred to them as 'penguins' if they were non-flyers). There are also Japanese informants and spies on the island. If the Dutch and Javanese do not fight on, then our position will become untenable.

8 March

The Dutch have formally surrendered (Tjarda van Starkenborgh, the Island's Governor General, to Gen. Hitoshi Imamura) at Kalidjati. At 1000 hrs, we ended up in Garoet, in the middle of Java, among rubber plantations. (This would become the main assembly point for prisoners of war before being sent, via rail or truck, to internment camps in Batavia.) [*Humphries: At 1200 hrs a rear guard, comprising three officers and fifty men, was posted to hold the road until 239 Bty arrived. This was withdrawn once the capitulation order came through. All light weapons destroyed (LMGs and sub-MGs).*]

9 March

At 1430 hrs Admiral Maltby and Maj. Gen. Hervey Sitwell surrendered to the Japanese commander at Bandoeng. Apparently the Japanese had threatened to flatten Batavia if the Allies failed to unconditionally surrender. There was little evidence of Japanese soldiers in our area at this time.

The regiment went to Tjisompet through mountain roads.

10 March

[*Humphries: Some men had made a break for it, causing a great deal of consternation. The situation was retrieved by Maj. F. Baddely, RA, before any Japanese reprisals could take place.*]

11 March

We were given orders to stack all weapons and ammunition for inspection (many weapons were rendered useless by their owners, in defiance of surrender terms, so that they would be of no value to the enemy) and be prepared for a big roundup. Battery unit diaries, codebooks, maps, etc., were destroyed. We had to set up a perimeter area, although there is still reasonable freedom of movement, providing a white armband is worn.

We are billeted in estate buildings and lorries on a Dutch rubber plantation at Tjisompet, near Garoet.

The occasional pair of Imperial Japanese Army soldiers appear, menacingly waving their rifles with fixed bayonets and sometimes hit and slap people for little or no reason. (This was our first indication of what was to come. Japanese soldiers were regularly beaten by their superiors. These soldiers viewed prisoners of war as subordinates and fair game for similar treatment.)

On a plantation in Java,
Far away from England's shore,

We lead a life of peace and quiet
After this stress of war.
When we were gathered together,
We learned the Glorious 77th
Had lost a Battery and a half
From its total strength of three.
And now we are prisoners of war,
On this plantation on a hill.
The Japanese may have taken our guns and arms,
But they will never take our will.

Gnr Henry 'Harry' Hamer

12 March

Formal Allied surrender to the Japanese commander, Gen. Imamura, took place at Bandoeng today. More Jap guards have appeared and we are all demoralised at the lack of a decent fight against our enemy, who are rather a diminutive and dishevelled-looking bunch of soldiers. There is general disbelief that we have surrendered to these characters.

[*Gen. Hitoshi Imamura of the 16th Japanese Army expressed surprise later that the Allies had made Wavell head of ABDACOM. He felt that the Dutch should have remained in command as they had the most to lose, commanded the largest army, navy and air force in the region, and knew the island's terrain best.*]

13 March

Over the next couple of weeks nothing much happened. It was a case of avoiding irritating the Japanese soldiers, finding enough cigarettes and fighting boredom. Food and water were OK at this time. (It would prove to be a very different case in less than three weeks.) We learned that the Japanese are predictably unpredictable! Japanese counterparts told our senior officers that Allied officers would be treated very well and would never be short of cigars, alcohol and man servants. What a sick joke that turned out to be.

14 March

Capt. Harold Davey (East Surrey Regiment) has been attached to our regiment as liaison officer.

20 March

The Japanese wanted us to march, on foot, to Batavia. The Japanese were informed that low water and food rations, plus the poor footwear of some of the troops, would make this exercise problematic. Amazingly they accepted this!

21 March

[*Humphries: The regiment set off in convoy with the 49th LAA Bty and 20th BOD to Trogong, where we stayed for two nights.*] Gen. Sitwell visited the regiment to raise morale.

'The perks for a captured British officer'. What a myth in reality! Illustration by Charles Holdsworth

23 March
[*Humphries: Proceeded to Tjibatoe and joined up with 239 Bty on route. Men housed in native huts for three to four days, while the Japanese organised transport.*]

28 March
We were rounded up by groups of uncouth Korean and Japanese guards and marched to a railway junction to board cattle trucks from Tjibatoe. It was fairly cramped inside these trucks and some prisoners were packed in like sardines. Although the train frequently stopped we could not get off. The heat was unbearable. Disposing of personal waste became an art in itself. Humorous initially, but it became extremely irritating and annoying to most of us before very long. We took two days' rations with us – thank God!

29 March
We arrived in Batavia and were frog-marched, with maximum degradation tactics, through the streets to Boei Glodok camp (a former Dutch civilian prison). Others, we heard, were marched to Tandjong Priok camp and a large Dutch Army barracks known later as Bicycle camp. (I would later get to know the latter camp very well!) At Glodok camp, Group Captain (Gp Capt.) C.H. Nobel (RAF) is the Senior Allied Officer (he later shared responsibility for the men with Lt Col Humphries).

[*My father was promoted to first lieutenant on 9 May 1942 in Boei Glodok, just before transfer to Priok camp. British junior officers received time-promotion, even in captivity, potentially up to the rank of captain.*]

Ronald was deeply demoralised by the lack of a concerted fight by the Allies, in the defence of Java, but felt that the unexpected fall of Singapore was the turning point that sealed the island's fate. He wrote that the Japanese were a merciless and determined enemy fighting an ill-equipped and disorganised multinational Allied force. Most British men would have fought to the bitter end if they had foreseen their ultimate fate.

The capitulation of the Allies remained a heavy burden to bear and a source of shame for Ronald. Gen. Hein ter Poorten, the Commander-in-Chief on Java, felt that the Allies would have been unable to rely on the local Indonesians, both civilian and the increasingly disaffected military, for support. The KNIL was, in large part, a colonial police force and not a modern fighting army. Ter Poorten was also aware the Japanese had spies and collaborators on Java.

After only a month fighting the Japanese there was an almost complete lack of air cover. The Allied fleet had been all but wiped out and too few infantry and tanks were available. Gen. ter Poorten had also been informed that no reinforcements would be forthcoming.

There were many stories of Japanese atrocities against Allied troops and civilians, especially where there had been a concerted and sustained resistance against the Japanese. In the circumstances, the Dutch surrender was understandable but, in my father's view, premature, although he had sympathy with ter Poorten's predicament.

Ronald was convinced that lessons should have been learned from the fall of Crete to the Germans, which should have provided military insight into defending an island of crucial strategic importance. Post-war evidence of the Japanese imperialistic campaign in the Far East indicated that a concerted and dogged defence of Java would have provided the Japanese with all manner of logistical problems.

My father remained unaware, during his lifetime, that Gen. Wavell had cabled Churchill on 16 February 1942, stating that the loss of Java, although regrettable, would not be critical to the war effort and any reinforcements would be diverted to Burma and India. In fact, Wavell described the impending situation on Java as 'hopeless'. It was surely a case of 'lambs to the slaughter' on Java. Gen. Wavell had also been the Allied Commander-in-Chief at the time of the fall of Crete!

Ronald made a note that armed Javanese plantation workers joined the Japanese guards early on after the surrender. He thought these men were members of a 'fifth column' that many suspected of being active on the island. However, it is more likely that these men were Japanese infantry disguised as plantation workers. This was a common ploy by advanced guards of the Japanese infantry to confuse the enemy. There are many anecdotal stories from South East Asia of Allied soldiers being unexpectedly fired on by local natives (Japanese soldiers in disguise). This had two outcomes: firstly, the element of surprise and confusion and, secondly, encouraging mistrust of the locals by the Allies. Unsurprisingly, innocent local natives were shot by the Allies who suspected subversion. In some quarters, this only fuelled resentment of the presence of the Allies in South East Asia.

Official records for the numbers of Allies and Japanese killed or wounded in action on Java are sparse. The Australians recorded thirty-six killed and sixty seriously wounded and 2,400 taken prisoner; the Americans 825 killed, including US naval personnel, and 900 taken prisoner. Casualties and losses for the Dutch, British and Japanese are not recorded.

Java and Madoera Island came under the control of the Sixteenth Japanese Army. Java's economic value to the Japanese was largely related to natural resources, a large workforce and a *developed infrastructure. The Japanese were reasonably tolerant of the Indonesian nationalists, seeing them as allies, but their behaviour towards the general population was harsh. There were terrible abuses of the civilians, including mass starvation. Several millions of the Javanese men (estimates vary between four and ten million) were forced into labour either on Java or the neighbouring islands. Many did not survive the war.]*

2: My Time in Japanese POW Camps around West Java

[The following are notes kept by Ronald Williams, on various scraps of paper, presumably written after the Japanese surrender in 1945.]

Many POW camps were makeshift and based in former civilian jails, schools or in newly built bamboo hut complexes called *bashas*. POW camps were often divided into sub-camps by barbed-wire divisions. POWs and camp guards moved regularly between camps both on and off Java, partly related to the use of forced labour and to contain perceived subversion. Movement between camps was often at very short notice. Prisoners were often marched to other camps but where the distances were great, such as Batavia to Bandoeng, POWs were transported in lorries followed by Japanese guards, often on bikes. Field-rank officers would be separated from junior officers and other ranks. Some senior officers were more than ready to stay in close contact with their men.

It was made very clear by the Japanese camp commandants that we POWs were a nuisance the Japanese had not expected to deal with: 'Nippon soldiers would not stoop so low as to be taken prisoner.' The Japanese soldier was expected to fight to the death; surrender was not an option for them. Thus the Allied POW was seen as the lowest of the low.

Boei Glodock camp in the old Chinese quarter was a nasty, filthy camp and former civilian prison for murderers and hardened criminals. It had high walls, watchtowers and cramped, bug-infested cells with concrete floors. There was very poor sanitation and water supply. Dysentery was rife. Little medication was available. Regular heavy work parties were taken from there to repair local airfields, such as Kemajoran. Many of the prisoners were RAF who had been transferred from Malaya and Singapore. The senior British officer was Gp Capt. Noble (RAF).

Tandjong Priok, Unikamptong POW camp, was mainly for British POWs. I arrived there on 14 May 1942. Half of 239 Bty and all 241 Bty had been in Priok camp from the beginning. This was a flood-lit camp with its own chapel (St George's) and was a large ex 'coolie's' camp containing about 3,000 men. We had to learn basic Japanese commands and how to count in Japanese, as Japanese numbers were used on parade (*tenko*). We also had to learn how to bow to the Japanese at *tenko*; bowing was from the waist, for at least five seconds, at an angle of at least 15°.

'Japanese camp guard'. Drawing by Karen Williams (Ronald Williams' granddaughter)

'St George's Chapel, Tandjong Priok camp'. Illustration by Charles Holdsworth.

The guards seemed to be less visible here; however, treatment in the camps became harsher as time went on. There were usually daily beatings, with fists, boots, rifle butts and bamboo sticks. The camp had a large number of medics and dentists but the Japanese confiscated much of the medicines and equipment for their own use. Hospitals were eventually organised in old Dutch Reform churches, Mater Dolorosa (infectious cases) and St Vincentius (surgical cases).

The best camp for food and climate was Bandoeng (a former Dutch infantry barracks), where we did occasionally have some meat and fish as well as two daily portions of rice, which elsewhere were largely inedible and contained maggots. This was often served up with watery vegetables (swill). In the early days following capture, Bandoeng gained a reputation for providing a full English breakfast with egg and steak. Sadly, this state of affairs was not apparent when I was transferred to Bandoeng in late 1944. Small amounts of tea, sugar and salt were occasionally available. Discipline was well maintained in Bandoeng due to firm leadership from senior British officers, with a continuing necessity to salute British officers as well as bowing to Japanese guards.

The key thing in camp was to avoid annoying the Japanese and Korean guards – never look happy or smile at them, do not to whistle or sing, unless in a concert, or provoke them in any way. Deliberate eye contact was not a good idea and they preferred men with short-cropped hair. On occasions, Allied officers were made to dig a trench to stand in when visiting high-ranking Japanese officers came to the camps, so that the diminutive Japs would not be overshadowed!

The Japanese had a tendency to pick on POWs who stood out physically, such as being very tall or very short, wearing glasses (not uncommon for the Japanese soldier), having tattoos (the Japanese viewed tattoos as a sign of criminality); beards and moustaches could be a problem if they looked more impressive than those worn by Japanese officers and camp guards. However, looking frail and weak could be an even bigger problem! [*Ronald remembered, as a POW of the Japanese, everyone had to accept that they had no rights and would not be treated as human beings. The Japanese never formally ratified the Geneva Convention of 1929 on conduct towards POWs. The barbaric way they treated their enemy, both military and civilian, bears testament to this defiance of international treaty.*]

Most personal possessions were quickly lost, although they could be used for bartering for food, cigarettes and medicines.

Sleeping was never easy. Men made bamboo platforms to sleep on, though in some camps sleeping took place on hard concrete floors or wooden floors covered in atap palm leaves. It was preferable to sleep off the ground and under mosquito nets to avoid the many bugs and insects crawling on the floors at night.

In April 1943, I was transferred to Bicycle camp, Batavia. This was the former HQ of the Dutch 10th Battalion (Bicycle Force) of the Netherlands East Indian Army and so named because of the large number of bicycles left by the Dutch. It was used as the main transit camp. Drafts of POWs were sent to other East Indian islands and Japan from here. These prisoner drafts began approximately twelve months after our capture. Living conditions were reasonably good compared to Boei Glodok and Priok, with showers, latrines, running water and lighting. We were housed, three to a room, in barracks with concrete floors, though Bicycle camp was often seriously overcrowded with drafts of POWS waiting for transfer. The accommodation was for 1,000 men but regularly housed 2,600. Men slept on rice bags with lice and fleas for company.

Sickness was high in this camp – malaria (Batavia had been built on malarial swamps), dysentery, beri-beri, diphtheria, tropical ulcers and avitaminosis were common. Lt Sonei, the camp commandant, who later terrorised the women and children at the Tjideng women's internment camp as the notorious Capt. Ken'ichi Sonei, was a very bad man with a vicious temper, particularly at full moon. Regular beatings occurred, even of his men! Some camp guards were equally brutal.

'POW camp personnel' by Flt Lt D.J. Dawson, RAF doctor, who was killed on a Japanese prison ship off the coast of Nagasaki, May 1944.

'Yamada' (probably a camp guard). Drawn by Geoff Tyson (2/40 Battalion AIF) in Priok camp.

A Typical Day

Time was Tokyo time, although we were in the wrong time zone, which meant very early starts.

The first obligation was to pay homage to the sons of the 'Empire of the Sun'. Roll call on parade *(tenko* or *kumpulan)* occurred twice per day. You got given rice with water twice per day if you were not ill; once a day if you were ill! Rice, rice and more rice was the staple camp diet. [*My father never touched rice after the war until, in the mid-1960s, we, as a family, visited Chinese restaurants.*] Occasional meat and greens were included with camp meals.

Patrols of the camp varied depending on the camp commandant and senior Allied officers' control of discipline. Guards searched for illegal papers and radios from time to time. If the *Kempeitai* (Japanese equivalent of the Nazi Gestapo) were called in, a prisoner death or two could occur.

Working parties happened most days, unless you were very sick. Allied officers were often beaten for sticking up for their sick men. Work parties were organised for planting castor oil seeds, salvage work and sisal (string) making. Other duties included burial parties and latrine digging. A work party could last for ten to twelve hours. Working in oppressive heat and humidity, particularly in Batavia, took its toll on the POWs.

[*Prisoner work drafts, 'slave labour', were sent to other East Indies islands, Burma, Siam and Japan starting in early 1943 and continued for most of the period of captivity. Lt Col Humphries, of the 77th, was joined by Lt Col Oakes, an Australian, to form 'H' Force. They were transferred to Singapore and in May 1943 sent to work on the Three Tier Bridge and Hell Fire Pass, staying at the notorious Hintock Hill and Kanchanaburi prison camps (camps where the death rate among prisoners was high).*]

Some camp entertainment and education occurred, depending on the talents of the prisoners.

The tolerability of each camp was highly dependent on the nature of the camp commandant. Often camp commandants would be away for days, leaving some obnoxious Nip sergeant, or even a private, in charge. There was a gradual de-sensitising process in each individual camp and death was never far away. In prison camps there was always a fluctuation of feelings of hope to despair.

Survival depended on a number of factors, not least was the quality of the senior Allied officer and the influence of the medics. Essential medicines were often hard to come by but this situation could be overcome by the senior Allied officer and medics persuading the Japanese that they would be better served by less sickness in the camps. [*Ronald told his wife that he was disappointed by the attitude of some of the more senior Allied officers, who seemed more concerned with their own survival than their men's welfare. It is interesting to note that, in the Far East, a disproportionate number of junior officers, NCOs and other ranks died in captivity, compared to the number of Allied Field officers who succumbed.*]

Slapping the faces of Allied officers was a favourite Japanese pastime. Although this was supposed to be only permitted by a Japanese officer, the rule was frequently broken in most camps.

Favourite Commands
Lekas – quick
Kura – hurry
Kioshi or ki-o-tsuki – pay attention
Keirei – bow
Kashira naka – eyes ahead

The Japanese regularly expropriated food and medical supplies paid for by the prisoner's fund and provided by the International Red Cross. [*The Japanese purloined American and Indian Red Cross parcels either for their own consumption or for the black market.*]

Food

The motto in some camps was 'No work, no food'.

Daily Rations – Ration statement issued by the Japanese (1g = 0.357oz)

	G	Oz
Meat		
Veg	526	18.5
Rice	170	5.9
Flour	300	10.58
Salt	20	0.7
Sugar	20	0.7
Tea/Coffee	0.5	0.18

Basic ranks were only entitled to 570g per day in total.

'Rice, rice and more rice' – the staple POW camp diet. Illustration by American Pat Trotta.

Pay

The Japanese eventually started to pay us, the pay being in line with their allowances. Most of us put a substantial amount of the payment into the prisoners' welfare fund to buy extra food and medicines, although after the war these contributions were deducted from our war pay. We found this to be a derisory response by our military paymasters to our horrific ordeal.

The total cash sum I received from the Japanese for the period from September 1942 to August 1945 was £546 cash, at least half of which was used by Wing Commander (Wg Cdr) Alexander for camp welfare funds (hospital and food) and troop welfare. Money issued by the Japanese, in both Japanese and local Dutch currency, was of low value compared to the American dollar and Dutch guilder. [*Ronald kept money in his Dutch book, some of which survived but was almost worthless in currency value. The Japanese advert for Jintan cigarettes can be seen clearly on the inside cover of his book containing 'camp dollars' (see colour plates). Two types of currency were issued, De Japansche Regeering in cents or Gulden, and Dai Nippon Teikoku Seihu in Roepiah.*

During the South-East Asia campaign approximately 180,500 Allied military were captured and approximately 100,000 civilians interned. It has been estimated that over a third of Allied FEPOWs, nearly 13,000 British, perished during internment (and the figure rose to fifty per cent or higher for those who were sent to slave labour camps). In comparison, it was less than two per cent for Allied POWs in other axis POW camps (Germany and Italy).]

Ronald Williams' Army payslip, at the end of hostilities, containing significant deductions because of payments made to POWs by the Japanese. That a large part of POW pay went into a camp welfare fund, for food and medicines, was of no interest to the Inland Revenue. This action, understandably, caused much resentment among former FEPOWs.

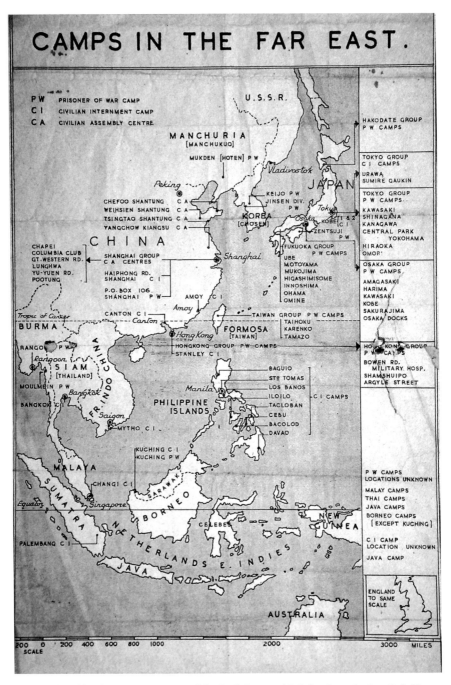

Map produced by the Far East Section of the Red Cross and St John Organisation, Park Place, London, in September, 1944. No civilian internment or POW camps had been identified on Java at that time.

List of POW Camps in which Ronald Williams was held

Tandjong Priok camp, Batavia: 10 May 1942–18 April 1942
Boei Glodok camp, Batavia: 29 March 1942–10 May 1943
Bicycle camp, Batavia: 18 April 1943-9 May 1943
Boei Glodok camp: 9 May 1943–12 February 1944
Bicycle camp: 12 February 1944–28 October 1944
Depot camp, Bandoeng: 29 October 1944–27 April 1945
LOG camp, Bandoeng: 27 April 1945–5 July 1945
Bicycle camp: 6 July 1945–24 September 1945

(POW camps on Java were designated by the Japanese with initials X, Y and Z according to which district the camp was in. Camps 'X' were POW camps in the Batavia district)

[*It was only in 1945 that the IRS (International Red Cross) had a reasonable idea of the where-abouts of POW camps on Java. The IRS was refused access to much of the Dutch East Indies. In fact, a team from the Red Cross was murdered in Malaya in 1944, almost certainly by the Japanese or by their sympathisers.*]

3: Records of Violations against POWs (Bandoeng Camps mainly) in 1945 and POW Deaths 1942–45

[*I presume that the following were the only written records my father kept, as they would have been fresh in the memory and written down after the Japanese surrender. These records were probably used for war crimes investigations. Also, it is likely that fellow officers would have kept records of other violations. Alternatively, records of worse violations were kept by the war crimes investigators; perhaps Ronald had already passed these on and not kept his own record?*]

April 1945, at Depot camp, Bandoeng
Violation: Starvation of whole camp for forty-eight hours, as a collective punishment for a minor misdemeanour. Supplies of tobacco were also stopped for three weeks. The Allied Commander was Wg Cdr G.F. Alexander.

Those were Colonel (Col) Anami, Sergeant Major 'Gunso' Mori M. (Masao), and Korean Private (Pte) Kasayama Y'kichi (Korean guards often had Japanese-sounding names). (Mori and Kasayama were known 'affectionately' as 'blood and slime', the two signs of dysentery!)

May–Aug 1945, at LOG camp, Bandoeng
Violation: Over-crowding and sordid living conditions. 3,800 Allied prisoners accommodated in a school reformatory (Landsop School) for 250 boys. Water and sanitation conditions were appalling. Food was grossly deficient. Allied commander and Japanese responsible, as above.

June 1945, at LOG camp
Violation: The senior British commander and most British officers badly beaten for failing to help the Japs obtain 'volunteers' from the British prisoners for work as motor mechanics. Allied commander as above and the Japanese responsible were Sgt 'Gunso' Mori M, and Pte Kasayama. It was witnessed by Lts Reardon-Smith, Collings and others.

1945, at Bandoeng camp
Violation: A British seaman, Erroch, of the SS *Empire Dawn* was made to kneel down on the ground and was brutally kicked about the head and shoulders by Japanese guards, Ptes Wusume and Sukiyama. The reason: Erroch had raised his fist to Wusume after being slapped about the face by this guard.

Most despised of the Korean guards at Bandoeng was Pte Harimoto. He took great delight in the daily beating of some of the Allied POWs. Others mentioned, without charges laid, were Kanamoto (Rudolph), Pte Kanai (Black BDT) and Sgt Wimoto.

June 25 1943, Glodok Jail, Batavia

Violation: All of the sick were compelled to leave hospital and stand (or collapse) on the camp parade ground. The scene was reinforced by machine guns and armed guards. Reason: One of the Japanese guards had found evidence of food being passed to two British officers who had been placed in the 'cooler'.

POW deaths in captivity recorded by RW and mostly referring to his old gun battery 239

Died at Priok and Batavia up until August 1943

Gnrs Hawkins and Thompson died very early on

Gnr L.W. Bricknell	239 Battery
Gnr C. Cook	239 Battery
Gnr Gibson	239 Battery
Gnr R.E.J. Norris	239 Battery
Gnr A. Owen	239 Battery
Gnr Pead	239 Battery
Gnr Plant	239 Battery
Gnr Tiffin	239 Battery
Gnr L.G. Smith	239 Battery
Gnr Sullivan	239 Battery
L Bdr A. Evans	239 Battery
Sgt L. Pugh	240 Battery
Sgt S. Street	240 Battery

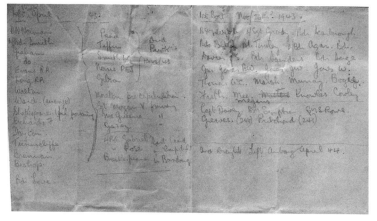

Part of a list kept by Ronald Williams on a secret scrap of paper, detailing the names of men from the 77th lost on prisoner labour drafts.

Died on Ambon or at sea; transfer of prisoners on the **Amagi Maru** to Ambon on 17 April 1943

Gunners (239 Battery):

Gnr B.N. Norman

Gnr R. Evans

Gnr E. Graham

Gnr G. Graham

Gnr M. Kennedy

Gnr R. Long

Gnr Walton

Gnr Ward (by aircraft)

Gnr F. Richards

Gnr Dayton

Gnr Tunnicliff

Gnr Brennan

Gnr Bishop

L/Bdr Shakespeare (fish poisoning)

L/Bdr J. Smith

Bdr Love

Majs L.N. Gibson and Mossford had left with this transfer of prisoners.

Lost on first transfer of prisoners returning from Ambon to Java (**Suez Maru** sunk on 29 November 1943)

Gunners (239 Battery):

Gnr L.J. Bailey

Gnr N.F. Baxter

Gnr J.W. Bogie

Gnr D.G. Coleman

Gnr T. Conley

Gnr J.S. Davies

Gnr J. Frith

Gnr B.W. Jones

Gnr J.W. Jones

Gnr W.J Jones

Gnr W. Garner

Gnr Hadley

Gnr W.R. Knowles

Gnr J.H. Lloyd

Gnr J.H. Marsh

Gnr J. Mee

Gnr R.P. Medway

Gnr D.T. Megins

Gnr H. Milner

Gnr A. Morrow
Gnr H. Mosely
Gnr J. Murray
Gnr J. Pike
Gnr I.A. Pope
Gnr R.C. Robertson
Gnr F. Robinson
Gnr Ronson
Gnr E.J. Stone
Gnr W.C. Thomas
Gnr H. Tucker
Gnr M.W. Wardell

Other ranks (239 Battery):
L/Bdr Agar
L/Bdr H. Guest
Bdr W.J. Whitman
Bdr W.H. Butler
Bdr J.S. Davies
Bdr C.W. Tinsley
Bdr H.T. Scarborough
Bdr N.E. Saunders
Bdr N.W. Sage
L/Sgt (Lance Sergeant) M.E. Grady
BSM Webb

Other Batteries: Gnrs G. Dawson, A. Hadley, L/Bdr J.T. Greaves, Bombardier (Bdr) K. Beard all from 240 and Gnr F.J. Pritchard, GMS R.H. Rowe, and BSM E. Sumption all from 241 Bty.

Officer: Capt. Harold Davey
Tragically, virtually the whole of the editorial team and many contributors to *The Jungle Journal* were lost in this unfortunate sinking of the *Suez Maru* by the submarine USS *Bonefish*.

A Johnston left Java for Malaya on 27 June 1944

Lost at sea, second transfer of prisoners (left on 7 August 1944)
Gnr Noakes
Gnr Elmes
Gnr DJ Evans
Gnr Norris,
Bdr Jenkins
Bdr DH Morgan, (all 239 Battery)

Survivors from Camp Eight, Fukuoka, Japan, 1945, who had been working in coal mines. Many had been drafted from Java and were members or associates of the 77th Royal Artillery Regiment.

Died in Java on return
Sgt G.W. Ball 239 Battery, drowned late 1944
L/Bdr T.J. Roberts 239 Battery, died Batavia, Oct 1944
Gnr H. Clare. 239 Battery

Capt. John W. Goronwy and Flt Lt J. Dawson, left on a draft of medics, by prison ship, from Bicycle camp on 14 May 1944; sunk and lost off Nagasaki in late May.

[*These deaths were recorded by Ronald in a notebook completed after the war. (Tony Paley, in his book,* The Sparrows, *has an almost complete listing of prisoners of the 77th who died in captivity, excluding officers.) There are no exact records of the numbers of men killed in action or during captivity, but it is estimated that nearly 400 men of the 77th lost their lives in these two ways. This was over a third of the regiment's total number of men who left for the Far East.*]

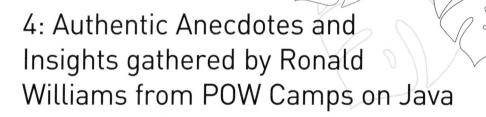

4: Authentic Anecdotes and Insights gathered by Ronald Williams from POW Camps on Java

A Promise Postponed

In 1942 the POW camp Tandjong Priok was divided into a number of sub-camps, and in one of these sub-camps, a number of men, of the 3rd Royal King's Own Hussars Regiment, were accommodated. One of the 'better type' Jap guards (if that is at all possible to state) had adopted them.

This guard did go out of his way to be helpful and was frequently the Hussars' escort on working parties outside the camp. When they returned in the evening, he was quite unperturbed when the Hussars drove any animals – goats, sheep etc. – which had strayed from a nearby native kampong, through the gates into the camp. Later, these strays would be slaughtered, cooked and eaten, to help down the unpalatable rice. The guard would also actively encourage the POWs to catch any fowl that had wandered from their runs.

One evening, the returning working party came across a cow grazing by the road-side. They pointed this out to the guard, who nodded approval and they drove the cow to the camp gates. Duty guards emerged from the guardhouse and after discussion with the work party escort, they insisted that one of the men go in to the camp to find a paintbrush and paint. On return, the prisoner was ordered to paint on the side of the cow, 'This animal belongs to the 3rd King's Own Hussars'. When he had done so, the guards said that he must let the cow go but it would be theirs (the Hussars') for keeps, after the war was over! Many a whetted prisoner appetite was left ruined.

A Misunderstanding

How we used to hate to *keirei*, which is bowing and saluting, to the Japanese! On every occasion a Jap came in our direction we had to bow – or else! What would happen if we refused to bow? Well, there were the cells, beatings, torture, starvation, and if you survived that lot – decapitation! Nevertheless, one tried to avoid bowing as much as possible.

On one occasion, a Jap guard appeared in our sub-camp in Priok; all the lads felt that they could not get away without the *keirei* with this particular guard and performed the necessary salutation, with the exception of one gunner, who was lying half-asleep on the veranda, keeping an eye on his kit drying in the sun, and who failed to jump to attention. The enraged guard cracked his rifle butt against the side of the poor man's skull.

From some distance, the prisoner's sergeant major could see that the man was in for a fearful beating and raced over to intervene. He attracted the guard's attention and pointed to the prisoner's ears to convey that the prisoner was deaf. A large grin spread over the face of the Jap guard, who gently placed his gun against the veranda and stood behind the prisoner, grabbed both his ears and proceeded to bellow in incomprehensible Japanese into both, while looking at the sergeant major for his approbation. Fortunately, 'ringing in the ears' was the prisoner's only punishment!

He, Who Laughs Last, Laughs Longest!

At Boei Glodok (*boei* is Malay for jail) in Batavia, most of the officers were accommodated in small compounds, consisting of a bit of ground to grow vegetables, and six small cells, in which three persons could live comfortably by Jap prison standards. I was in a cell with AJ (Alec Jardine, a Canadian) and Doc G. (Goronwy). Near our cell were three cells occupied by Aussies. They were great big chaps, with one, JF ('Jack' Frost), a Tasmanian sheep farmer, being at least 6ft 6in tall.

Now Doc G. (RAMC) was a mischievous little Welshman from Pontypridd who was never averse to playing tricks on people. The Aussies were much the same and they and the Doc vied for the most outrageous trick to be played on each other.

One time the good Doc was in arrears and he was just waiting for the right opportunity to play a wicked trick on the Aussies. Fortune would have it that the Japs had suddenly become inoculation mad and sent all kinds of anti-this and anti-that to be stuck into us POWs. We were lined up almost daily for injections. On one occasion, an odd type of serum arrived and our MOs (medical officers) decided that they did not like the look of it.

However, the Japs always made sure that whatever was supposed to be inoculated was given. Our MOs poured the serum away, and we were ordered to attend for our 'mock' injections. We lined up in the usual way, in the sick bay, and the MO pretended to inject us with sterile water. If a Jap guard became too inquisitive, the poor POW being inoculated would receive the full shot of sterile water.

Doc had noticed that the Aussies had not turned up for this 'mock' injection parade. He thought that this was an opportunity to get his own back. He enlisted the services of four MOs to carry trays with the usual injection paraphernalia, and headed off to the Aussies' quarters. Most of the Aussies were together when the Doc and his retinue arrived. The Doc apologized but stated that the Nips had noticed that some of the men were absent. He was ordered to go and find them and give them the proper injection. They readily agreed, not wishing to offend the good doctor, and he proceeded to inject them all with sterile water, but only after dipping the needle into strong surgical spirit. The air was blue and the Aussies, to a man, said that the injection felt worse than being shot. The Doc told them that it was a life-saving injection.

By chance, a few days later, the Aussies had been chatting to one of the less intellectual of British gunners about their experience with the injections, and the gunner said that this was odd as the Doc had only pretended to inject him! I returned that day to find the Doc minus his eyebrows and half his head shaved.

The Joke is on the Doc?

In the early days, whilst there was still some semblance of normality, meal times could be amusing. Doc G. was very keen on his food but equally fussy about whom he sat with at meal times. On one particular evening, a group of five, two from the 77th (including myself) and the three Aussies, were keeping a seat for the Doc at our table. We had supplied his place with a knife and fork, which would fall apart on use, and a mug with no handle and a hole at the bottom.

The stage was set, but where was the Doc? The CO came in and was preparing to sit at our table when he noticed some strangers a little further down the hut and enquired who they were. On being informed, he hesitated, sat down at our table but then promptly changed his mind and went to sit with the strangers. We breathed a massive sigh of relief because the CO would not have appreciated our antics.

Still no sign of the Doc! Next, the Unit Dental Officer went to sit at our table but we told him the place was reserved and he carried on. Following on came the second-in-command and we said the Doc was sitting at our table and he passed on.

Now the Doc was usually very prompt at meal times, and we began to be concerned that some misdemeanour had befallen him. Perhaps he was ill? We would surely have heard if the Doc was ill. Perhaps he had been detained by an irate camp guard? At last, he appeared and was dashing toward our table, when he halted abruptly at another table and proceeded to talk to the occupants. We called to him, to remind him that we had a place reserved at our table. After a few minutes, the Doc came over to our table and was preparing to sit down when, to our surprise and annoyance, he said that he had better sit with the CO to talk over a few matters, and promptly left.

Our schoolboy prank had come to nought! However, the Doc, who seemed to have prescient insight when it came to practical jokes, would be caught again. We vowed to persevere and think up a more elaborate trick for the next occasion.

Surrender Against the Odds

A small, and inadequate, Australian force (2/40th Battalion) had been sent to Timor to defend the island against the Japanese. The first attack came from Jap paratroopers, who had descended, like 'gorillas', out of the sky. The Australians were well positioned for this type of attack and wiped out most of the enemy paratrooper force. However, the Japanese then landed battle-hardened troops and light tanks which gradually over-powered the Australians.

The Aussies fought heroically for three days and nights, with little sleep or food and low on ammunition, until a Japanese tank squadron broke through into their jungle position, the leading enemy tank bearing a white flag. A Japanese officer descended from the tank, with an interpreter, and approached the Australian position. A group of Aussie officers led by Lt Col Leggatt, including their own interpreter, Capt. Terry East, met the Japanese advance party.

The Japanese officer commenced jabbering in unintelligible Japanese, in a very excited manner. The only word East recognised was 'surrender'. Eventually, in frustration, he said, in Japanese, to the Japanese commander, 'You want to surrender?'

'Yes! Yes!' replied the Jap officer.

'Then hand me your sword,' retorted East.

At this the Jap officer jumped almost six feet in the air, shouting, 'No! No! No! You must surrender!' and so it was decided.

The 'Brigadier'

There was confusion about some of the Dutch military rankings. When the Aussies arrived on Timor to assist in the defence of the island, the senior Aussie officer was in discussion with his Dutch counterpart about troop deployment. The Dutch commander said that he had four brigades locally. The Aussie commander looked at him in astonishment and asked, 'Why have we [*the Australians*] been asked to reinforce the island, if it already has so many Dutch troops on it?'

The Dutch commander looked most offended, and informed the Aussie that a Dutch brigade was only twenty men, under an NCO called a brigadier!

English as She is Spoke

At Bicycle camp there was a large separate barracks for new POW arrivals, who were kept in isolation. This was mainly to stop the rest of us getting up-to-date news about what was going on in the outside world. The Japs were unaware how much information was getting through, particularly from secret radio sets; the operators, who maintained a very tight system of cascading information to other prisoners, cleverly disguised these sets. Some camps were better equipped with radios than others were.

One time, a group of recently captured British Indians arrived in the over-crowded isolation barracks. Twice a day the Japanese made a head count of prisoners on *tenko* and the assembled prisoners had to '*bango*'; that is, number off in the usual military fashion, but in Japanese. The Jap commander of the isolation area was prepared for newcomers to use their own language until Japanese numbering had been learned. He had reasonable understanding of English numbering himself. The Indians commenced numbering off and things were going well until a group of Indians with limited English, well down the line, were reached. Numbering went 'thirty-eight, thirty-nine, thirty-ten, thirty-eleven,' etc. The Japanese commander was not amused and thought that these Indians were deliberately insulting his intelligence. The Indians learned Japanese numbering very quickly after that!

No Escape Clause, 1941

Around July/August 1941, Allied POWs were all compelled to sign a 'no escape' clause, which for us on Java was probably inconsequential as escape was almost impossible. However, on mainland Malaya, Burma and Siam, the opportunities for escape were more realistic and resistance to signing this oath of good behaviour was very determined. The signed oath was to obey <u>all</u> orders of *Dai Nippon (teikoku riku) Gun*, including no attempt to escape.

In August 1941, Col Fukue (appropriate name!), Japanese commander of prison camps in Singapore, insisted that all Allied POWs, of all ranks, must comply with the individual signing of the 'no escape' clause. Every man refused to sign. As a result, all Allied POWs were taken to Selarang barracks square, Changi, in Singapore, where 16,000 men were squeezed into barracks fit to house 850 men.

The men were herded every day, for four days, to the camp parade ground, by guards with fixed bayonets, and covered by machine gunners. Finally, with Japanese patience running out, they made all sick POWs join the daily parade. They executed some prisoners on the pretext that they had tried to escape, but everyone knew this was untrue. Eventually all POWs signed the oath but indicated that this declaration was signed under duress and, therefore, invalid. The POWs returned to their own camps on 6 September. [*The Japanese officers responsible for this action were sentenced to death in 1946 by the War Crimes' Commission.*]

An Eye for an Eye?

In Java many natives are Hindu-animistic and the waringin (banyan) is considered a holy tree. If it is ever necessary to cut down or severely prune these trees, a special ceremony needs to take place, performed by the local holy man to appease the spirit of the tree.

We had one of these waringin trees in the central compound at Boei Glodock and the Japanese commander, Yamamoto, gave orders for the tree to be severely pruned. At that particular time I was working in the spinning factory and watched this activity unfolding. Knowing something of Javanese legends, I flippantly remarked that Yamamoto was taking a big risk chopping off big limbs from this tree, without bringing in the holy man.

About a year later, when I was at another camp in west Java, news came through that Yamamoto had been involved in a serious road accident and had lost one of his legs! This was definitely a case of a 'limb for a limb'.

There is One Born Every Minute

The following conversation took place on the island of Ambon, where prisoners were forced to build aerodromes and runways. A Japanese army driver, who had been brought up in the USA, was driving a British POW to pick up supplies. The Jap spoke perfect English with an American accent and the conversation eventually worked its way around to the war. At that moment, they passed a group of Japanese soldiers resting at the side of the road. The POW asked 'Who do you think will win this war?' The Japanese-Yankie driver retorted, pointing in the direction of the resting Jap soldiers, 'Those suckers think they will!' and gave the POW a big grin.

Fair Play

In a camp in Batavia, the prisoners were of mixed nationalities, including many Dutchmen in their sixties and seventies, who had been members of the Destruction Corps. They had helped to destroy anything deemed useful to the enemy immediately prior to the Japanese invasion.

The elderly Dutch did not fare well in the harsh prison conditions and many of them died. A senior Japanese medic visited the camp one day and, after inspecting the conditions and the camp records, demanded to see the senior Dutch, Australian and British officers and MOs. He gave them a severe dressing down, describing the deaths of the elderly Dutch as scandalous.

However, he was not so much outraged by the deaths themselves but that the British, Australian and younger Dutchmen should take their turn in dying! He hoped that, on the next occasion he visited, the deaths would have equalised.

Down on the Farm

This is a true story, which gives the reader an insight into the incomprehensible workings of the minds of some of our camp guards.

At the Bandoeng camp a Japanese guard had in his charge a number of ducks and pigs in a pen. The ducks dutifully laid eggs and the sow delivered nine piglets for Japanese consumption only. Over a period of time, the egg production reduced and some of the piglets disappeared. One day, the irate guard was observed muttering to the animals and threatening them with his bamboo stick. Things did not improve and eventually he lost his marbles and went in the pen bashing all before him. The survivors had food and water stopped for three days. Needless to say, the little farm did not last much longer and, unfortunately, the prisoners lost their supply of extra foods.

No Exit

One of the first animals that caught our attention when we arrived in Java was the little lizards called tjit-tjak or chichak. These were seen scampering across walls and ceilings in most buildings and were especially prominent against light fittings at night. They were harmless and were actually encouraged because they fed on all kinds of insects, including the dreaded mosquito.

There were also larger lizards called tokas, because they repeated the call 'tokay' many times. There was a superstition in Java that a tokas that croaked seven or twelve times would bring good luck. I did hear one croak thirteen times, but this was exceptional. A friend told me that he was in a nightclub in Soerabaja, before the Japanese invasion, when a tokas suddenly started up; the whole place went very quiet and there was a great cheer when it stopped at seven. Many thought that this was a sign that the Japanese invasion of Java would not take place.

I also heard a story of a British colonel, who had gone up country from Batavia, writing to complain that he was woken most nights by these wretched croaking things. His CO wrote back, stating that if he kept counting the number of croaks, he would soon fall asleep.

However, my story relates to a good friend, Ken Taylor. We had not been prisoners for very long and it was still possible to obtain little luxuries. Ken sold some articles of clothing to buy a tin of condensed milk and that evening he decided jubilantly to have some milk with his tea. He bored a small hole in the top of the tin and poured a small amount into his tea mug, then placed the tin on a high shelf so that ground bugs would not be attracted.

In the morning, after polishing off a meagre portion of disgusting-looking rice, Ken grabbed the condensed milk for its second outing into a mug of tea. He tipped the can but nothing came out! He shook the can, muttering that it still felt full, but after several unsuccessful attempts at pouring milk decided to open the top of the can. To his dismay he found two half drowned and bloated tjit-tjaks inside the can. He had not thought that these creatures could possibly squeeze through such a small opening. They probably would have got out again if they had not been so greedy.

Radio Broadcasts

The Japanese allowed the names of surviving Allied POWs (six to ten at a time) to be broadcast as a gesture of good will to the IRCC (International Red Cross Committee). Japanese radio technicians would visit the camps and record selected POWs for radio broadcast. Officers were most likely to be chosen for these broadcasts. The recording would be limited to no more than a minute and a half, supervised by the camp interpreter and a camp guard. These broadcasts started in March 1943 on Java. Prisoner broadcasts were received on public radios in the southern hemisphere, particularly Australia, New Zealand, and South Africa. [*Surprisingly the IRCC did not have Ronald listed as missing and initially doubted the radio message's authenticity! Only sporadic news came through from Ronald after this broadcast, until the Japanese surrender in August, 1945.*]

Camp Sport and Entertainment

In the early days of captivity we were generally physically fit; certainly fit enough to play games of 'rugger' and football. Such games as 'Officers versus the Sergeants' and 'Army versus the RAF' would take place. Whilst we were playing a game of rugby, refereed by Welsh rugby international Wilf Wooller, I asked a group of diggers (Aussies), at half time, what they thought of the game so far?

'Awe, I dun-no sport,' said one of them in a very derogatory tone. 'It seems to be all whistles and 'arse-up' to us!'

It is interesting to note that after the war both the Japanese and the Australians took to rugby and football like ducks to water.

Camp entertainment was very varied, and depended on the talents of the prisoners. There was the inevitable good musician around who could sing and play a musical instrument, when available. The Dutch were good at organising the 'concert party' with either a band playing or multiple acts. Even a Shakespeare theatre group was formed, who put on several of the Bard's great works, and very good performances they were too.

The Americans were good entertainers, particularly with harmonica and guitar and the Australians had raw humour which kept us amused on many occasions.

Of course, with the beginning of drafts and mass ill health, the will and spirit to put on entertainment became seriously muted. [*The chapter on* The Jungle Journal *will expand on matters of camp sport and entertainment.*]

Escape

One of my Welsh brothers-in-law asked me after the war why I had not tried to escape from Java and I replied, 'Java was an island, surrounded by shark-infested waters, under military occupation and miles away from anywhere. We were white skinned and hardly inconspicuous. No POW who tried to escape ever lived to tell the tale.' Locals would also be given cash rewards by the Japanese for reporting any escape attempts or the whereabouts of escapees. Escapees were usually shot or beheaded. (In fact, soon after capture, in my first POW camp, several RAF personnel were summarily executed for attempting to escape in a Japanese plane.) There were also serious reprisals against any remaining POWs from the same camp enclosure as the escaped prisoners. This proved a major deterrent against escape attempts.

There were rumours that some men survived in the jungle, under the protection of friendly Javanese, until the end of the war. This has never been confirmed.

Propaganda generated for the Japanese media depicting Christmas dinner at UBE camp, Japan. The food and drink (the bottles were empty) were taken away after the photographs were taken. The Japanese photographer took over three hours and the food was not to be eaten. The men sang 'There will always be an England' with much gusto. The Japanese demanded a translation and, according to Lt Cecil West of the 77th, 'were pretty pissed off when they got one'. (Lt Cecil West)

Christmas Review at UBE camp, Japan in 1944. The fittest POWs were used for this propaganda photograph. (Lt Cecil West)

Japanese Propaganda

The Japanese were great at propaganda. They would take a party of officer-prisoners to a local golf club and take pictures of the prisoners playing golf; then the officers would sit down to a splendid meal that would be whisked away uneaten as soon as photographs had been taken. Similarly, they would take prisoners to the local newspaper offices to show prisoners producing their own newspaper, and prisoners would be photographed fishing and swimming in the sea.

Photographs also went into Japanese newspapers showing Allied prisoners having life-saving surgery from top Japanese surgeons – these were all fakes. A very attractive and immaculately dressed Japanese female nurse met one of our lads, who had broken his leg, in the sick bay and gave him a large glass of milk. A photographer appeared and took a snap and then the nurse and the milk disappeared in a flash. The poor chap was left to drag himself back to his mates untreated.

On another occasion, a number of us were marched off to attend a so called 'memorial' service to our war dead. When we arrived at our destination in a field behind the Catholic hospital, which was now a Japanese guardroom, we came across a huge white cross. From a distance it looked like stone but close up we could see it was made from tea chests. On its base was inscribed, 'Lest we forget'. Most of us muttered under our breath, 'We won't, you can count on that!'

We were formed up in neat lines in front of this abomination, then some smartly dressed Japanese soldiers formed up in front of the cross, bowed their heads and lowered their guns in a deferential manner. Japanese officers saluted, and then followed a multitude of clicking and flashing cameras recording this event, with Japanese journalists also taking copious notes. Then we were marched back to camp.

A 'memorial' service on Java with Japanese officers in the background. This was another propaganda exercise which disgusted many of the POWs present.

We were ashamed to be part of this charade. On return to the camp, we were instructed to write down our impressions of this special event laid on by the Japanese Imperial Army. Most of us wrote down one-liners, such as, 'Thank you Imperial Japanese Army for mocking our war dead.' Surprisingly, there were no repercussions regarding these expressions of disgust. [*A similar episode was described by Gp Capt. Noble in Lord Russell's,* The Knights of the Bushido.]

Some commentators have stated that the Japanese military behaved in a brutal way because 'Bushido' stated that a soldier who allowed himself to be captured by the enemy was worth nothing and deserved total contempt from family and State. Why then did they try so very hard to cover up their vile behaviour through outrageous propaganda?

Having unwillingly assisted in propaganda work, we had no illusions when reading Japanese newspapers and magazines. I remember being nauseated by a propaganda magazine, which contained numerous pictures of Japanese soldiers showing affection and devotion to animals, particularly dogs. It was quite absurd because we knew, as

POWs, that the Japanese, almost without exception, would show extreme cruelty to dumb animals; so much so that we considered animal baiting and cruelty to be a regular pastime of the Jap military. Whether it was solely to offend us British, knowing that we loved animals, especially dogs, we could never fathom out.

George and Others

Animal atrocity stories came from every quarter where the Japanese had been. These are but a few examples of their cruelty. One dog, suspected of carrying messages outside the camp, was tied between two posts outside the guardroom, where it could not move, eat or drink, and was kicked by all the passing Nip guards until it died. Another dog was caught by guards and was slowly hacked to death for no apparent reason. Jennie, a harmless lovely big black and white bitch, whilst passing the Nip cookhouse, had a pan of boiling water chucked over her, leaving her with terrible scalds.

Then there was Pete, a dog that came into the camp following a small draft of men. Pete was most welcome, as we had been dog-less for several months following a Jap purge. Unfortunately, he was scratching so much that several of us grabbed him and gave him a good wash. He forsook our friendship after that, probably fearing another washing! Pete readily accepted the other men, who had not been involved with this cleansing act. He was no trouble but, whilst following a work party of men through Batavia, one of the guards took exception to his presence and ran him through with his bayonet. I can still hear the poor dog's pitiful cries whilst he lay dying.

Another typical story concerns one of the camp cats, who was caught taking the entrails of a gutted fish from the cookhouse. The punishment was one eye cut out and her lips cut off. Monkeys came in for similar treatment if caught.

Here I would like to pay tribute to one camp dog, George, who behaved as if a typical English master's dog and hence the name. In fact, when we threw the last shovelful of earth onto his final resting place, I was moved to tears and vowed vengeance against the perpetrators of his demise. He was only a mongrel, of a typical mixed kampong breed, but he quickly attached himself to us POWs and clearly showed as much hatred towards our captors as we tried to.

'George, a favourite POW camp dog'. Illustration by Charles Holdsworth.

We could picture him parading around the camp dressed in a Union Jack, and being very proud of the honour. We did fear for his future because he challenged Jap guards with a stare and the occasional growl. We would have been goners for similar behaviour. Our men tried very hard to stop George having confrontations with the Japanese military but it was, generally, to no avail.

Behind the Japanese barracks, in Priok, was a large field mainly used for storing heavy petrol drums and timber. It was from here that George emerged one day as a pup. POWs who were part of a working party, loading some of these petrol drums onto lorries can remember him frolicking around with his mum and siblings.

Then the usual Jap fun started, with soldiers catching and kicking the young pups into the air. One of our boys at the end of the work party managed to catch a limping and bleeding George and conceal him under his clothing. Thus, George was adopted and taken back to the camp, where he was presented to Wilf Wooller.

Wilf knew a thing or two about training pups. This was the first time we had such a young dog in the camp. The young pup was full of tricks and kept us all amused. He lay down in a most curious position; the Docs suspected this to be the result of a dislocated hip from the guards' kicking. This is probably why he showed his resentment towards the guards from the beginning. He would annoy them and avoid their kicks and stoning.

One day a Nip guard ordered us to take George to the guardroom for inspection. We knew this would be for his disposal, so we pretended that George had run off. Fortunately, the guard seemed to forget about his command. Soon after, we were moved to another camp and smuggled George along with us.

George continued to grow, and this camp had plenty of other dogs around and many trees. He was very happy. When we were on parade, we could watch George and the other dogs having a right good 'mess-around'. George was becoming the 'king of the castle' over the other dogs as gradually he defeated all the aggressive dogs in typical dogfight fashion, and beared the scars to prove it.

We moved on again to a native jail, taking George with us. It was much harder to control George's natural instincts in this camp. The living accommodation was cramped and the guards were much closer at hand. George resented their presence and would have bitten them, if given half a chance.

There were companions for George – Jennie, a black bitch, a smooth haired mongrel, whose name escapes me, and a small dachshund looked after by the inimitable RAF pilot officer Paddy Creegan, a mad but loveable Irishman. The dogs were great fun; they kept us amused and raised our spirits. George's prone posture was becoming more eccentric and we were all amazed that he could be so agile when up and about.

George had a great liking for shaving soap; he would always seek out the man having a shave and enjoyed nothing better than to have a handful of shaving soap placed on his nose.

One evening there was an announcement that 'High Nippon' officers were coming to inspect the camp. The camp interpreter announced that any dog that interfered with this inspection, in any way, would be killed. This placed us in a dilemma, as we could not be with George whilst the inspection took place and he was almost certain to make a nuisance of himself. With great relief, we learned that one of the working parties would not be involved in the inspection. George was cleverly secreted out of the camp the following morning.

However, George was not too far away; in fact, on the other side of the high wall with a garden working party. The inspection began with the Japanese officers strutting around in an inscrutable manner moving from cell to cell, barrack to barrack and then to the factory. As they passed our group, we stood impassively to attention. Our minds were thinking evil thoughts but we were now well used to disguising our inner emotions. The guards accused us often of having no inner feelings. If only they knew what we were thinking about!

Eventually the Japanese procession reached the cookhouse. As they walked through, they were interrupted by a horrendous animal noise; the like of which we had never heard before, which visibly disturbed the Japanese officers. They carried on, not to appear perturbed, and disappeared from sight. Yes, it had been George, who must have sensed the presence of these 'High ranking Nips'.

Unfortunately, some of the guards suspected that George had been the culprit and later stoned him whenever he appeared near them. Amazingly, George managed to avoid significant injury including bayonet thrusts because of his keen sense of survival.

There was one Korean guard, the only Korean to show any flicker of humanity in the time I was on Java, who came to warn us that some of the other guards were planning an horrific demise for George the very next day, so we discussed the options and decided that we should humanely put down George. We knew the alternative of trying to encourage him to escape would end in failure. He was so loyal that he would return, almost certainly, to meet his fate, which would be a slow and lingering one if meted out by the guards.

Doc Goronwy managed to obtain some morphine, sufficient to kill a grown man, and injected George. He did not die for ages, although unconscious. One of the men eventually could not stand it any longer and bashed George over the head with a blunt object. We buried George the next day with almost full military honours.

I thought that he had been such a brilliant inspiration to the POWs that I went back, on POW release, to find his grave which was covered with pretty flowers (poor man's roses). [*There are many anecdotal stories of POWs eating dog meat, with dogs' chances of survival in POW camps being very low! This was clearly not the case with George.*]

Ode to George

When we buried him beneath that burning tropic sun,
And the hot soil fell upon his morphine-stricken limbs.
Bitterly, with tears, I swore that e'er my day was done
I'd tell the world about him and his deeds.
An outcast from the kampong, nought but mongrel dog was he,
Yet he had the strains of hunting dogs that in the Java
Jungles of the south, savage Steen breed fearlessly;
'George' we called him, and we loved the brute.

Almost De-'Livered'

A working party of Dutchmen went, from Bicycle camp to work at a local Japanese barracks. One of the Dutch junior army officers had the job of supervising a small party of fellow prisoners in the cookhouse, where he managed to pilfer or 'liberate' a piece of liver and conceal it under his hat.

On returning to the camp, the prisoners paraded as usual in front of the guardhouse, to be counted. For some reason the head 'hancho' (guard commander) took exception to the junior Dutch officer and clouted him several times across the face; perhaps the Dutch officer had a smirk on his face because of what he was concealing under his hat? The force of the blow to the officer's face dislodged the liver and it started to weep blood! Red juice proceeded to run down the forehead and face of the Dutchman.

The 'hancho' looked shocked and rapidly became penitent when he had seen what he had done. (At this time only Japanese officers were allowed to strike Allied officers across the face.) The 'hancho' insisted that he take the 'wounded' Dutchman straight to the sickroom. The Dutchman equally insisted that he was all right and that he would have to report the incident to his senior officer if he were to be taken to the sickroom. Fortunately, the Japanese never discovered the truth of the 'bleeding' forehead, or the fat would have been well and truly in the fire!

Come Rain or Shine ...

There was one Japanese guard in Boei Glodok camp who was a funny little fellow, and relatively harmless, who behaved a bit like Dopey from the Seven Dwarfs. At Boei Glodock we had to spin cord from sisal, to be woven into rice bags. 'Dopey' was an ineffective guard and allowed poor-quality cord to be made. There were regular beatings from the 'hancho' for both 'Dopey', and us, for this act of defiance. We were not too bothered, as we realised that our lack of effort did not really undermine the Japanese war campaign and so they were unlikely to behead anyone for their lack of effort. We did agree though that if we had the chance we would make extra strong string to hang the blighters when the war ended.

One day, two of our junior officers, who were supposed to be encouraging the men to produce better string, absented themselves from the factory. For this act, they were thrown into the cells on short rations. Sometime during the afternoon, someone dropped bananas through the cell opening. The skins were not properly buried and one of the more obnoxious camp guards discovered them. We were all called out on parade in the middle of our evening meal. These sudden parades usually spelt trouble. (We gave the sobriquet 'yella-fever' time to these sudden parades, because there would inevitably be a great deal of yelling, and at a fever pitch, from our Japanese 'friends'!)

When we arrived on the parade ground grumbling, fixed bayonets and light machine guns confronted us. This was a bit 'heavier' than usual and we expected some really bad news. Yamamoto, the camp commander, appeared and ordered everyone from the sick bay to be paraded as well. Reluctantly, they were brought out and, as expected, many patients collapsed to the ground.

Then the interpreter, Kanamoto, alias 'Rudolph', because of his long sideburns, took centre stage. Rudolph was quite insane, but very proud of his command of English. (He would go around the camp asking POWs how they were coping without women and what they did to alleviate sex problems. Some men told him 'tall' stories wondering whether he would go and try out some of these methods on himself!) Kanamoto addressed us: 'Unless the one of you who passed bananas to prisoners in cell make full confession; ALL men will stop on parade one month, two month, I repeat, one month, two month … rain or shine!'

Luckily, this bad situation was eventually resolved and we did not have to stay on parade for one or two months … rain or shine. Kanamoto was obviously impressed with his little speech and 'rain or shine' became his watchword for many a day. [*Les Spence in his book,* From Java to Nagasaki (*edited by Greg Lewis), records that the 'Banana Incident' occurred at Boei Glodok on Friday 25 June 1943. He records also that a number of Allied officers were badly beaten up by the Japanese.*]

Who is There?

Before paper and pencils were unobtainable in POW camps, we managed to produce a number of camp magazines. One of the regular columns was entitled 'Was my face red!' in which contributors would write about any embarrassing experiences encountered since they had been at war. I was too embarrassed to submit the one I am about to relate.

When I was younger, I had looked at spiritualism, because I thought that there was something in it, but I lost interest in the subject. However, in the prison camps, my interest was rekindled and I managed to find a book on this subject. I was trying to discover if we could communicate with our folks back home through a medium.

One night I managed a long read on spiritualism and felt quite upbeat about succeeding in my quest. I retired under my mosquito net and went to sleep. My bed, apparently moving, suddenly awakened me. This was very odd as there was no one else in the vicinity in my room. My heart leapt into my mouth and I thought honestly that I had awoken some spirit through my reading. The bed moved again and I asked, 'Who is there?' There was no reply. Then the bed really did move and I shot out of it like quicksilver. I could hear a commotion across the camp and shouting from the local native kampong. Outside it was apparent that we had suffered an earthquake. This event shattered my faith in spiritualism.

Little Green Shoot

I had been very ill with 'blackwater fever' (malaria) but was, fortunately, helped through this illness by Wilf Wooller and my Aussie friends, particularly George Gunn.

On one of my rehabilitation walks, George and I spotted a green shoot, which we kept quiet about, thinking that it would be a worthwhile plant to eat at some stage. We watched it and nurtured it, with dilute urine, for a number of weeks and eventually, to our huge disappointment, it grew in to an inedible loofah!

Lt Sonei

Sonei, alias 'Sunnyboy', was a nasty camp commander, but some of his actions occasionally amused us. He had a caged pet monkey which had seriously displeased him on one particular occasion. Sonei decided to cut one of the ropes which operated the monkey's swing. The monkey seemed to prefer this change and played up even more! Sonei was enraged, but could not see a way to stop the monkey's irritating antics. Fortunately, the monkey was not summarily despatched; this was Sonei's preferred method for dealing with delinquent behaviour.

Sonei was quite proud of his increasing ability to speak English. One day he was overheard berating some of his guards, thus, 'Now men, you must do as your good commander tells you and be very good boys.' This was quite laughable coming from a man like Sonei.

Sonei was executed by a Dutch firing squad on Java. His death sentence resulted from his treatment of internees in the Tjideng women's camp. His level of nastiness, and the numbers of atrocities committed, had increased since his transfer from Bicycle camp to Tjideng. Dutch women nicknamed him 'Syphilitic' Sonei as they were convinced that venereal disease had made him insane. It was rumoured that some of Sonei's body organs were removed and used for medical student teaching back in Holland.

Camp Specimen Orders

POW camps had their own individual specimen orders, depending on the camp commandant's preferences, as well as general orders. For example, no POW was permitted to grow a beard bigger and longer than Col Anami's. Other orders were:

No whistling or singing permitted
Bow to Japanese soldiers at all times
POWs congregating in groups of more than five are banned
No religious services, unless supervised by a Japanese officer
No prayers for an Allied victory
Learn Japanese commands and numbering
No escaping – on penalty of death!

[*The Japanese were fearful of POW revolts. At times, it would have been possible to overpower the immediate guards, but a major camp breakout on Java would have been fraught with problems, which have been alluded to elsewhere.*]

Japanese Hell Ships

Many POWs suffered from the indescribable horrors of the transport 'hell' ships. Not only were the conditions on board horrific, but there was the ever-present threat of sinking from bombs or torpedoes from Allied planes and submarines.

One typical story that came back with the survivors of one 'hell' ship, which returned to Java, regarded the death of a young RAF corporal. A drunken Japanese sergeant went berserk and, for no particular reason, detailed his men to strip the poor young man and beat him with iron bars. Amazingly, the young man was still alive after this vicious beating. The Japanese sergeant then coolly and callously beheaded the RAF man. Fellow POWs were forced to witness this barbaric act.

Camp Bibles

We were all issued with Bibles before going overseas. I received mine, a small New Testament version, on the 2 December 1941, through the Bible Society (The Naval and Military Bible Society of Scotland). The inscription inside the cover read, 'Be strong and of good courage, for the Lord thy God is with thee whither-so ever though goest'. This did not mean a lot to me at the time but became more meaningful after the war.

Bibles were not always treated with reverence in captivity and pages were sometimes used to roll cigarettes as they made great 'fag-paper'. I was not particularly religious during my time in captivity although I always retained the usual military bearing for camp services and religious occasions and I kept my Bible intact. I used it for pressing small flowers and leaves. The Bible is still with me and contains over thirty named and pressed flowers. When I returned home and realised that it was the faith and prayers of loved ones that had sustained me through three and a half years of hell my attitude to religion changed and I became a Christian, which enriched my life and removed much bitterness and hatred from me. When I was on my way back to England I wrote in the back of the Bible, 'Our faith never faltered'. The following was one of our camp prayers.

Give us courage Lord
To endure this bitter time
Of tribulation. Give us strength
To withstand disease and death,
And the degradation of captivity.

Give us courage Lord
To hold high our heads,
Never forgetful of our blood
Which flows from our motherland
Rich, strong and enduring,
A battle cry to endeavour.

Give us courage Lord
To wait with patience for that day,
When the ebb and flow of war
Shall encompass us again,
For that hour when we will know
'We did not fight in vain'.

Boei Glodock camp, 1942

A Little Angel

I befriended a young Javanese girl whilst in camps in Bandoeng, who managed to pass me vegetation containing caterpillars and some food through the barbed-wire fence. Depending on my state of hunger, I would either eat the caterpillars or observe them develop into butterflies. I made a study of the different types of butterfly and recorded them in notes and drawings assisted, in my learning, by a number of Dutch biologists. The caterpillars turned, via the chrysalis stage, into some amazing butterflies, e.g. six inch wing span. The young girl was exceedingly brave as both of us would have received a fearful beating, or worse, if caught by certain camp guards.

Camp Diaries

Most senior Allied officers frowned upon POWs keeping an open camp diary. Japanese military searchers in the camps would be looking for anything remotely looking like a diary. The main problem with a diary, if discovered, was the close scrutiny the camp interpreters would subject the diaries to. Any information, which might suggest the presence of a short-wave radio in the camp, possible information from outside informants or the planning of subversive activities and records of Jap violations, would be eagerly sought. Information in a diary could easily be misinterpreted and lead to an unwelcome visit from the dreaded Kempeitei.

In the early days, one English NCO who kept an open diary listing, with daily entries, complaints about food quality, hygiene and accommodation, was made an example of by the Japanese. He had a spell in the 'cooler', with little water, no food or sanitation and only the clothes on his back to protect him against the rough concrete floor.

I chose not to keep a diary in camp during captivity although I kept, initially, shorthand notes to remind me of events, particularly names of men leaving on prison drafts and wrote these up after the Japanese surrender in 1945. On one occasion, a Jap guard found some of my short hand notes and he believed he had discovered a spy in the camp. Fortunately, these were some of my attempts at journal writing and the Jap camp interpreter had, amazingly and fortuitously for me, a copy of Pitman's short hand in his possession. I decided, after this incident, to incorporate items of interest in my poetry, in alternative coded form. [*Unfortunately, my mother destroyed all of my father's notes and letters, containing coded material, after his death, as they contained some very personal information.*] I was acutely aware that some POWs kept diaries, either in coded form or well concealed – usually buried in the ground in containers.

At this point it is pertinent to state that the Japanese 'kindly' allowed us to send a message home indicating that 'our health was excellent' and we were 'being treated very well by our captors'! Jap propaganda pictures supported this outrageous notion.

Playing Dead for Real!

We were going out on an early morning work party from Batavia, when we passed the sick hut and sitting outside was a young Australian who had picked up a fever. He was propped up against the hut side with his bush hat drawn over his eyes. As we passed, some of us gave him a friendly pat on the head and hoped he would be better soon. We returned in the early afternoon and were amazed to see the young Australian in an identical pose. One of the men stopped to check on him and on shaking him the Australian toppled over, stone cold dead. This was camp life! However, we were all shocked that we had failed to recognise that he was probably already dead when we had left earlier in the day.

A Sudden Change of Heart!

Towards the end of the war I was moved to LOG camp, Bandoeng – an old reformatory originally built to hold 250 boys, but which during the war held 3,800 POWs at any one time. We were crammed in like sardines. News came (through the secret radio sets) of the Japanese surrender (although the Japanese in the camp did not admit to this) and caused great excitement in the camp. Shortly after, a large cartload of fresh-looking meat arrived at the cookhouse. This was the first meat that many POWs had seen since capture.

'Slimey' Kasayama, an artful and thoroughly wicked Korean private, was actually in charge of the camp with the bloodthirsty S/M 'Gunso' Mori Masao as, by this time, camp commandants had largely lost interest in their jobs and were spending more and more time with their 'comfort' women.

Kasayama was a particularly malignant piece of work, who was responsible for many prisoner deaths on the outer islands of the Eastern Archipelago while building aeroplane runways. Hearing the commotion, Kasayama appeared and asked the senior Dutch officer what was going on. The officer did not want Kasayama to know that the prisoners were aware of the Japanese surrender, fearing instant reprisals from Kasayama and his cronies. The Dutch officer said that the sight of the meat, that had just been brought in to the camp, excited the men. To which the evil snake Kasayama replied, 'Why you did not tell me that men like meat? I could have got plenty every day!'

Radio News Item, After 7 September 1945

POWs from Rabaul said that the attitude of the Japanese changed immediately after the surrender was confirmed on the radio. The Japanese began bowing and smiling to all the Allied prisoners. Some even crawled in front of senior Allied officers. A lot of the Japanese were visibly crying and one committed suicide in front of the prisoners by slitting his throat.

Several prisoners asked their senior officer where Seac was on the map, as they could not find it anywhere, and it was receiving a great deal of publicity on the radio. SEAC is the abbreviation for South East Asia Command!

5: Verses in Captivity, 1942–45

I am not going to claim that what you are about to read is great poetry. In fact, I do not claim that it is poetry at all; that is why I have entitled this chapter 'Verses in Captivity'. However, the circumstances in which these verses were written should be of general interest. Incredibly, I managed to hang on to most of my verses throughout captivity. The Japs did not seem to view them as a threat and most probably thought them to be the scribbling of a deranged man! Other POWs were less fortunate, some having considerable portfolios of art and written work taken and destroyed following Jap searches of POW quarters. The Japanese were terrible at confiscating and destroying written material produced by the prisoners. We heard after the war, that POWs' work, some of which was of a very high standard, was sold to rich Japanese for their delectation. I was truly amazed by the fortitude of some POWs, who kept up their writing, drawing and painting, knowing that it could all be taken from them at the whim of some jealous, spiteful or ignorant Jap or Korean guard.

Geoffrey Crump in his book, *Speaking Poetry*, states that the world of 1939 created no poetic awakening as did the First World War and suggests two main reasons for this. First is the very different tempo of modern warfare; the days of trench warfare, described as long periods of unutterable boredom punctuated by periods of extreme terror, were gone and, with that change, the opportunity to ponder and reflect on the capricious nature of trench-warfare, as described by the likes of Rupert Brooke, Siegfried Sassoon, Ivor Gurney and Wilfred Owen.

Second, in the Second World War, there was much greater screening of military personnel and any person with established credentials in the arts or theatre would find themselves in offices, particularly back room jobs in the Ministry of Information, or script writing for propaganda films, rather than in front-line military action.

POWs though, most certainly, had plenty of time to ponder, although writing one's thoughts down whilst in captivity could be difficult. Paper was often difficult to come by – although we made some of our own – and the first call on paper was to be cut-up and used to roll cigarettes with cheap foul-tasting native tobacco.

I wrote a poem in appreciation of our wonderful treatment in South Africa, two months before our surrender on Java.

The Convoy

We came in tall, grey ships
From the rain and gloom of the North;
Soldiers from the motherland,
Sons she had sent forth
To be worthy of her noble name,
Regardless of glory or fevered fame,
That peace and honour might reign again
On this sad, tortured earth.

The sea had been our mistress
An infinity of days,
With the vicissitudes of a maiden's smile
And the mystery of her ways.
Tired were we of the ceaseless motion,
The wide expanse of immeasurable ocean;
We gazed on your land with sweet emotion,
Whilst sailing through the Bay.

You treated us like heroes –
Through wide hospitable doors.
We forgot the war and the stormy seas
In the warmth of the welcome of yours.
We shall ne'er forget your smiling land
Of mountain, valley and silver strand,
And we thank you all for being so grand.
Au revoir, South Africa.

'Empress of Australia' *Convoy WS14, January 1942* ('The Convoy' is included in
The Jungle Journal No. 1)

The first in the series of verses whilst in captivity is entitled, 'To a Sparrow'. I was in
a native prison in the Chinese quarter of Batavia. I had been very ill with malignant
malaria and nearly died, but quinine saved the day. After my recovery from this illness,
I remained very depressed and the humiliation of our surrender was uppermost in my
mind. I was struck one day by the busy chirpings of a sparrow in one of the camp trees,
which made me realise that I needed to snap out of this dark introspection, and start to
appreciate the good things in my surroundings.

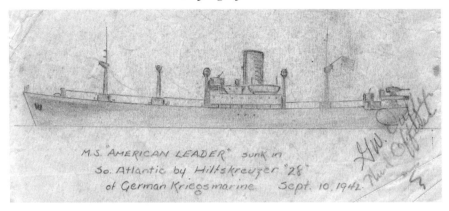

'*American Leader* sunk in the South Atlantic by the German auxillary cruiser *Michel* in September 1942.' The survivors were eventually handed over to the Japanese, off Batavia, in November 1942. Drawing by merchant marine third officer, George Duffy, in Priok camp.

'Lieutenant Ronald Williams recovering from malaria in Boei Glodok prison in 1942.' Illustration by Charles Holdsworth.

To a Sparrow

Come hither, little sparrow,
Come hither here to me,
And tell me what the world is like,
And how blue is the sea.

Tell me what the people do
At their work and play;
And all the little children –
Are they as happy as the day?

Do the sails still flutter
When the ships put out to sea,
And the nets come up sparkling
With fish to eat for tea?

Do the winds still bustle
And make the forest dance,
And mountain streams come tumbling
From peaks of high romance?

O sparrow, happy creature,
Were I as free as thee;
Nor pent up in these prison walls,
T'is woeful hard for me!

Into the bright blue sky I would fly,
And set my course for home;
And when I reached that joyous place,
Oh! Ne'er more would I roam.

Boei Glodock camp, April 1942

The next is '*Nil Desperandum*' or never despair, in sonnet form, which is a very personal one for me, reflecting my mood during times of despair and how I coped.

Nil Desperandum

I could never endure this bitter fate – these hours
That creep in endless dirge of Despond's strife,
Were it not for the thoughts of you – my wife,
Who waits, I know, a lovely springtime flower
With head uplifted for the cooling April shower

Of hope divine and love's eternal life.
She, who conquers fears and rumours rife,
With faith sublime, the good Lord made her dower.

Dear God! If you can wait with courage rare,
Must I falter – of sterner stuff – A man?
Bow low my head; my heart filled with despair,
As though of life I had drunk the final dram.
God forbid! For your dear sake I'll share
Invincibly the care and be a MAN!

Boei Glodock camp, 1942

The next camp I 'visited' was in Tandjong Priok, in the main port of west Java. We were housed in temporary 'coolie' quarters. The Chinese had been used for general labour duties across the Dutch East Indies. Here I continued a camp magazine, managing to make six editions. There was still an old typewriter in the prison which was in working order. We initially called the magazine *The Jungle Journal*, later changing it to *Yasume Times*. *Yasume* is the Japanese for 'day of rest', although this was a rare event in captivity. [*Ronald produced the first two editions of* The Jungle Journal *in Boei Glodok camp. Editions 3 to 8 were produced in Tandjong Priok camp. Five of these editions survive in the Imperial War Museum, in London. (No. 7 is missing.)*]

Several of the following items were written for inclusion in the magazines, including this verse of mine called 'The Last Cigarette'. This may have no impact on the non-smoker, but a cigarette was a major source of comfort for many of us during our long captivity. Some prisoners took up smoking whilst in captivity. The smokers tried to dissuade the new smokers because of the shortage of tobacco, but usually with little effect.

The Last Cigarette

I look at you longingly and despairingly,
'My last cigarette'.
Almost afraid to light you up,
For you may be my last. We prisoners cannot get
Supplies of your seductive, aromatic weed.
Yes – you may be the last – perhaps for years?
Indeed, for ever? Please excuse my tears.
You have been a good friend!
I remember a bad smash and bloody head,
Almost unconscious, but I said,
'Please have you a cigarette?'
Then there was the roar of guns
And scream of bombs, too near,
And in the stunned silence that followed,

Your sweet vapour helped me to smile,
And look at my men with confidence and good cheer.
I remember youthful days in callous company –
I should have blushed deeper than my tan,
But, I took you from my silver case,
And you helped me to act as a man.
Yes, I am grateful, and the parting will be sad!
Still, perhaps I will not smoke you now
But keep you hidden, lovingly.
And when times are really hard you will comfort me,
And your sweet memories make my heart less sad.

Tandjong Priok, 1942 ('The Last Cigarette' is included in *The Jungle Journal* No. 2)

I took up smoking (much to my wife Margaret's disgust) shortly after the war began. I did keep that cigarette, wrapped it in silver paper and put it into a tin; when my craving finally became too great I slowly undid the tin – only to find that the cigarette was no longer in there. It had been pilfered!

At some time or other, I suppose everyone, including the fighting man, realises the utter futility of war. My next verse, 'The Curse of Cain', reflects this feeling.

The Curse of Cain

God is good! He gave me the good earth,
And freedom to roam over mountains,
Where the pure snow glistens in the sun;
Through valleys with cool, flowing streams;
By woodlands where trees reach to heaven;
To the shore where the sea leaps in exultation
Or mirrors the azure of the bright sky.

God is good! He gave me the good things of the earth
To eat that I should not go hungry,
And to be happy, healthy and strong.
Covering He provided, that I should not be naked
But warm, when strong blew the storm.
He gave me a house – a haven of rest,
And a garden, where sweet flowers bloomed for joy.

God is good! He gave me an intellect
To enjoy art, good books and music.
He gave me the will to toil and pride in the sweat on my brow.
He gave me joy in harmless fun;
But greatest of all He gave me love –

Love of life, love of nature, love of home,
And that wonderful emotion, love of wife and child.

God is good! It seemed he gave me all –
Everything to satisfy the most heart felt desire,
But what did I, and millions of my compatriots do?
We took up arms to kill each other too!

Tandjong Priok, 1942 ('The Curse of Cain' is included in *The Jungle Journal* No. 3)

Many nights in captivity were dominated by difficulties in getting to sleep, because of concerns about what was happening back home and the missing of loved ones. These concerns never lessened and, if anything, became progressively worse as time went on. The lack of mail from home and no photographs of loved ones, prime targets for removal by the malevolent camp guards, were hard to bear and a constant source of worry. [*My mother sent my father a number of photographs, all done professionally as she did not have a camera, of herself and my older brother Barrie. None of these reached my father and were, presumably, removed by the Japanese censor.*]

Most of us presented a very brave face, but it was difficult. Some said not knowing what was happening to loved ones was better than receiving bad news. Bad news could mean giving up the will to live. I was over the moon to receive my first mail from my father, some eighteen months after I had embarked, from Gourock, giving me the home news. Fortunately, this appeared to be good news, although the Jap censor had obliterated several parts of the letter with black ink. The next verse is self-explanatory.

How Long?

How long, O God, will be this night
Of utter darkness and despair;
Of aching hearts that strive to wear
A jester's mask of laughter light?

How long before the break of day
Must we, beset by restless dreams
That mingle past and future schemes,
Yet for that brighter dawning pray?

How long before I see the shine
Of love in her, my dear one's, eyes,
And feel sweet passion gently rise
Within her heart close pressed to mine?

I'll thank thee then despite the past,
And laugh at dangers met and won,

For that sweet moment when I run
To her and say, 'Dear heart, at last!'

Tandjong Priok, 1942

We played games to keep up our spirits including, in the early days, physical games like rugby and football. POWs made their own packs of cards and some carved their own chess pieces. These were mostly quite crude because of a lack of suitable implements to carve them. The next verse is entitled 'Chess' and, again, is self-explanatory.

Chess

The courtyard, sunlit, was hushed despite the throng
Of courtiers, richly robed, who stood about the two,
Who, with eyes intent, stroked their beards in contemplation
Of the chequered board, where each piece, like a warrior, at its station,
Stood resplendent – King, Queen, Castle, Bishop and Knight –
Playthings of striving minds in a keen but friendly fight.
Thus from Wisdom's womb for weal or woe
Was born the royal game of 'Chess' some 2,000 years ago.
'Landlord, more canary,' roared jovial Sir Charles,
Shaking the olde inne's rafters with his lusty voice.
'This chess 'tis sure a thirsty game, what say ye Ned,
Was there ever such as to keep a man from his wife and bed?'
But soon the room grew quiet and still
As each Noble, suddenly sobered, bent his will,
And with rook and pawn, and gesture grand,
Played chess, while good Queen Bess ruled the Land.

Beneath a tropical sun, in nook and shade,
Groups of men, some barely clothed and some unshaved,
Sit, a board between, upon the ground or on rough-hewn stools,
And with concentrated effort renew the fight of
Kings, Queens, Bishop and Knight pieces hand-carved,
Some crude, but fit to lull these men, half-starved,
With mental distraction from thoughts of feasts;
Thus in 1942, British prisoners played chess in the far-off East!

Tandjong Priok, 1942

I could have called this next verse 'Floating' relating to a most memorable experience we encountered whilst in Priok camp in 1942. For a few weeks, with no fathomable explanation given, the Japs allowed us to bathe in the sea in the afternoons. This was great fun, although one had to put up with the stings of the innumerable small jellyfish present in the water. We were also conscious of sharks being in the water and some of the pranksters would shout out, 'Sharks!' This most enjoyable bathing experience was never to be repeated. I was not aware that photographs were taken of us swimming, but this could have been a propaganda exercise after all.

Brief Escape

I lay back and looked into the skies,
Watching the fleecy, fleeting clouds,
Until the sun's bright stare,
Dazzled and closed my eyes.
My head was cushioned as tho' in down;
Gently was I cradled to and fro.
I felt the warm breeze caress my face,
And salt spray spatter over my brow.
No sound I heard save distant voices,
That seemed so many miles away.
This was freedom and peace entire.
O, could I thus forever stay!
But time and tide relentless flow;
Each happy moment fades in the insistent roar
Of a thousand mundane needs –
I turned, and swam back towards the shore.

Tandjong Priok, 1942

The next verse is named, '*Hiraeth*', a Welsh word meaning a longing for home, family and country. I am English but my wife is Welsh, and Welsh speaking, and many of my men were Welsh. I had spent many years in Wales, working and tramping around the countryside in my free time. I felt that I had a great affinity with the Welsh, except when they played rugby against the English!

Hiraeth

O Land of ancient castles whose strength hath passed
And resolved itself in the fiery ardour of thy sons;
Whose old grey walls stand as mute monuments
To those days when strife rode through the Land,
And Norman Barons sought thy fathers to enthrall;
Whose hateful frown the centuries have smoothed away,
Leaving naught but romantic beauty, and
idyllic peacefulness.

O Land of sweetest song and perfect harmony,
Thy singer's fame has been acclaimed throughout the World.
Even the darkest valleys sing with melodies, as of angels' voices,
Which surge re-echoing amongst the ageing hills,
Where in troubled times thy bards sought sanctuary,
And with impassioned harp wrought runes of prophetic fire,
This set alight the torch of freedom to go flaming through the Land.

O Cambriansis, when shall I see your welcoming shores again,
And gaze upon thy pleasant pastures from some rugged peak,
And watch a meandering river's silver stream
Reflecting sunbeams from a summer sky serene?
And hear the swelling chorus on a Sabbath eve
Reverberating from the House of God, and at dawn
A feathered choir singing sweetly in Dewi Sant's
secluded Palace?★

Boei Glodok camp, 1943

★ The secluded Palace of Dewi Sant is in Saint David's, Pembrokeshire.

We are back in Boei Glodok camp again, where I wrote another sonnet, 'Perchance', which dwelt on the grim possibility of not surviving captivity. This seems a suitable moment to emphasize that most prisoners rarely showed abject despair and tried to avoid discussing the possibility of not surviving. We had absolute conviction that the Allies would eventually triumph, even in our darkest moments; perhaps it would take twenty years or more? Of course, we could not guarantee our own survival, but the defeat of the Axis countries was very important to us.

Perchance

Perchance should I not leave this awful place alive
To live again a life of every day,
Nor see open spaces where happy children play,
By pond or lake where ducklings learn to dive,
Whilst in the bright summer sky, larks strive
To out-sing the angels with immortal lay.
Nor in the cool of evening make my way
Shoreward, where the white sea-horses drive,
Then grant my restless spirit grace to roam
Beyond this land where I, a prisoner, lay;
To ride the wildest wind, which leads me home

To where my loved ones wait for me and pray.
And let me irk them, not with shriek or moan,
But with sweet whisperings of love alway.

Boei Glodok camp, 1943

This is a piece I included in *The Yasume Times*. This was written in Boei Glodok camp, where most of the prisoners were either British or Australian. The piece attempts to convey what the Australians and English POWs missed about their own countries.

November 1943

Another month has passed on golden wings,
How else but golden that brings
Us, like a tribe of prodigals,
Nearer to the homely hearth –
The haven of all our yearning,
The mantle of our strength and
The very substance of our being?

In England, the trees have shed their summer splendour
In showers of rustling, russet leaves,
Which the wild west wind scatters down the winding lanes,
Startling wool warm sheep and rousing cudding cattle from their knees.

'Ploughing the Fields'. Illustration by Charles Holdsworth

Night early drops her curtain and the labourer in the fields
Unharnesses his heavy horse from the attached plough,
And wends his way homeward to the cheery fire
With pearls of perspiration, on his furrowed brow.
And, as he shuts the stable door, free at last to take his ease,
He breathes the pungent smoke, of a wood fire, wafting along in the breeze.

In Australia, summer imperceptibly approaches, while
In the Blue Mountains, the air yet retains the exhilaration of crystallized ice
To stir the blood of healthy hikers roaming the heights,
Where nature, a wanton nymph, ever paints fresh pictures to entice.
And at the Melbourne races the crowds converge from every quarter,
For the city is all a bustle, with excitement surging up.
There will be a galaxy of splendour and a symphony of speed,
When the proud aristocrats of the turf line up for the Melbourne Cup.

Boei Glodok camp, November 1943

We often wondered at the night sky in Java, which reminded us of home. By the end of captivity, most of us could recognise the major constellations in the southern night sky. However, we could not see one important star! I wrote this next piece for the camp journal.

'The Melbourne Races'. Illustration by Charles Holdsworth

'A Star Unseen'. Illustration by Charles Holdsworth

De Profundis (Contemplation)

The night sky is a dome of black velvet on which are set millions of shining jewels, some scintillating like diamonds and others possessing the quiet pallor of ocean pearls. To the south lies the Milky Way, with its great clusters of star cities – a huge area of foam covered magic and mystery. Yonder lies the Southern Cross with its pointer to the Pole.

Orion the Hunter is midway in the heavens with Sirius the dog, the brightest star of all, stalking at the Hunter's heels. Many constellations look down upon us but, alas, the one that we know well, the North Star, is far, far away from our gaze. We hope one day to look into the heavens and see our dear old friend again.

Boei Glodok camp, 1943

The following poem is dedicated to Capt. John W. Goronwy, RAMC. Capt. Goronwy was drafted to Japan, from Java, in May 1944. Actually, by the end of hostilities there were not a huge number of British prisoners left on Java. Many had been shipped all over the Far East; to Japan, to work in the mines and factories, and to Malaya, Burma and Siam to build railways or to the smaller islands of the East Indies to build airfields. I was lucky to remain on Java because no major work to further the Japanese war effort was required on the island.

The men were usually drafted in units and administrative groups, although the officers were often picked out on parade for these drafts. I seemed always to be ignored; perhaps I looked too sickly? On the particular occasion that my best friend Doc 'Grony' was detailed for transfer, the request was for British doctors. I did not want to be separated from Doc 'Grony' and did my utmost to get on his draft, but without success. When I set about tracing the Doc after the war, I discovered that an Allied submarine had torpedoed his transporter ship off the coast of Japan. [*This was the sinking of the* Tamahoko Maru *by the US submarine* Tang *off Nagasaki.*] Many men drowned, including my good friend. Initially, I had hoped that the Allies, as happened in some cases, might have picked him up, but this, sadly, was not to be the case for the good Doc.

I visited Carreg Cennen Castle in 1947, on one of my tramping trips to the Carmarthen van, West Wales, and remembered Doc 'Grony' describing to me the underground tunnel leading to an ancient cave beneath this castle and the eerie nature of the castle perched on a precipitous limestone rock. We had many interesting talks about Welsh castles while in prison camps in Batavia. I managed to find the tunnel to the cave by a partly concealed crevice at the base of Carreg Cennen Castle and, as I walked through the tunnel with a torch, I could just imagine the dear little Welshman telling me the story of the castle in his, at all times, cheerful voice. I shed a few tears in his memory on that cold, wet day in 1947.

Dear Departed Friend

Now you are gone my dearest friend,
Companion of my every hour.
Gone into the dark unknown
And left my heart a withered flower.

Your footsteps follow blindly on
Those who wraithlike went before,
Fading from our consciousness
Like ships that drift beyond the shore.

So many drafts have marched away,
Composed of men with whom we fought.
Bravely they went with a farewell smile,
Jesting as though their fate meant naught.

But you were more, far more to me;
Our bond was cast in precious gold.
You were the star that lit my life
With sympathy that ne'er grew cold.

Your presence made this life worthwhile –
Each weary and dreary prison day,
Where only friendship has the power,
Despair's dark tempest to allay.

We parted with a grasp of hands:
I swiftly turned to hide my tears,
And strode away unseeing, numb,
My heart weighed down with nameless fears.

Where you are now, I do not know.
We dance to the tune our captors play.
I only know that I cherished you so,
And curse the day that you were sent away.

Java, June 1944

(I wrote this before I learned of the sad death of Doc 'Grony')

This is another sonnet about England, written in 1944. If we should die that others
might live in freedom from tyranny, this would be a cause worth dying for.

'Home'. A drawing of Exeter by POW Lionel Stanton in November 1942.

To the Motherland

O England, mother of my youthful days,
Who shaped with patient hand my mind and soul,
As oft I walked your distinct and charming ways,
And pondered on the grandeur of thy role:
And when 'To arms' became the clarion cry,
That thou should live, I prayed for strength to die.

I care not what the suffering may be:
The pain and protracted agony of death,
Her name will I utter with my parting breath,
For she is most worthy of the best in me.
And if, indeed, it should be fate's decree
That never more her beauty I shall know,
Though sad the parting, I'll not fear to go
If she remains, inviolate and free.

Bandoeng, 1944

This verse I had to commit to memory, until it was safe to write about such things, without the Japs accusing me of treachery. I composed it several months before we learned of the Jap surrender, although, from our secret radio broadcasts, we knew that the Allies were winning the war.

Freedom (1)

Each night I lay abed and thought of you,
While tossing on my bed of heartless stone.
I heard the restless prison's spirits moan,
Not those alone who lingered on – I knew
The mournful cry of those departed too.
Ne'er more on earth will you by them be known,
Though perchance, they'll gain a heavenly throne.
May we yet live to see this penance through?

Oh, Freedom, none has beauty such as you:
No other virtue can with you compare.
The flowers of joy and love, they cannot bloom;
And all things we love are absent too,
If they may not your faithful friendship share.
Pray, Freedom, take us to your bosom soon.

Batavia, 1945

The following poem I wrote in 1947, two years after release as a Jap POW. This is what freedom meant to me.

Freedom (2)

Not a care have I, in this great wide world,
As I wend the country ways.
Not a pang in my heart,
Not a pain nor smart,
Not a blot on these gladsome days.

Away from the town, the crowd and the din,
Away from the narrow street
To the wood and the flower,
To quaint church and old tower,
To the air that is pure and sweet.

There is a blue sky above untouched by a cloud;
There is birdsong in meadow and tree;
There are cool shady nooks,
And the chatter of brooks,
As they jingle along to the sea.

These are the things, for which I thank God,
Thank him on bended knee,
For the valleys and tor,
For the woodland and moor,
For the joy of just being free.

Cross Lane, Pembrey, 1947

While in prison camps, I spent many an hour composing verses and poems for my dear wife, Margaret. This was very important to me, to retain my sanity in such violent living conditions. These are some of my efforts.

Margaret

Marigold clusters art thy hair:
Angel's halo hath thou there.
Roses' sweetness paints thy lips.
Graceful art thou as a sailing ship.
Apricot texture hath thy skin.
Rare beauty sways thy figure slim.

Eyes so bright like stars at night,
True and sweet art thou my heart's delight

Java, 1944

I Would!

Who would not fight for eyes so bright,
As those that you possess?
Who would not dare for your Titian hair,
Which I alone may caress?
Who would know fear when you are so dear,
Nor laid low for less?
Who would not die for the sake of your cry,
If you were in distress?
Who would seek rest on your sweet breast?
None 'til we've won and the warmongers gone,
And the evil are under arrest.
Then we will be happy, and the world will be free,
A fine place for all those children you promised me!

Java, 1944

Many Happy Returns of the Day

Today is your birthday, sweetheart mine,
And from my mountain eminence of time,
This Eastern land the rising sun awakes,
Eight hours before the English hour he takes,
I have watched, in spirit, some moments of your special day.
I saw your curls like gold upon a drift of snow,
And then, your eyelids flickered, opened and your eyes began to glow,
Child like with anticipation as you realized the pleasure the day would bring,
Greetings from friends, from loved ones tokens, each little thing,
A precious link, in the chain of happiness, and self-esteem.
For loving is giving and giving is loving – So it would seem,
Then, suddenly, your face clouded as you thought of me,
Your husband and lover, when again would you see?
Would I not take you in my arms and say?
'Dearest wife, many happy returns of the day'?

Bandoeng, 4 February 1945

We first received news that the Japanese had surrendered to the Allies on 16 August 1945. I found a quiet corner in the POW camp in Batavia, sitting on a rough-hewn stool in the blazing sunlight and naked, except for a loincloth, I composed the following lines for my lost friends.

To the Dead

Comrades, had I but the power
I would paint your names in flaming gold
Across the skies, that man should honour you.
And never forget, as I shall not forget,
The part you played and the way you died.
You died in pain and anguish on a far tropic Isle,
With your last thoughts of home and a loved one's smile.
Died that we who remained should not be for ever enslaved,
But should build that brave new world that all of us have craved.

You gave, gave your all, willingly and unafraid.
How can we ever thank you, and this debt ever be repaid?
Will your sacrifices be allowed to count for naught?
Your ideals and the dreams forgot, for which you so nobly fought.
O comrades, from your Valhalla, help us to remember thee,
And hold that memory sacred for those that died for our liberty!

Batavia, 1945

Many of my comrades I knew were dead or likely to be dead. They had been scattered all over the Far East, as slave labour in making aircraft runways on islands in the Flores and Banda Seas, working as 'coolies' in Sumatra and Malaya, on the 'Death Railway' from Thailand to Burma, and some in Japan working in mineral mines. They had died from malnutrition, starvation, tropical diseases, beatings and deliberate 'cold-blooded' murder for failing to work or lagging behind on death marches, and because of a raised fist in retaliation to an insult, or attempts to escape. The excuse for killing POWs could be quite trivial. Life hung by a thread in many prison camps.

I wrote the following on the way back to England, and this portrays my enjoyment of the flora and fauna on Java, particularly the great trees. A number of eminent Dutch biologists, who were civilian internees, helped me in the identification of plants, trees and insects.

Enchanters Three

Now at last that I am free and need your kindly shade
No more. Do I forget? O, no! For when
My eyes are closed I see you yet again,
A dancing, dancing in the breeze,
Rhythmically swaying your regal crowns,

As gusts dart sudden from the Java Sea.
Each fluttering leaf reflects the sun serene:
Each twig and branch joining in symphony.
Can I forget when you entranced my heart –
Gave pleasure where it seemed that none could be?
O, who but one in prison pent can really love a tree?
You danced and pranced, and waved your supple limbs,
Shaking your heads in unsurpassed glee,
And brought a glimpse of heaven to that so hateful prison;
Though, hell unholy it was meant to be.
Dance on, you tropic trees, now I am free,
And live so far from your romantic home,
I know that others still have need of thee.
So dance on, dance on, you enchanters three,
Tamarind, Mango and Mahogany.

Gibraltar, 1945

'Churchill inspecting the Fleet', drawn by Sgt Herbert Clifford for *The Jungle Journal*. (Courtesy of Mrs Adèle Barclay)

Sergeant Clifford Herbert (77th Welsh RA) drew a cartoon with Winston Churchill smoking a large cigar and wearing his seaman's peaked cap, standing near the stern of a battleship where the White Ensign was prominently displayed. In the background, other warships were in line astern. The caption was, 'Leave it to the skipper'. The last sonnet is dedicated to the man we all had great faith in, 'The Leader'. I had started this verse in 1941, but left it. I had the greatest of pleasures completing the verse under the noses of armed Japanese guards, after the formal Japanese surrender. Churchill was a figure of hate for the Jap soldier.

The Leader

Dark clouds gathered and glowered over this Isle.
Hateful hounds of war have escaped their leash,
And snarled their threat at many a sea beach,
Scarce guarded sands, mile upon endless mile.
Our eyes, by fearful hearts propelled the while
For winged death, did scan heaven's furthest reach.
Our Allies fell – alone we did beseech
That God our fate and will, would reconcile.

Dark days, dread nights until our prayer was heard.
Then came a man, who struck a mighty flame,
With hope and courage in his every word.
Winston Churchill was the great man's name,
And with his fire the Nation's spirit stirred,
He led us forth to victory and fame.

Batavia, September 1941 and 1945

The concluding item I wrote in appreciation of a small band of Australians, *[from 2nd/40th AIF and 2nd/1st Royal Australian Infantry]* many of whom I became very friendly with in Java camps who, for a few days, had held Timor against overwhelming odds. Eventually, utterly exhausted and outnumbered at least twenty-two to one, they had little option but to surrender. For this last verse, an Australian private, who regarded the Australian 'outlaw' Ned Kelly as a national hero, inspired me.

O Aussie

O Aussie, you're a fine fella with all yer carefree ways,
Yer comes from God's own country or so at least yer says.
Yer never gives a damn an' swears like bloomin' 'ell,
Though 'twas good to 'ear yer cursin' when the bombs soon fell.
Yer were 'coo-ee-in!' like demons when you charged into the foe,
But tell me Digger, dinkum, what I really want to know –

Who's this man, Ned Kelly, Australia's uncrowned King,
Whose pedigree an' praise yer so often 'eard to sing?

O Aussie from the cattle lands where life can be all alone,
Where yer rides away into the 'blue', far away from 'ome'
Where yer chases up the 'beefers' an' gives 'em soppy names,
Which would make a trooper blush, an' bring smiles to ol' dames.
Where yer does a really tough job it takes a man to do,
But tell me, Mr Drover, for I'm no buckaroo –
Who's this man Ned Kelly, Australia's uncrowned King,
Whose pedigree an' praise yer so often 'eard to sing?

O Aussie from the wheat belt, where the paddocks stretch for miles,
Where yer don't go in fer 'edgerows or little country stiles.
Where the tractors throb a tune of toil ploughin' up the land,
An' then emerge the 'arvesters where golden wheat does stand.
Where mistress weather is yer dame – she can make or break yer too,
But tell me Mr Cockey, O tell me straight an' true –
Who's this man Ned Kelly, Australia's uncrowned King,
Whose pedigree an' praise yer so often 'eard to sing?

O Aussie from the outback, where the virgin forests grow,
Where you've got to be a bushman if yer 'ope to make a go.
Where the boomer is the monarch an' the kookaburras jest,
An' a possum or a bush rat may disturb yer well earned rest,
Where yer may just meet those brumbies or a bunyip any day,
But tell me straight ol' timer, before yer on yer way –
Who's this man Ned Kelly, Australia's uncrowned King,
Whose pedigree an' praise yer so often 'eard to sing?

O Aussie you're a fine fella with all yer carefree ways,
Yer comes from God's own country, that's what the 'old un' says;
Yer never gives a monkeys an' swears like bloomin' 'ell,
I believe you'd shame the Devil, an' 'e do pretty well,
But there ain't no 'arm in swearing when you've got an 'eart of gold,
So tell me dinkum, Digger, if I may be so bold –
Who's this man Ned Kelly, Australia's uncrowned King,
Whose pedigree an' praise yer so often 'eard to sing?

Batavia, 1945

[*As a teenager, Ronald had spent two years in the Queensland bush, Australia, working as a 'jackeroo' farm hand. His father took him out of public school at sixteen, before he could go up to university, with a view to toughening him up for life's hardships. Frank Senior wanted his oldest* son to become the 'finished article', ready to take over responsibility for the family business, and so sent him 'down under'. This was seriously detrimental to Ronald's education but this tough experience may have been instrumental in saving his life in POW camps.

Most of the poetry, verses and prose in this chapter were in a typed manuscript form produced by my father with the intention of either producing a short book of poems or as part of a larger book about his experiences in captivity. Recently, further verses and prose that he wrote while he was in captivity have come to light. These are handwritten in pencil on very thin paper.

The first prose is called 'Wedding Anniversary' and would have been written in October 1942. He had married in St Martin's Church, Roath, Cardiff, in October 1940. His bride was a staff nurse in Cardiff Royal Infirmary and he a sergeant major in the Royal Artillery. Fortunately, the bride's elder brother was an ordained priest and he managed to arrange a special licence, otherwise the wedding could not have taken place as neither the prospective bride or groom were from the parish. Ronald's parents were present at the wedding, but neither of the bride's parents could be there. Her father had recently died of pneumoconiosis and her mother had to tend to the family farm in west Wales.]

Wedding Anniversary

Two years ago my dearest, two years ago
You and I were wed. Two years ago to
This very day and hour.
I led you by your trusting little hand
In mine, to the altar, where stood the
Blacked-robed priest, who recited over us
The Christian marriage rite.
We were pronounced man and wife before the world.
We were made one; two hearts to beat as one;
Two pairs of lips to kiss in unison.
He sanctified our primeval love,
And I swore to love and cherish you forever,
And no less will I do for you.

We were one, yet far apart, separated by
Many thousand miles of tumultuous oceans.
Eleven long months have dragged on since last
I saw you and thrilled by the softness of your lips.
And by your side was our little son,
Whom God had sent to comfort you in your sorrow.
For you know not whether I am alive or dead,
Unless your heart can feel mine pulsating
With love for you through these inimical climes?
A captive, behind barbed wire, held by the war-like Nippon.
Despite the dangers we have met
And the countless all-consuming fevers,

My heart beats strong for you.
And you my love, where are you?

I picture the little farm on the brow of the hill,
And the cosy warm kitchen where you sit and sing
To the little lad in your arms, about his missing father.
Though your heart remains sad and will strong,
Day follows day and still no tidings come ...

Tandjong Priok, October 1942

[*St Martin's Church, Roath was largely destroyed by a German incendiary bomb soon after the wedding in 1941.*]

Sergeant Major Ronald Williams and Staff Nurse Margaret Williams (*née* Davies)
in November 1940.

[*The next piece, written in Java and undated, is dedicated to my elder brother Barrie. This must have been written fairly shortly before or after my father had been taken prisoner in 1942.*]

To my Son

I have seen you but once, my son,
On the day following your grand entrance
On to life's implacable stage.
Just once, and who can tell whether
The first time will be the last?
For where I am, the wings of death
Hover over us like vultures,
And fate plays chequers with our very lives.
Yes, I may never see you again – a sad thought
For I have much love to give,
And would delight in seeing you grow
From young sapling, into a strong and healthy boy.
I can only dream of how you are growing up
And pray for the day, we will be united again.

Java, 1942

[*The next poem was written for New Year's Eve 1943 and conveys the feeling that not all needs to be doom and gloom. True British grit and a sense of optimism are called for in coping with the stresses and strains of being a Japanese POW.*]

New Year's Ode

There's a bright new moon in the sky tonight,
A ship that sails the ethereal seas.
We've turned our money 'neath its gleaming light
And wished our luck would better be.
For its New Year's Eve, m'lads, m'lads
New Year's Eve, nineteen-forty-three;
And we are prisoners of war, m'lads,
All praying to be free.

There's a rushing wind in the tropic night,
Which makes the palm trees sway,
Like the whisper of wishes ever bright
In the thoughts of our dearest ones, far away.
For its New Year's Eve, m'lads, m'lads.
At night we do wish to stay,

For we are prisoners of war, m'lads
With hopes for a brighter day.

We know there is many a day to wait
Until the long drawn battle is won
We know its no use bemoaning our fate
And cursing at what's been done,
For is New Year's Eve, m'lads, m'lads
And we resolved to let the slow sands run,
Just like Britishers should, m'lads
And grin and bear as though it were fun!

Boei Glodok, 1943

Java Moon

I stood entranced watching the moon,
Rising in the Java sky,
Casting beauty as it did loom
Up and up on high.
Its colour was the purest gold
That ever I have seen,
Filling the eastern sky so bold
With a shimmering disk shape so keen.
In glory and delight
Robbing thus, the black robed nightlight
Of its sceptical sway.
Even when I go away,
My thoughts will always incline
To the splendours of this tropic sublime,
Rising o'er the distant Java hills.

Boei Glodok, 1943

[*The following is a rhyming verse on the subject of death and patriotism, with some of the vigour and simplicity of lines from an earlier, perhaps even Medieval, time.*]

Oh England

I care not what the suffering may be,
The pain and perhaps the agony of death.
Her name, I'll utter with my parting breath
For she is worthy of the best in me
And, if indeed, it be my fate's decree

That, ne'er again her beauty I shall know
Though, sad at the parting, I'll not fear to go,
If, she remains inviolate, and devil-free.
Oh England, mother of my youthful days,
The patient sculptor of my heart and soul
I learned to love your lovely ways
And gleaned the grandeur of your regal role
And when, 'To Arms' became the clarion cry,
I prayed that you will live, if I should die.

Bicycle camp, Batavia 1944

6: End of the Nightmare and the Journey Home

No. 1 Bicycle camp, Batavia, Java

Diary 1945

14 August

At approximately 1300 hrs, the first Allied plane we had seen since March 1942 flew high and fast over the camp. The experts identified it as a de Havilland Mosquito. This produced a great deal of excitement, particularly from the Jap gun battery, which opened fire on the aircraft, but the Jap gunners had really no idea how to aim due to years of inactivity! This is certainly very encouraging and we hope to see increasing Allied activity, so long as they do not bomb or shoot us instead of the Japanese.

15 August

At 0400 hrs the working party that has been going to Priok early every morning, ostensibly to repair Jap motor vehicles, was cancelled without explanation. At reveille, we saw Jap guards patrolling the roadways inside the camp. This is most peculiar and raised speculation that something major had happened. Then all outside working parties were cancelled! The optimists think the war is over, while some of us think there is to be an attack on Java by the Allies. However, we do not want to raise our hopes too high.

16 August

The war is over indeed! A message, on our secret radio, has come through telling us of the Japanese surrender. The Japanese had surrendered at midnight on 14 August.

In the evening, whilst I was working in the barrack room office, I was nearly brained by a drunken Korean guard who suddenly loomed in the doorway with a large bamboo staff, charged at me, and brought the staff crashing down towards me but, fortunately, the overhead lights deflected the blow and they smashed to the floor. I beat a very hasty retreat and the idiot guard then went on a rampage in several other huts, until a fat Japanese sergeant caught him and was last seen jumping on the Korean's head.

People in isolation were released today, including a draft from Makassar and the crew of an Australian bomber, who had been shot down quite recently. They gave us an update on what had been happening in the war in the Far East, including the dropping of atom bombs on Japan. [*Hiroshima and Nagasaki on 6 and 8 August respectively. There were 140,000 British and Commonwealth, 20,000 American and 60,000 Dutch, POWs in the Far East at the time of the Japanese surrender, including civilians. Many had to wait until late September to taste real freedom.*]

21 August
A small draft, under Maj. Clive Mossford, arrived from Makassar into Bicycle camp. Some of them were in very bad nick indeed and the major was only skin and bone. I had known the major as a big solid chap, so his appearance was a great shock to me. Seeing these men with legs and arms like matchsticks and horribly swollen joints made me feel quite sick. I had to restrain myself from rushing up to one of the Japanese guards and slitting his throat though, fortunately, I had no weapon to hand. Mossford said that they had been told on the 15th that the Japs had surrendered, but our dear guardians had still to inform us.

22 August
The entire English-speaking group, comprising British, Australian and American, about 800-odd, arrived from Bandoeng, including my old pal George Gunn. He immediately took up residence with me. The Nips have started dishing out proper food, clothes, blankets, mosquito nets, cigarettes, etc. We can see that many of these items (British Red Cross) have been stored away for some considerable time – this is truly despicable. Obviously, the Japs have the wind up and are trying to create a good impression; however, the physical state of the men will tell no lies.

26 August
We hold a Thanksgiving Service and there is a strange lack of outward emotion. However, during the singing of 'God Save the King', I choked up and had to stop singing. I do not believe that I was alone. I wrote long letters home. This is the first time that I haven't had to use set phrases dictated by the Japanese which included, 'My health is excellent' and 'Our daily life is pleasant'. The Japanese censor will also be a thing of the past.

1 September
We picked papayas from the outside garden today. Memories of comrades sent away on work drafts, not to return, start to flood back. We try to block out negative thoughts as much as possible.

2 September
First time out of camp today – we went with PO (Pilot Officer) Paddy Creegan to the Convent Hospital where Squadron Leader (Sqn Ldr) Shoppee is seriously ill. We both donated blood, but the Doc does not think things are too hopeful for the squadron leader.

The Japanese who took us tried to be friendly. We saw a white woman for the first time for over three years. She did not seem to want to acknowledge our presence – maybe she was German! There are Indonesian Nationalistic slogans written in English all over the place, calling for an end to Dutch rule. The trams seem very overcrowded with natives and some whites. [*The Japanese signed the unconditional surrender.*]

4 September
Several Dutch Mitchells fly over Batavia. Planes had been over previously, but not as low in the sky.

5 September
We have the camp radio blaring out calling the Japanese everything under the sun. We are still under the protection of the blighters and have not even a single bayonet between us. Some of the Nip officers know that they are in for serious punishment and we are a bit worried that they may turn on us, so this is a rather an unpleasant and unpredictable time in some respects. Also wrote a letter to Mrs Johnson at Tjiden. [*Mrs Johnson was married to Johnnie Johnson. Both were civilian internees. My father had befriended them on Java before the Japanese invasion. Ronald had stayed in the same cell in Boei Glodok camp with Johnnie Johnson and Doc Goronwy. I cannot find out any more details about the Johnsons and, surprisingly, my father did not appear to keep in contact with them after he arrived back in England. Les Spence, in his book,* From Java to Nagasaki, *mentions that in June 1943 in Boei Glodok camp, Wilf Wooller had a falling out with a Mr Johnson, an English civilian Wooller thought was being too helpful to the Japanese in factory production, and seemed to have forgotten that he was working for the enemy. This may be the same Mr Johnson, as time and place both tally.*]

7 September
Two Dutch Mitchells flew around, quite low, for about three quarters of an hour. Sqn Ldr Shoppee is making good progress; he has now had the blood of ten different people – and what an assortment! It would be interesting to see whether he has a personality change when he recovers – he could become a real all-round eccentric. We heard that the Liberators had been dropping medical supplies and food parcels over Batavia. Apparently one of the boxes hit an elderly woman and killed her. I received a reply from Mrs Johnson.

8 September
A Liberator has flown low followed by a Mitchell over our camp. A British major (Maj. Greenhalgh, I believe) of the Parachute Regiment dropped in on us this afternoon and asked us to be patient and take no chances. His actual words were 'Don't muck about', as if we would and could! The Indonesian nationalists are becoming restive under their leaders, Sukarno and Hatta, and are an added danger. (It transpired subsequently that although the Indonesian nationalists hated the Dutch colonialists, by the end of the war they hated the Japanese Imperialists even more.)

9 September

A B-25 and a Dutch Liberator flew over today.

10 September

Went to a camp concert this evening; the first for about a year.

12 September

Our first film show – *Snow White and the Seven Dwarfs* – was set up. Many breakdowns occurred, but what a welcome change.

14 September

Wrote letters home. I mentioned that I had received two letters from Dad in 1943, but first letter from Margaret in May 1944. Also, said that I hoped to be home by Christmas at the latest. We are hearing more about Japanese atrocities on the radio.

15 September

We have now had a long month of waiting, but things seem to be happening at last. HMS *Cumberland* has docked in Tandjong Priok and many Liberators are flying around. I wrote another letter home. How wonderful it is to write as a free man again, but I have had no news from home for seven months. I heard yesterday that some of our lads, including Wilf Wooller, a damn fine fellow, who went to Singapore two years ago with 'HRH', are on their way back home. [*Col Humphries – 'HRH' – left at the same time and took back with him a roll of honour of the regimental dead carved on a large piece of jungle timber. This was later presented to the Dean of Llandaff Cathedral, Cardiff. He also took back a plaque designed by Charles Holdsworth, which became an iconic emblem for the 77th Artillerymen in captivity. The plaque was illustrated in* The Jungle Journal, *and is included within the illustrations.*]

This affair has been a surreal experience and I am most fortunate to come out of it in one piece. Many of my good friends are dead and many more, we have not heard news of; I suspect they have suffered a similar fate. They are as good as murdered by the Nips. I will endeavour to expose the individual horrors of the camps, at the first opportunity.

A Mr W. Ballinger, of the *Western Mail* newspaper, South Wales, has caricatured certain officers of the 77th, which should be published in the paper. The artist is Flt Lt Audus, a lecturer from Cardiff University. I have been caricatured examining a flower!

Java is really a wonderful island, or was before the Japanese arrived and messed up the place. I am sure it will be again once things settle down. It is full of fantastic jungles containing tigers, rhinoceros, wild cattle, and very old Hindu temples – Java has been Mohammedan for nearly a thousand years. These are interesting people living in wonderful mountain scenery with active volcanoes. I should love to come back when the situation is better.

[*Leslie Audus (RAF) sent Ronald a Christmas card in 1946 with a caricature of him examining a caterpillar, while sitting semi-naked and cross-legged on a rattan mat, deciding whether to*

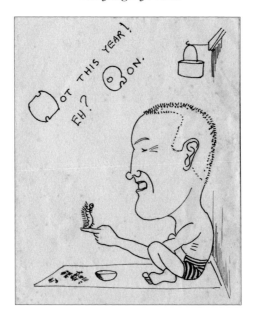

eat it or not (above)! Leslie Audus became Professor of Botany at the University of London after the war. He wrote a book, Spice Island Slaves, *in which he recounted how he made vitamin-rich potions from yeasts, which saved many a prisoner's life.*]

16 September

Admiral Paterson visited the camp and addressed us, complimenting us on our bearing and patience.

17 September

The few New Zealanders (about twenty-two) flew out, followed by most of the Americans. The first mail is dispatched today, so I can get on with letter writing again. I wrote another letter home, saying that I had started a book in captivity, but the Nips kept taking papers and pencils away. However, I said that I managed to conceal all my poems in my Dutch books, in which they did not seem interested. For the past twelve months, I have been typing away on an old battered typewriter and re-editing a camp journal, *The Jungle Journal*. This has been good for morale but production of enough copies has been a headache.

18 September

Maj. Mossford and his party flew out today. Some of the RAF had managed to arrange flights to Singapore on flying boats.

20 September

I went with George Gunn and a working party to the women's camp at Kramat. The women have had a terrible time of it, probably worse than we had. It was nice to hear children's voices again. One part of the camp was separated for the women, mostly half-castes, who had voluntarily cohabited with the Jap soldiers, and those who had been forced into prostitution (the 'comfort women'). We were told one gruesome story of a Dutch woman who was continually pestered by a Nip officer but rejected his advances. He finally laid in to her in front of women and children, tied her hands together, placed her thumbs on a table edge and smashed them to pulp with a metal bar. She died later from malnutrition and infection. I hope the perpetrator rots in hell.

21 September

After yesterday's mixed experiences, we went to visit the Naval Fleet at Priok. I went with a party of twenty officers to visit the *Cumberland*. I was just into my second gin when the ship's chaplain announced that an invitation had come from the captain of the frigate, HMS *Kale*, for five officers to join him and his crew for drinks. I volunteered immediately! We wiled away the afternoon chatting, drinking whisky and soda and smoking. It was a wonderful experience. My body was not quite up to the drinking, but I managed to leave standing on my own two feet and as happy as Larry.

22 September

Letter arrives from Dad. Everyone is well, although brother, Hugh, had a lucky escape when his bomber crashed in Tripoli and burnt out. He thought that Hugh might be flying out to the Far East to pick up POWs; it would be a funny thing if he comes to Java to pick me up. We have been issued with new 'bush' wear, but it is miles too big. One little Aussie captain told me that the trousers he was first given tied up over his head; he could see out by peering through the fly holes. One's sense of humour is gradually returning! I realized that I had only laughed at the antics of the Aussies and Capt. 'Grony' in three and a half years and nothing much else.

Later went back to the tempal [*sic*] factory.

23 September

I went to Tjideng (women's camp) to see Mrs Johnson. Found her to be well but anxious for news of Johnnie. I spent a pleasant afternoon with her and chopped wood for the cooking stove.

24–27 September

Embarked on an LCI No. 3 (landing craft) at Priok. At 1400 hrs, we set sail, about 300 of us, in three LCIs escorted by HMS *Kale* for Singapore. The Fleet, comprising HMS *Cumberland*, two frigates and five minesweepers, lined their rails and gave us a great send-off. We are away from Java at last under the White Ensign. During captivity I kidded myself that once we were released I would remain on Java for a few months to discover its beauties, but now I cannot wait to get away.

However, I feel very concerned about the Dutch women and children who remain holed up in prison camps in very precarious circumstances. Surely, something should have been done for them first. I do not think we would feel as vulnerable as the Dutch if we had to wait a little longer to travel home. There are many armed Jap soldiers, criminals and nationalists (*pemuda*) roaming around west Java.

Units of the Dutch Fleet had accompanied *Cumberland* into Priok, including the refurbished Dutch cruiser *Tromp* (HMNS *Tromp* had escaped the carnage of the Java Sea Battle and reached Fremantle, Western Australia for repairs).

En route from Java to Singapore, the weather was dull and showery with the occasional squall. I was seasick the first night and the following morning, but did not care too much. A bad squall the second morning made the barge toss and turn quite dramatically. I lay on my bunk hoping that the pork and beans I had for breakfast did not reappear; I just managed to keep them down.

There was little of interest to see apart from porpoises and flying fish. The flying fish fascinated me; some flew for great distances and left interesting trails in the water before take-off, while gaining momentum by rapidly flipping their tails in the water. In a calm sea, this left incredible symmetrical ripple patterns. There were also sea birds and coast swallows.

We seemed to be taking a long course, presumably to avoid minefields, and went through the Strait of Karimata between Billington and Borneo. We passed in sight of Billington and the Karimata Islands and the Islands of the Riouw Archipelago. The *Kale* left as our escort the second morning and was replaced by a frigate from Singapore.

We entered Singapore in darkness on the evening of the 27th. It took a long time to enter port and we did not drop anchor until midnight. We passed a maze of brightly lit shipping, including the flagship HMS *Nelson*, an escort carrier, and other Allied boats.

28 September

Officers proceeded to the Sea View Hotel; this had been used by military flyers, British and Australian, before the Japanese had overrun Singapore. In my haste to leave the docks in the first truck, I managed to miss Lord Louis Mountbatten, who addressed the disembarking troops at the quayside. The men said that he was full of admiration for what we had been through and that we had fought valiantly against the odds.

This was a bit of a blow as I had also managed to miss seeing Lady Edwina Mountbatten when she visited Batavia, being with a work party that had gone to Kramat women's camp on that occasion. We received rations of cigarettes, chocolate, soap, etc., besides a large pile of kit. The kit was not much better than that issued in Batavia, being much too large. I had a stroll to the nearest shops in the evening.

29 September

We went aboard the MV (Motor Vessel) *Cilicia* – a nicely appointed ship and late-armed cruiser. No shore leave was granted and we spent the day uneventfully.

30 September

Shore leave granted from 1400 hrs to 2359 hrs. Spotted my old friend Johnnie and his wife down on the quayside and rushed down to meet them. Mrs Johnson had managed to get a flight from Java a couple of days earlier. I had not seen Johnnie for several years and was glad to see him in reasonable shape. I arranged to meet them in the Raffles Hotel, famous for its Gin-Slings, in the afternoon and we sat chatting about old times and our mutual acquaintances.

Col Grafton joined us for dinner. Afterwards we made our way by taxi to the New World amusement palace. It comprises many Chinese theatres, one Malayan theatre, several cinemas, small stalls and restaurants. We went to a small Chinese place that sold beer and had some real Chinese chow, but no rice! The Chinese fascinate me, especially the women and children. The women are industrious and the children amuse themselves very easily. The women had braided jet-black hair with a wonderful sheen like satin. Nearly everyone speaks very well of the Chinese, who are loyal and hard working. I have great admiration for them – they suffered horribly under the Japanese.

I wrote letters home to Margaret and Mum and Dad when back on board ship.

Life at the moment doesn't seem real and I have to pinch myself that I am not just having a rare happy dream only to wake up to a Jap guard's rifle butt bashing me in the head! The stories coming through about the war in Europe, describing the fighting in Italy and Germany, fill me with a sense of frustration and failure. We really had rotten luck being sent to the Far East, where we achieved very little.

1 October

I went into town immediately after lunch (also, I managed to extract $50 from my old pal the paymaster!). Went with Griff Davies and met up with Johnnie again at the Raffles Hotel, where many different people were coming and going. [*Lt G. G. Davies had been recommended for the MC for his courageous work as gun position officer during a heavy enemy bomber raid on Tjilatjap on March 5 1942.*] One such we bumped into was the Australian, Bradford Potter, of the yacht *Fram* fame. He told us that the Japs had nearly executed him after he was caught in Javanese waters with papers, signed by the Admiralty, stating that he had permission to fly the Blue Ensign. The Japs took a lot of persuading that Potter was not a spy.

I strolled through the streets in the evening and bought stamps and a camera. I saw some beautifully carved Bali heads in ironwood, which I could not afford. I feel like a child again – things are captivating my attention and trivial things thrill me: the wooden carvings, the pictorial stamps I bought, and the sight of young very attractive Chinese women and beaming Chinese children. Oh, what joy! Just after sundown, I passed a large tree full of sparrow-like birds making a tremendous din.

I heard, during the day, some of the terrible stories about the Japs' crimes in Singapore. Hundreds of Chinese, deemed pro-British, were rounded up and herded into a barbed wire playing field enclosure, in front of the Government buildings. They were kept without food or water for three days, and then massacred. The Nips took others out to sea in barges and killed some on the boat, but others were thrown live to the sharks.

The most appalling case was of a Chinese businessman who was hung upside down on public display while a small tube was connected to a vein and blood was slowly drained from his body. It was indeed a gruesome and bestial death. I had seen some photographs at the BMA Information Bureau showing Jap soldiers using live Indian prisoners for bayonet practice; some were also used for rifle target practice. (This was part of the *Sook Ching* 'purification by elimination' massacre. It has been estimated that 50,000 Chinese from Malaya and Singapore were murdered by the Japanese *Kempeitai* under Col Tsuji.) There were some presentable pictures of POWs filling in sandbags for air-raid shelters around Government House. Our people, I understand, are treating these crimes as serious war crimes.

I am not aware that there has been any physical violence towards the captured Japs so far, but I did learn that our guards at Changi jail are teaching Gen. Saito, 'Shito' to us Brits, to bow so low that he bangs his head on the ground. He was in charge of all prison camps in this part of the Far East, including Java. When he took over in Singapore, he addressed the prisoners at Changi by saying 'I am the successor to my predecessor. Good day.' A bizarre and profound statement indeed!

I have seen pictures of England, which fill me with ecstasy and longing. The tears are not far away. 'Oh England, how I love thee; no suffering would be too great that thou are freed from tyranny.' Later in the evening, I went with Johnnie, his wife and staff, to the cinema. This was the first proper cinema visit since Cape Town in January 1942. We saw *Victory in Tunisia*. It was war, bloody war, including heavy artillery, naval bombardment (the Navy are a grand bunch of lads with plenty of guts), aerial bombing, and terrific tank battles with advancing infantry; a tremendous combined action with British, including the magnificent Eighth Army, American and Free French forces.

The Nazis were well and truly licked and it was grand to see. I just wish I had been part of it! I do become very discouraged and helpless thinking of our floundering efforts in Java. I keep telling myself that we could not be blamed for our predicament and it was like 'lambs to the slaughter'. We are the same flesh and blood as the Eighth Army for goodness sake!

2 October

I have been placed in charge of military personnel on my troop deck. It was raining heavily when we woke up this morning and the outlook is dull for the rest of the day! I went out with the camera, but the light was poor, so only took three snaps. I visited the Raffles Museum, which has quite a good natural history section, particularly ornithology. I spent only about an hour in the museum, but could have spent at least a week.

I met Schoulie and Sen Jull for tea; after Schoulie went home, Sen and I met up with Johnnie and wife, by chance. Of course, Johnnie would invite us to dinner so, to square things up, I bought Mrs Johnson a set of embroidered handkerchiefs, which she very much appreciated.

Before dinner, Sen and I visited an Indian barber's shop. A funny old man cut my hair and took great pains about it. It is obviously an art to these people. He did try to leave me with a hair parting but, after years of camp 'convict' cuts, this was nigh impossible. We had a very pleasant evening, marred only by the taxi driver dropping us off at the wrong dock. We could see the *Cilicia*, but several stretches of water were between her and us. We circumnavigated one dock and, fortunately, a passing truck driver picked us up and took us to our boat.

On returning, I heard from one of the lads that Lt Ken Taylor had died in Siam. This was very sad news to me – I was very fond of Ken, who had been like a brother to me in the early days of captivity; nothing was ever too much trouble for him. He leaves a wife, and a son whom he has never seen. I can well remember Ken's prophetic line in my autograph book: 'We have but little time to stay and once departed may return no more.' Ken had written these words four days before we embarked from Glasgow in December 1941. Back on the *Cilicia* quite a number of civilians, men, women and children, are coming aboard and more are expected tomorrow. The result is that most of us, except senior officers, have been kicked out of our cabins onto troop deck D, in the forecastle. The accommodation is now lousy, which has led to a great deal of discontent amongst the soldiers. Initially, I resented this but when I considered that a number of the civilians had had an awful time of it, I resigned myself to roughing it back to England. This is still a palace compared to Bicycle camp.

Lt Alan Reardon-Smith (AR-S whose family owns the Reardon-Smith shipping line) related a good story – he was looking for one of his family ships in Singapore harbour and found one quite by chance. He made his way up the gangplank to be confronted by a burly ship's mate, who told AR-S to 'Bugger off!' AR-S, who was looking somewhat dishevelled at the time, rose to his full height and said, 'I am Alan Reardon-Smith and I own this bloody ship.' Alan was quickly ushered on board.

We heard that Japanese military flags remained flying in parts of the Far East until the middle of September and that Gen. Yamashita had continued to fight in the Philippines until 8 September.

4 October

Set sail at 1400 hrs for home unescorted – whoopee! Unfortunately, the CO decided to have a conference at this time and I missed all the sights leaving the main dock. I did take some photographs, although the weather was bad. I really enjoyed my last day in Singapore, although I ended up rather the worse for wear! My head is suffering today!

Yesterday, first thing, I went to the cable office to send messages home about our imminent departure, then proceeded to the museum to take a closer look at some of the stuffed exhibits. I was impressed with the black Sumatran rhino and the saladangs, the wild cattle with very large heads, orang-utan, cobras, sharks, local crocodiles, which seemed to be as long as the pythons on display, about twenty-four feet. There were also examples of swift birds' nests, used by the Chinese to make their famous soup.

After a good look around, I went off to Raffles for a free tea. I had considered going to the cinema, at about 1930 hrs, but went into a café/bar for a drink of lemonade first. Three Allied army officers on a nearby table invited me over to join them. We had many beers and ended up in a Chinese restaurant to sober up. I managed later to feel stable enough to go and say a fond farewell to the Johnsons.

22 October

Quite a long gap since my last entry, but things on my troop deck have kept me busy. On about the 9th we called in at Colombo, Ceylon, and had a few pleasant hours ashore. On the 10th, I went down with a fever and I was admitted to the ship's hospital on the 11th. I am now recovering after about ten days completely 'out of it'. This was quite ironic, as I was supposed to be looking after the sick and crippled on my troop deck. A fat lot of good I was to them! The weather is getting colder and we may need overcoats by the time we reach good old England. The weather remains dull. Hopefully, we should be arriving home in England in about a week.

23 October

It is a beautiful and warm day and the sea is a real Mediterranean transparent blue. This morning we passed very close to the fortress island of Pantellaria, 'the Italian Malta', and our course is heading for the North African coast. We are encountering increasing amounts of shipping. I had intended writing up many notes on this trip but the fever scuppered that idea. I have managed to obtain some copies of the *Western Mail*, the Welsh paper in English, in which 'HRH' has been shooting a 'hell of a line' about Welsh POW treatment by the Japs.

A young Dutch boy came over to chat to us. AR–S asked him what he wanted. The Dutch lad said in half Dutch and English that his mother was busy talking to two gentlemen, and could he go and play with the soldiers. This certainly put us in our place!

24 October

The African coast is still on our port side, with quite visible mountains. We passed Algiers at 1100 hrs, but could not see much of it. A little while later the White Star Cunard, *Mauritania* passed by on our port side. I used my last exposure to take a snap of it. Schools of porpoises now regularly pass the boat and this has caused quite some excitement for the children, especially when they leap out of the water. The weather is good and the sea calm. The children are amusing to watch; many of them will be visiting England for the very first time. A lot speak half-English and half-Dutch lingo. My understanding of Dutch is much better when reading the language rather than listening, although the children do seem to speak a language I can comprehend.

25 October

Arrived in Gibraltar at 1300 hrs and lay off until 1600 hrs. A large number of launches pulled up alongside and parties of officials ascended onto the ship, followed by bags of mail. I received a rather puzzling letter from Margaret, who was expecting me home last Tuesday. I hope she has not gone to Weston-super-Mare because I have reserved the train for Burry Port, South Wales. Still, I am sure it will work out all right in the end. I hope Margaret will not be dashing around the railway stations waiting for someone who is not going to arrive!

Gibraltar is a most impressive sight with houses scattered on the lower slopes of the 'Big Rock'. Many of the buildings appeared very grand with inverted casement windows. A number of boat vendors rowed out to the ship with odds and ends for sale, but no one appears to have much money. The captain of the ship did not see them as welcome visitors and got the crew to turn water hoses on them.

The gulls seem a lot sleeker than the ones back home. The weather remains good, but for how much longer I do not know. I will have forty-two days straight leave when I get home. I am seriously considering publishing a book about my experiences in captivity. When I get home, I shall go down on my knees and thank God that I have survived this terrible ordeal, while so many others have perished. It is truly a miracle.

28 October

Capt. Stormont, the ship's master, provided a very successful farewell dinner for the ex-POWs and civilian internees on board, in recognition of our forbearance and cooperation during the trip home.

We docked at Liverpool on Tuesday 30 October. I took the train to Bristol and then Weston-super-Mare. Dad managed to alert me by mail that M&B [*Margaret and Barrie*] were staying in Weston and I arrived in a gale to meet them. Apparently, these were the worst storms for some years, with promenade benches being tossed into the air by the strong westerly winds and a high tide. Dad was away on business in Manchester. I spent a week recuperating at Sydney House, my parents' home, before heading back, with Margaret and Barrie, to Pembrey, South Wales. [*My mother said recently that she did not recognise my father at Weston railway station. He was out of uniform, smoking dreadful Semangat Japanese cigarettes, looked haggard and appeared at least ten years older than she had expected. Son Barrie, aged four, could not comprehend that the man they had met was his father.*]

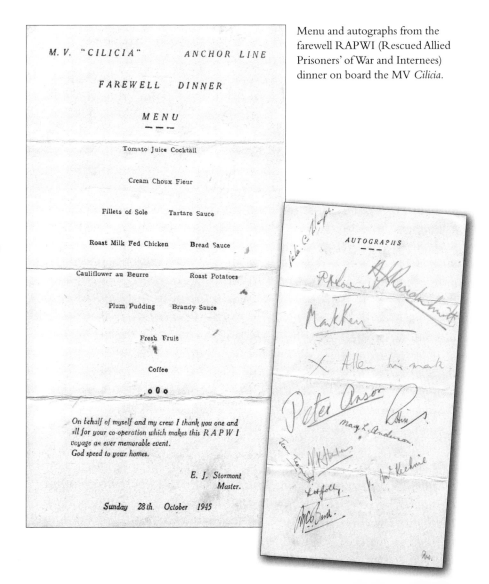

Menu and autographs from the farewell RAPWI (Rescued Allied Prisoners' of War and Internees) dinner on board the MV *Cilicia*.

M.V. "CILICIA"   ANCHOR LINE

FAREWELL   DINNER

MENU

Tomato Juice Cocktail

Cream Choux Fleur

Fillets of Sole   Tartare Sauce

Roast Milk Fed Chicken   Bread Sauce

Cauliflower au Beurre   Roast Potatoes

Plum Pudding   Brandy Sauce

Fresh Fruit

Coffee

o 0 o

On behalf of myself and my crew I thank you one and all for your co-operation which makes this R A P W I voyage an ever memorable event. God speed to your homes.

E. J. Stormont
Master.

Sunday 28th October 1945

AUTOGRAPHS

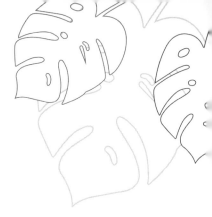

Part II: Appendices

1: Volunteering for Military Service

This account is based on notes kept by my father, written and oral recollections of family and friends, and personal accounts of fellow artillerymen.

Ronald volunteered his services for the military just before the outbreak of war in mid-August 1939; war was declared against Germany on the 3 September. He was keen to join the RAF as an air gunner, but did not succeed as RAF recruitment was popular at this time. This did not prove a problem, some months later, for his brother Hugh (a flight engineer) and brothers-in-law, Bruce Rowe-Evans (a Lancaster bomber pilot) – later to win a DFC (Distinguished Flying Cross) and Lewis Morris (RAF administration).

As Ronald was living and working in South Wales, he volunteered for the 77th Welsh Anti-Aircraft (AA), Royal Artillery (RA) Regiment based in Cardiff. He was, in all probability, influenced by his father, Frank Snr, who had been an artillery sergeant during the First World War. Frank Sr survived a bad mustard-gas attack in France in 1917, was later mentioned in despatches and was due to start officer training when the war ended.

The 77th was a Territorial Army regiment, established for the air protection of Cardiff, Barry and the surrounding districts. Many well-known Welsh sports stars, including rugby internationals Cliff Jones, Wilf Wooller, Les Spence and Kenwyn Street, also joined the regiment. Ronald was allocated to 239 Battery and became Gnr Williams on the 20 August 1939. He was actively manning anti-aircraft guns during the last week of August 1939.

Incidentally, Ronald had been keen to fight in the Spanish Civil War in 1938, for the International Brigade against Franco's Fascists, but his father would not allow him to leave the family business. His father concurred with Winston Churchill that Britain was in imminent danger of becoming embroiled in a war with Hitler. He argued that if Ronald had been killed or seriously wounded in Spain this would not have helped Britain's likely war prospects, or the family business!

New Gunners! Ronald Williams is in the centre and Moss Simon to his left in September 1939.

Sergeant Frank Williams (Ronald Williams' father) of the Royal Artillery in the First World War, 1917.

Gun emplacements in Cardiff were based at Llanishen, Cardiff Docks, Ely Race Course, Penylan, Maerdy, and Western Avenue. 239 and 240 Btys were barracked at the Drill Hall, Dumfries Place, Cardiff; with gunnery lectures taking place at the City Hall. In 1940, 239 Bty was protecting Barry Docks and the Bristol Channel.

Ronald was based at the Bulwarks, Barry at a fixed gun battery, in a line of artillery defence with Lavernock Point, Sully. He records in a diary that two enemy 'visitors' (Heinkel 111s) were shot down on 4 November 1940 and another the following night, with help from the 'Sully boys'. The planes fell like 'flaming balls of fire' into the Bristol Channel.

Members of 239 Battery training on a fixed 3-inch anti-aircraft gun in September 1939.

Lance Bombardier Williams (doing a Nelson impression, far right) on a 3-inch fixed gun in 1939.

A new 3.7 inch mobile anti-aircraft gun at Porthkerry, South Wales, in 1940.

3.7-inch guns firing at night, Porthkerry, South Wales, 1940.

Although there were no other records of action in Ronald's papers for this period, he wrote after the war to the WO (War Office), on behalf of his regiment, about the WO's refusal to present the Defence Medal to the surviving 77th members, stating:

> We were actively manning artillery around Cardiff from the end of August 1939 till mid 1941. We shot down many German raiders during that time, and we were given a Civic reception by Alderman Walter R. Willis, on our return from the Far East in recognition of our sterling defence of Cardiff.

George Thomas, MP pursued an inquiry on behalf of the regiment but my father does not have this medal because the Defence Medal was eventually only awarded for non-operational service.

During the period that Ronald was involved in the protection of Cardiff, and later Barry Docks, he rose rapidly through the ranks to battery sergeant major. He told me that his army bosses were impressed with his typing and shorthand skills! I am sure other, more important attributes would have been considered in his promotion.

In August 1941 the regiment was transferred to Blandford Camp, Dorset, and 239 Bty was sent to Headingly, Leeds. On 10 October 1941, 239 Bty was transferred to Crewe, Chester, and joined up with 240 and 241 Btys, to protect the railway. Soon after this, on the 29 October 1941, the regiment was called to Glasgow and based at the old Drill Hall, Merryhill (home of the 80th Field Regiment, Royal Artillery).

Ronald's first child, Barrie, was born on 18 November 1941, in a Cardiff nursing home. He managed to obtain a special twenty-four-hour warrant and transport to see his new son. He travelled to Cardiff, and found the nursing home, but only had about an hour with mother and first born, before returning to Glasgow.

Ronald Williams' Military Record

(77th HAA Royal Artillery Regiment)

Gunner: August 1939

Battery Sergeant Major: July 1940

Second Lieutenant: 5 February 1942

First Lieutenant: 9 May 1942 (while a POW)

Captain (T): November 1945

Army discharge: July 1946

Officers and senior NCOs of 239 Bty before travelling to the Far East in 1941. BSM Ronald Williams is in the front row to the right of Maj. L.N. Gibson (Battery commander). Captain Sir William Thomas is to Gibson's left.

Senior Regimental NCOs with Regimental HQ officers Lt Col H.R. Humphries, Capt. Mossford and Lt H. Clatworthy. BSM Ronald Williams is fifth right, front row.

Senior officers and NCOs of the 77th Royal Artillery Regiment. Lt Col H.R. Humphries is in the centre with riding boots and shooting stick. Also present in the front row are Maj. Mossford (RHQ) and Battery commanders Majs L.N. Gibson, L.J. Street and Gerald Gaskell. Ronald Williams is fourth right, second row.

2: A Dark Night Descends over the Dutch East Indies

[*The following is an account written by Ronald regarding the bravery of the Dutch East Indian Fleet, who, assisted by British, American and Australian ships fought the advancing Japanese, despite being heavily outnumbered. Ronald was on Madoera Island, Java in a forward observation post, during the time of the sea battles. He would have been witness to some of the actual sea battle action and party to radio information on the progress of events. I can only assume that he was sent to Madoera Island to advise on artillery positions, as the island had a number of anti-aircraft batteries. He left no diary record of this period, but did write a play about Madoera – One Came Back Home.*]

I had contemporary knowledge of many of the events described in this true story. I have based most of this account, for factual accuracy, on an article which appeared in the Dutch newspaper, *De Pen Gun*, on 1 March 1946.

The struggle the Dutch Navy maintained during 1941–2 against the Japanese in the defence of the Dutch East Indies, culminating in the Battle of the Java Sea, was a heavy price to pay to protect the 'Insulinde'. Much of the Dutch Navy was destroyed during this period and the splendidly wealthy and culturally diverse Dutch East Indian islands, with a population of over 70 million inhabitants, fell prey to the Japanese invaders. This event was perceived by the world's news reports at the time as little more than a sideshow to the German occupation of Europe.

However, this event was no sideshow as the task faced by the Dutch Navy, with help from the British, American and Australian navies, was formidable from the outset. The Allied Military High Command was well aware that the superiority of the Imperial Japanese Navy would overwhelm the Allied fleet. Yet this hopeless situation was pursued. One must question: why?

In the first place, it was of the utmost importance that the enemy be engaged and impeded for as long as possible (the importance of this will be explained later). Secondly, the Allied Fleet stayed to fight as a retreat to Australia could have been counter productive and, ultimately, a disaster for the Antipodes. Many Dutch and Javanese sailors did not want their beautiful islands to fall into enemy hands. During the whole of the conflict, there were very few Javanese naval desertions, a relatively easy option for the Javanese sailor whilst in dock, which spoke volumes for their commitment to the cause. The land forces were not as fortunate with this level of commitment from the Javanese.

This is the brief story of a small Dutch East Indian fleet, assisted by American, British and Australian ships, which fought to the death in the seas of the East Indian Archipelago against the tide of a superior Japanese force which were numerically much larger, better armed and had predominately modern warships.

It was a heroic and brave struggle, dogged by misfortune and lack of air cover. It was hopeless from the start – from the High Command to the lowest naval rating, they knew that the odds were stacked against them, but a fight to gain time was the goal. The goal was to gain time for Australia and British India to prepare them for possible invasion. Time was never more precious – the enemy had to be delayed, and delayed it was by the magnificent sacrifices of this small Allied fleet.

In order to gain a clearer picture of what occurred in the Dutch East Indies in late December 1941, and the first few months of 1942, it is necessary to return to the night of 7 December and the day of 8 December 1941. The Japanese committed an act of treachery, without provocation, by attacking Pearl Harbor, Manila and Hong Kong, enraging the Americans and much of the rest of the world in the process.

At Pearl Harbor, eight of the US battleships were sunk, or severely damaged; a crippling blow for the US Pacific Fleet. The Dutch declared war on Japan and within days Japan began to cast its shadow over the East Indies. On 10 December 1941, a fresh blow came when two battleships (one a battle cruiser), the HMS *Prince of Wales*, and HMS *Repulse*, only recently arrived in the Far East, were sunk by Japanese torpedoes off the east coast of Malacca. Japanese transporters successfully landed troops on the Malayan coast, via the Gulf of Siam, in preparation for the invasion of Singapore.

The Dutch naval force, which opposed the invaders of the East Indies Archipelago, included the following:

- Three light Dutch cruisers – the *De Ruyter* (Rear Admiral Doorman's Flag Ship), the *Tromp* and the *Java*
- Seven destroyers – the *Van Ghent, Kortenaer, Piet Hein, Banckert, Van Ness, Evertsen,* and the *Witte de With*
- Twelve submarines – K10–K18, O16, O19 and O20
- Twenty-seven flying boats

The submarines had moderate success in harrying the Japanese convoys and sunk a number of troop transporters during this naval campaign, with the loss of two of their own. However, this hardly curtailed the Japanese advance towards Singapore.

After the loss of the *Prince of Wales* and *Repulse*, British naval power in the Far East was greatly reduced and, in consequence, the naval forces that could be mustered by the Allies were not great. The British had:

- One heavy cruiser – HMS *Exeter*
- Five light cruisers
- Thirteen 'dated' destroyers
- Twenty-seven submarines.

The strength of the Japanese 'Southern' naval force, uncertain at the time, was thought to be:

- Three battleships
- Nine battle cruisers
- Forty-eight destroyers
- Eighteen submarines

In reserve there were:

- Fourteen cruisers
- Twenty-one destroyers
- Forty-four submarines.

Most of these were modern, unlike the Allied fleet, which had ships dating back to the First World War.

How many were used is uncertain, but the easy passage the Japanese had before reaching the Dutch East Indies made it likely that most ships were available. The Japanese had considerable advantage in the air and were able to maintain reconnaissance over the entire operational field. The Allies had no such advantage and relied on guesswork based on scanty reconnaissance information. What information they received came from the Dutch Marine *Luchvaartdienst*, who did what they could with few airworthy planes, and flying around the clock.

The defence of the Dutch East Indies depended, principally, on the great naval base at Singapore, which had been subject to heavy bombing by the Japanese. The loss of this key base would prove to be the undoing of the Allies and the Dutch occupation of the East Indies. Moreover, Singapore could not possibly hold out unless her sea communications remained open.

The Japanese closed these rapidly and by the time Java came under serious threat only the Sunda Strait between Java and Sumatra was open to Allied shipping. Thus, the defense of Java was essential for the whole future of the Dutch East Indies and so spirited and energetic preparations were made for action in Java. The combined Dutch, American, British and Australian naval forces worked tirelessly together, although seriously hampered by disparate signalling codes.

The first landings on the East Indian Archipelago occurred on British North Borneo and, despite regular submarine attacks on Japanese ships, the invaders continued to make rapid advances. On 10 January they landed on Tarakan, a small Dutch island off the east coast of Borneo and rich in oil; the following day onto Celebes, the Minahassa, and soon the mainland of Dutch North Borneo. With great speed, they lay down airfields and, profiting from their great air superiority, were in a position to bomb Java and regularly attacked ports and airfields. Allied submarines were also regularly targeted.

The continued American resistance at Corregidor on the Philippines did not delay Japanese progress appreciably and large Japanese troop movements headed for

New Guinea via Ambon. However, it had been hoped by the Allied command that Singapore and Java would hold out and many Allied troops were transferred to shore up these key positions.

This weakened resistance on some of the smaller islands. In the middle of January, the American, Vice Admiral T.C. Hart, took over the command of the Allied fleet (named the ABDA fleet because it included American, British, Dutch and Australian ships).

On 20 January Dutch reconnaissance aircraft reported a large concentration of Japanese vessels in the Makassar Strait between Borneo and Celebes. Allied warships went into action. Four weathered, but battle-hardened, American 'four-stacker' (four-funnel) destroyers equipped with torpedoes managed to inflict quite severe damage on Japanese ships in the Makassar Strait. Such was the cunning of the attack that not one of the American destroyers was hit.

On 1 February a strike force of ships, not needed for essential convoy work, was formed under the Dutch naval Flag Officer, Rear Admiral Karel Doorman, based at Soerabaja naval base, Java. From the first days of the strike force's existence it met with ill fortune, which was to continue throughout the naval campaign. The fleet was assembling just north of Bali when it came under sustained attack from Japanese bombers in which the American cruisers USS *Houston* and USS *Marblehead* were put out of action. The *Houston* was able to limp back to Soerabaja; the remaining ships dispersed into the Indian Ocean.

On 13 February, the Japanese landed on Banka Island and launched an air and naval invasion on Sumatra, intent on seizing the oil installations at Palembang. The next day Admiral T.C. Hart was recalled to Washington and supreme naval command of the ABDA force was handed over to Dutchman Rear Admiral Conrad Helfrich, based in Batavia. A day later Singapore surrendered to the Japanese. Java would now be in the direct firing line of the Japanese advance!

Rear Admiral Karel Doorman battled courageously against the odds during the Battle of the Java Sea. He went down with his flagship *De Ruyter* on 26 February, 1942. (Courtesy of *De Pen Gun*)

The threat to Sumatra by the landings on Banka had become very serious and the Allied strike force was brought into action. The intention was to send a raiding party from the Sunda Strait northwards, between Banka island and Billington, through the Banka Strait, in an attempt to sink as many Japanese troop transporters as possible. Doorman had only five light and heavy cruisers, the *De Ruyter, Java, Tromp*, HMS *Exeter* and HMAS *Hobart*, at his disposal, plus six American and four Dutch destroyers.

This sortie occupied the days of 14 and 15 February and was beset by problems from the start. The Dutch destroyer *Van Ghent*, whilst passing through a narrow section of the Sunda Strait, ran aground in the pitch darkness. The *Banckert* stopped to take off the crew of the stricken Dutch destroyer and, in consequence, lost touch with the rest of the squadron.

Early next morning, enemy reconnaissance planes sighted the squadron and from 0900 hrs Japanese bombers pummelled the naval squadron for most of the day. The Allied naval squadron pressed ahead but, eventually, became widely dispersed whilst taking evasive action from the enemy bombs. Doorman decided that the squadron was not in the best condition or position to continue and signaled to return to base. Amazingly, due to good seamanship, the squadron suffered little serious damage.

The Japanese now had an easy passage through to Sumatra and by 20 February had a firm grip on lands north of the Sunda Strait. The Dutch fleet suffered two serious losses in quick succession when the destroyer *Van Ness* was sunk by air attack near Banka, whilst escorting evacuation ships. The coastal defence ship the *Soerabaja* was sunk, ironically, in the harbour with the same name.

It was now clear that Java was in imminent danger of invasion from the north, west and east. A Japanese convoy had been sighted south of Celebes, sailing in the direction of Bali. The remains of the Dutch and British air force managed to hassle the convoy for most of the day.

The naval strike force received orders to attack. Doorman had split his squadron: on the south coast of Java, based at the naval base of Tjilatjap, were the cruisers *De Ruyter* and *Java* and destroyers *Piet Hein, Kortenaer* and USS *Ford*; based at Soerabaja, on the north east coast, was the cruiser *Tromp* and the four American destroyers, *Stewart, Parrot, Edwards* and *Pillsbury*.

The attack by the Allied strike force, starting on the 19 February, was designed to be two pronged. Unluckily, the *Kortenaer*, on leaving Tjilatjap, ran aground and was left behind. The remainder sailed full steam towards Bali to intercept Japanese troop ships.

The Japanese appeared to have been taken by complete surprise initially; in the early exchanges, several Japanese transporters were sunk, and warships damaged. However, the superiority of the Japanese naval vessels soon started to inflict terrible damage on the Allied squadron. The destroyer *Piet Hein* was hit in her engine room and then unmercifully pounded to oblivion by enemy gun batteries. The *Java* was moderately damaged and the destroyers *Ford* and *Pope*, who had joined in the action, lost contact with the squadron. The remainder made their way back to Soerabaja for repairs, refueling and re-arming.

A few hours later, the northern group went into action. The four American destroyers took the lead and raced through the Bandoeng Strait, which was well lit with burning debris and guns blazing away. The enemy was now fully prepared for action. The Dutch battle cruiser, the *Tromp*, ran the gauntlet of Japanese firepower and received eleven direct hits. She made it back to Soerabaja but was considered too damaged to take any further part in engagements and sailed for Australia to undergo substantial repairs. This was her good fortune. She arrived in Darwin on 27 February, on the very day that her Dutch sister ships were wiped out in the Battle of Java Sea. Thus, the *Tromp* was the only Dutch surface warship in the Far East to survive to the end of the war.

Once again, the enemy had been delayed, but not deterred, and quickly Bali and Lombok were seized. However, the four American destroyers returned to port with only a few battle scars.

The last phase of the battle for the East Indies was now at hand. With Singapore lost and Borneo, Celebes, Sumatra, Bali and Lombok all but overrun, things were looking desperate for Java. However, there was still a slim chance that a miracle would save Java and every effort was being made to shore up Java's defences and a final naval engagement was being planned.

Two strike forces were organised, one based in Tandjong Priok, Batavia, the western strike force, and the other at the main Dutch Naval base at Soerabaja, the eastern strike force. The Batavian port was being subjected to intense bombing and it was decided that the western strike force would make haste to Soerabaja. Some smaller ships were left behind in Tandjong Priok for anticipated transport escort duty. The heavy cruiser *Exeter* and HMAS *Perth* with destroyers *Jupiter*, *Encounter* and *Electra* set sail for Soerabaja to join the cruisers *De Ruyter* and *Houston* and destroyers *Witte de With*, *Kortenaer* (since refloated), *Banckert*, *Edwards*, *Alden*, *Ford*, *Paul Jones*, and *Pope*.

USS *Houston*, known affectionately as the 'Galloping Ghost of the Java Coast' due to the number of times the ship had been reported sunk. She did eventually sink in the Sunda Strait while running into a major Japanese landing force. The artist is a *Houston* naval carpenter, L.E. Biechlin (Priok camp, February 1943).

On the 26th information was received that the Japanese had a large convoy in the Java Sea proceeding straight for north Java. At noon, Doorman held his last council with his naval commanders, where it was decided to make sweeps along the northern coasts of Madoera and Rembang until contact was made with the enemy convoy.

By this time, there was no Allied air reconnaissance. *Banckert* had taken direct hits during bomber raids on the port of Soerabaja and was considered too damaged for action. Other ships had also taken hits during the bombing raids but committed themselves to a last-ditch naval battle.

The striking force put to sea for the last time. After cruising throughout the night and following morning due north of Madoera Island, Doorman received messages that Japanese troop ships were passing east of the Bawean Islands. Doorman gave orders to intercept the ships at full speed ahead. At 1615 hrs the enemy convoy was sighted. However, no troop carriers could be identified as this was in fact a covering squadron consisting of two heavy and two light Japanese cruisers and twelve destroyers.

A gunnery duel commenced but, unfortunately, the range was too great for the Allied cruisers and they were ordered to close the distance. The *De Ruyter* and *Java* were hit but not seriously. Two Japanese destroyers took direct hits.

Suddenly, six Japanese destroyers launched a torpedo attack. It was repelled successfully by the Allied squadron, who managed to sink one of the Japanese destroyers. The remainder of the enemy destroyers retired under a smoke screen.

An hour later the squadron had its first major setback as *Exeter* took a direct hit in her engine room, killing many of the engineers; she was ordered back to Soerabaja with the *Witte De With* as escort. A smoke screen was used to conceal the withdrawal of these ships.

Soon after, evidence of Japanese submarine activity was observed and at 1715 hrs the *Kortenaer* received several well-directed torpedoes and broke in two. Some of her crew were picked up by *Encounter*. Coming out of the smoke screen, the destroyer *Electra* encountered four Japanese destroyers. She went down with all guns blazing and one of the enemy destroyers eventually sank from the effects of *Electra*'s firepower.

The crippled *Exeter*, along with destroyers *Witte de With* and *Jupiter*, had their own little naval battle with a Japanese heavy cruiser which they eventually managed to drive away from the retreating *Exeter*. An attempt was made to reform the squadron and present a more concerted front to the enemy. However, the lack of air cover was a key disadvantage, and having little clear idea where enemy ships were positioned would prove very costly for the Allies.

Attacks on the enemy troop transporters became ever more difficult. Night fighting was also a mismatch as the Japanese Navy was very experienced at fighting in the dark and made use of magnesium flares to great effect. At 1930 hrs, Doorman signalled that the enemy appeared to be retiring westward, but there were no sightings of troop ships, which was their main target. None of the Allied naval commanders were any the wiser.

At 2030 hrs, there was more exchange of gunfire but little damage to either side. The squadron commanders decided to commence a sweep along the north coast of Java to exclude the possibility that troop transporters had slipped through unnoticed.

By this time the destroyer *Encounter* was out of touch with the remaining squadron and the smaller American destroyers were forced to return to Soerabaja to refuel.

Japanese submarines took advantage of the depleted squadron and sank the *Jupiter*. The strike force at this time consisted of only four cruisers who were now up against a force at least ten times stronger. The cruisers *De Ruyter*, *Java*, *Houston* and *Perth* decided to head north to move away from the submarine threat. The Dutch sailors had the traumatic experience of passing survivors of the *Kortenaer* thrashing around in the water. They dare not risk stopping to help, as they would become easy prey for enemy submarines.

At length, in the middle of the Java Sea, the last act of this great naval drama was played out. The Allied cruisers encountered two heavy Japanese cruisers and a number of destroyers. A fight to the death occurred with hits inflicted on both sides. Unfortunately, at 2315 hrs, the Dutch cruisers *De Ruyter* and *Java* were torpedoed with Rear Admiral Doorman going down with his flagship. The two remaining cruisers, heavily outnumbered, escaped back to Tandjong Priok.

Two days later, USS *Houston* and HMAS *Perth* made an attempted breakout through the Sunda Strait, hoping to fight on after much-needed repairs in Australia, but they ran slap bang into the Japanese fleet disembarking troops to attack west Java. They put up a brave fight but enemy torpedoes and gun battery fire sank both. Unfortunately, the ships' captains had been misinformed about Japanese positions and had only enough ammunition for a minor skirmish.

The battle was lost, but there were a number of Allied ships still afloat. The heavy cruiser *Exeter*, destroyers *Witte de With* and *Encounter* had made it back to Soerabaja. Unfortunately, *Witte de With* was bombed and sunk in the docks. *Exeter*, and the

'The end of the USS *Pope* during the Battle of Java Sea'. Artist unknown.

destroyers *Pope* and *Encounter*, decided to make a run for it out to sea because of the intense aerial bombardment, but they too ran into a Japanese squadron.

The *Exeter* was already seriously disabled and did not stand a chance, while the destroyers gave as good as they got but, ultimately, succumbed to superior fire power. The Dutch destroyer *Evertsen* tried the same route as the *Houston* and *Perth* and suffered the same fate in the Sunda Strait.

The four old American destroyers *Edwards*, *Alden*, *Ford*, and *Paul Jones*, due to their shallow draughts, managed to outflank the Japanese warships, although they had to fight their way through the shallows in places. They eventually broke through the Bandoeng Strait and made it to Australia. The American destroyers *Parrott* and *Whipple*, and the light cruiser *Marblehead*, also survived the action in the Java Sea and returned to the United States via Ceylon.

The Japanese were already landing on Java while, at sea, the Dutch submarine *K15* sank a Japanese fuel tanker. This was the last Allied success in these waters for some considerable time. On 8 March 1942, the Dutch announcer, Bert Garthoff, on Radio Bandoeng soberly gave the last message about surrender and played the Dutch National Anthem. He later paid with his life for this act of defiance. The night had indeed fallen over the East Indian Archipelago. The Japanese took just over three months to conquer South East Asia, but it took the Allies over three years to free the area from Japanese occupation.

3: Camp Journals Produced in Captivity, 1942–45

The Jungle Journal Part 1: Editorials and Captivity

Ronald wrote:

> To maintain the morale of the men and to keep minds occupied, I and some of my fellow POWs interested in producing a camp magazine set about organising such a venture. There was no shortage of expertise to write articles, poetry and amusing items. There were also those who could draw cartoons and illustrations. One of the main problems was finding enough paper, pens and pencils. On occasions, these were non-existent, after being taken from us by our guards.
>
> We managed to produce six editions of *The Jungle Journal* in Tandjong Priok camp and, later, a number of *The Yasume Times*. Great care was taken to avoid the wrath of the Japanese camp interpreter and camp commandant in what was written down (or typed, when a typewriter was available). A great deal of clever innuendo and subtlety needed to be employed!

As far as my father was aware, there were no original copies of the camp magazines surviving – although he had the originals of some of the cartoons, drawings, and poetry from the journals in his collection (these are included in this book). However, research by Lesley Clarke and Margaret Martin of the Java FEPOW Club 1942, with help from the Imperial War Museum's Far Eastern prisoner of war expert, Roderick Suddaby, established that the family of the late Maj. Gerald Gaskell, 240 Battery Commander in the 77th HAA, had deposited, on permanent loan, six issues of *The Jungle Journal* in the Imperial War Museum in 1998. A further edition came to light through Bill Marshall, Chair of the Java Club, who had a photocopy of the No. 2 edition. Therefore, editions No. 1 and 2, produced in Boei Glodok camp, and editions No. 3, 4, 5, 6, and 8, produced in Tandjong Priok camp, are extant. Greg Lewis, in his book *Java to Nagasaki*, based on the wartime diaries of the late Les Spence, describes that Les Spence had also deposited copies of *The Jungle Journal* with the *Western Mail* newspaper. Unfortunately, these copies are lost.

Ronald's papers indicate that detailed contributions had been identified for a total of eleven *Jungle Journal* editions. It seems very likely that editions No. 9 to 11 were never completed, or even started. One can speculate on the reasons why, but paper shortages, illness and major journal contributors being sent on labour drafts to other lands early in 1943 would be likely reasons for the demise of this journal. In fact, by 1943 in some camps in the Far East, the Japanese severely curtailed POWs' recreational activities, although Roderick Suddaby states that this curtailment was not universal.

Ronald managed to recruit over fifty officers and men, mainly from his regiment, to contribute to these camp journals. Contributions could be in the form of poems, verse, prose, short stories, anecdotes and articles of general interest. Cartoons and drawings were popular. My father recorded two hundred separate items for the journals in his notes. Major contributors were Sgt George Ball, Sgt Clifford Herbert, Gnr Charles Holdsworth, Lt Noel James and Bdr Michael J. O'Mahony for cartoons and illustrations. Gnr Daniel Evans, Bdr Frank Fryett, Gnr Edward Graham, Gnr T.G. Lewis, Bdrs Brian Norman and Norman Saunders, and Ronald himself made up the core of the journal writing. Officers Harold Davey, Herbert Lloyd, and Wilf Wooller were also regular contributors.

It appears that Ronald was the principal editor, with editorial assistance from Frank Fryett, Brian Norman, Norman Saunders, Norman Sage and T.G. Lewis.

The copies of *The Jungle Journal* at the IWM are all typewritten on various kinds of paper (all of A4 size) from letterheaded Dutch Rubber Company (N.V. The Estates Supplies Co., Ltd., Batavia) notepaper to very thin copying paper (*The Jungle Journal* No. 8). The contents vary from twenty-two pages in length (*The Jungle Journal* No. 1)

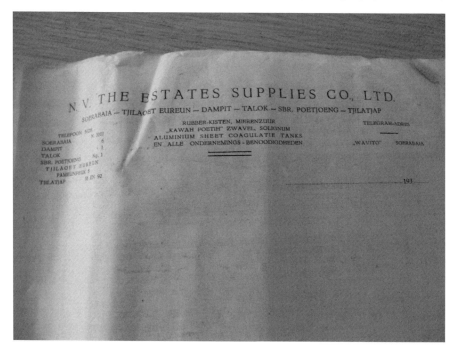

'N.V. The Estates', Batavia. The headed notepaper used for the first edition of *The Jungle Journal*. (Courtesy of Mrs Adèle Barclay)

Paper used for JJ.

to fifty-five pages (*The Jungle Journal* No. 6). Most of the contents of the surviving journals are readable, although some of the copies are in a parlous state through regular handling by their original readers. Illustrations are in both black and white and colour (crayon). There were instructions in some of the journals to pass copies on for others to enjoy and not to stow them in kitbags. A number of the contributors used pseudonyms, partly for effect. My father wrote as Lt Ron Williams, 'Sirius' (dog stories), 'Hot Stuff' (a sports reporter), 'Guner' (deliberate misspelling) 'Puddleberry', 'M.O. Ack' and 'Ronwil' and, with others, 'Bookworm'; Gnr Brian Norman was also 'Old Nore'.

Wilf Wooller wrote under the *nom-de-plume*, 'Turkeyneck', Col Bob Humphries as 'Gnr Marhen', and Harold Davey used various Malay words to sign off articles, such as '*Telur Bebek*' (duck eggs) and '*Sekolah Budak*' (schoolboy).

The contents of *The Jungle Journal* are a mixture of the light-hearted and serious, with an emphasis on POW activities, including sports reports, for example, officers *versus* sergeants soccer matches. Wilf Wooller was a regular contributor of sports reports. Regular features included 'My Corner of Britain', 'Local Customs' and 'My Most Embarrassing Moment'. Titles such as 'Born in Zunny Zummerst by Gurt Turmut', and the 'Surreyman's Tale' were included in 'My Corner of Britain'. 'Local Customs' included 'Roll out the Barrel'. Hobbies were included such as stamp collecting, chess, angling, model making and catching rabbits!

A number of articles had a distinct military theme, both factual and fictional, such as 'The Convoy', 'Return of the Soldier', 'Retreat from Tjilatjap', and 'Air Activity over Java'. A sense of escapism is conveyed in much of what was written, which is not surprising considering the circumstances. The short stories were mostly fictional, but written by those with inside knowledge of the workings of the central plots. These included journalists, lawyers and historians.

Humour was an essential attribute to maintain the POWs' spirits. However, some of the contents of cartoons and articles produced showed a cynical form of humour, which was, again, unsurprising in the circumstances. Titles included 'Come and get it!' – a reference to rice meals, 'Santa was a POW on Java', 'Spend a Vacation on Sunny Java', 'Can I go home Sir? I have done my Time' and 'A Dissertation on Fictional Food', a reference to the poor POW diet lacking in protein, vitamins and minerals.

There were also more wistful short stories and poems, for example: 'Little Lady Waiting', a reference to a prisoner's yearning to get back to his wife, 'I wish I had Something to Occupy my Mind' and 'Thoughts in a Malarial Ward'.

A typical list of items for *The Jungle Journal* issues:

Cover:
'Prison Scenes' (Ft Lt D.J. Dawson) 'Flyswatter' (No. 5 issue) (Charles Holdsworth)

Poems:
'The Last Cigarette' (Ron Williams)
'The Curse of Cain' (Ron Williams)
'Retreat from Tjilatjap' (T.A. Griffiths)
'In Memoriam' (D.J. Evans)
'Longing' (D.J. Evans)

Cartoons:
'Air Activity over Java' (G.W. Ball)
'Londoner's Dream' (G.W. Ball)
'No thanks I'd rather a Kensitas' (G.W. Ball)
'Home on the Range' (G.W. Ball)
'Emergency Rations' (Clifford Herbert)
'Leave it to the Skipper' (Clifford Herbert)

Sports Report:
Officers *v.* Sergeants (Hot Stuff)
Drama reports: Shakespeare by the St George's Players (John Forge)

Short Stories:
'Life's Ledger' (Frank Fryett)
'Priok Church' (Charles Holdsworth)
'A Close Shave' (Capt. Herbert M. Lloyd)
'Glodok' (N.E. Saunders)
'The Memory' (Wilf Wooller)
'The Sting' (B. Norman)
'Sunshine and Shadows' (G. Jones)
'Metacrania' (Frank Fryett)
'The Umpire's Decision' (Ken Vick)
'A Convivial Evening' (Robin Charles)
'Retribution' (Brian Norman)

Articles:

'My Corner of Britain: Bath' (Ron Williams)

'Evensong' (John G. Howell)

'Eyes Brown, Frightened Four' (Frank Fryett)

'Twelfth Night' (Norman E. Saunders)

'Service Traditions and Practices' (Col Humphries)

'Madurese pre-History' (Michael J. O'Mahony)

'Java Notes' (Capt. H. Davey)

'Sportsmanship' (Norman E. Saunders)

'Dissertation on Food in Fiction' (Brian Norman)

Others:

Astrology Corner ('Old Nore', Brian Norman)

'This is our Heritage': Included here are well-known poems such as 'If' by Rudyard Kipling, 'Remember Me' by Christina Rossetti, and 'The Soldier' by Rupert Brooke, which provided a certain resonance and meaning for the POWs. The appended explanation 'In the exigency of our present circumstances, this poem is reproduced without the permission of the executrix, etc.' was added.

'Your Health in the Tropics' ('M.O. Ack', Ron Williams)

'Silly Symphony – The Dufftown Monarch' (Edward Graham)

'Letters Home from Guner [*sic*] Puddleberry' (Ron Williams)

'Bookworm – Gems of literature' (various contributors)

'Dog Stories' ('Sirius' Ron Williams)

'Canary Breeding' (Reginald A. Avriall)

There was also reference to a list of Christmas presents to be sent to camp guards and Japanese cooks as follows:

Kasayama: pack of razor blades to commit HK (hari kari? Japanese ritual suicide)

Mori: bottle of Guinness for maintaining jet black hair

Pte Y: Bovril to put in the rice for flavour with a caption in Dutch: 'Fer rijst de piggy swill – Fer de flavor de Bovril'.

Pte U: Maclean's toothpaste for maintaining the sparkling teeth of this viciously grinning guard.

The following are pertinent extracts from extant issues of *The Jungle Journal* that emphasise the real dilemmas faced by the POWs. I have made some grammatical corrections and removed racial terms, which would have been acceptable military parlance in the 1940s, from a number of the articles.

The Jungle Journal No. 1

Somewhere in Java, 1942

You are now reading the first issue of *The Jungle Journal*. This paper is produced in the hope that it may help pass the time for us. Facilities being what they are, don't expect too much. If this production can help one gunner forget, for five minutes, the disappointments and discomforts of his present situation, then our editorial efforts will not be in vain.

The editorial policy of this paper is very simple. We try to entertain. The only promise we make to our readers is that this journal will remain free and independent or cease publication. There will be no propaganda matter printed under the present editorship.

Will anybody and everybody who has a story to tell or a verse to work off please submit it for publication. Like the Salvation Army, we say 'All contributions will be gratefully received'. We will endeavour, however, in this world to give some reward – maybe a packet of rokkos [*rokok cigarettes*]? This means YOU!

We ask that you give us a frank criticism of this issue and tell us what to do with future issues. But not too frankly please!

There follows a dedication:

This space in our first issue is dedicated, in true humility, to the memory of gentlemen of this regiment who died in active service on this foreign soil.

The first edition of *The Jungle Journal* was relatively slim compared to later journals produced in Tandjong Priok camp. The first edition was a 240 Battery, 77th HAA production with five contributors and, in all probability, was produced both in Boei Glodok camp and during confinement after surrender. This edition was signed off as being printed and published by 'The Jungle Press Ltd, a subsidiary company of 240 Bty, RA, in captivity as Prisoners' of War in the Java jungle'.

The second edition of *The Jungle Journal* was produced in Boei Glodok camp, Batavia in April 1942 with extracts from the editorial as follows:

Just over a month ago you were reading the first issue of *The Jungle Journal*. Remember? A lot of water has flowed down the drain since then. The environment has undergone a metamorphosis. Not so the Journal. We are still trying to entertain. But we still need contributions … We ask every man to write a description of the job he did in civilian life or, in the case of a sergeant, a description of the labour exchange from which he drew his dole! THIS MEANS YOU … The man who has never made a mistake is the man who has achieved nothing. Please send us your contribution.

Many sick men in the hospital would be only too glad to be fit enough to go out on a working party. Do you ever think of dropping a tin of milk or a

2. Ronald Williams' POW camp number.

1. This Dutch book, *En Euwig Zinge de Bosshen*, was Ronald Williams' constant companion n POW camps and contained nuch of his written material and lrawings.

An example of a pressed anese flower in the book, *En uwig Zinge de Bosshen*. Ronald illiams learned to read Dutch m books such as this. This ok and its contents proved be of no great interest to the anese, possibly because the ide covers were covered in erts for Japanese cigarettes d propaganda material for an's Great Asia war effort.

HOOFDSTUK XXIX

Nacht over de bosschen van Bjørndal; nacht, die naar grauwige morgenschemering toegaat — met duizenden sluipende dieren, op weg naar de grasvelden, of op roof uittrekken... die naar grauwige morgenschemering toeg... en en over de oude hoeve.

In de... ertrek vlamde het vuur van pijnboomen... gcheelen nacht had gebrand. Bij de tafel... nken. Mejuffrouw Kruse had den geh... nch aangedragen en daartusschen... Zoolang er menschen op waren, moest zij... en, zooals het het lot van de vrouwen, die vo... houden zorgden, in die dagen was, maar zooiets... vannacht was nog nooit voorgevallen. Het waren de... Dag en de kapitein, die in het voorvertrek zaten, en het... het bezoek van den overste.

Kapitein ...inge ...d in het leven schipbreuk geleden. ... de hand gewezen, en *dat* was ...en, die het meenden te weten. ...den een man, en er waren misikken in Klinge's leven geweest. Hij was in zijn jeugdjaren een zoo warmhartige vriend geweest voor zijn vrienden, en tot dank was hij op bedrieglijke wijze zijn geld kwijtgeraakt, en zijn meisje. En aan vrienden, die hij geholpen had, had hij die beide dingen te danken. Zoo had hij het geloof in de menschen verloren en zijn troost bij het drinken gezocht. Zóó luidde, volgens majoor Barre, zijn levensverhaal.

335

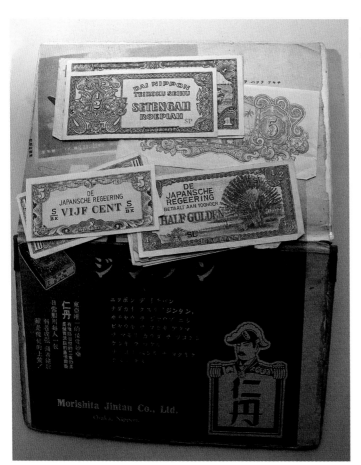

4. 'Camp dollars'. Money used to barter for goods and medicines.

5. Japanese cigarette packets also proved useful as writing paper.

6. In a Japanese POW camp in 1942. Illustration by Charles Holdsworth.

7. 'Get rid of that rice belly!' A cartoon by Sgt Herbert Clifford, drawn in a POW camp and displaying a touch of sarcasm.

New
Year Greetings

BOEI GLODOK 1944

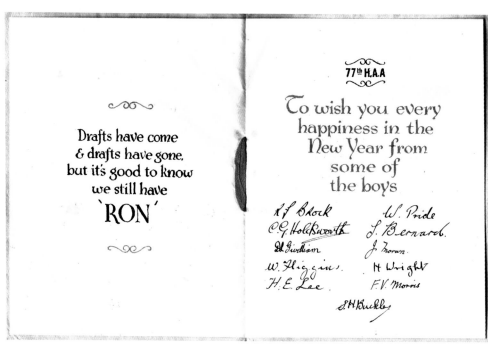

77th H.A.A

To wish you every
happiness in the
New Year from
some of
the boys

Drafts have come
& drafts have gone,
but it's good to know
we still have
`RON`

R.f Brock   W. Pride
C.G. Holdsworth   S. Bernard
H Gwilliam   J. Moran
W. Higgins.   H Wright
H.E. Lee.   F.V. Morris
        S.H Buckley

8. New Year's greetings card for Ronald Williams from some of his men, made in Boei Glodok camp, 1944. They had managed to avoid transportation to other islands.

9. A Dutch POW camp concert party in 1942. Illustration by a Dutch Army POW, E.E. Kloen.

10. Examples of poetry kept in the book *En Euwig Zinge de Bosshen*.

Central Panel, St. Georges' Church. Tandjong Priok.

11. Central glass panel design by Lt Noel James for St George's Chapel, Tandjong Priok camp. This was submitted as part of a competition but was not the winning design.

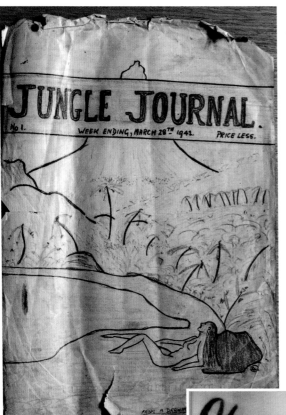

12. Front cover of the first edition of *The Jungle Journal* drawn by Ronald Williams. (Courtesy of Mrs Adèle Barclay)

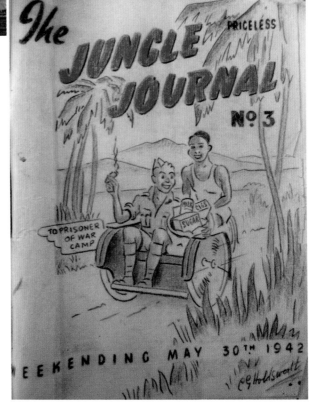

13. Front cover of *The Jungle Journal* No. 3, drawn by Charles Holdsworth. (Courtesy of Mrs Adèle Barclay)

14. Front cover of *The Jungle Journal* No. 4, drawn by Noel James showing Gnr Brian Norman beavering away writing for the journal. (Courtesy of Mrs Adèle Barclay)

15. Front cover of *The Jungle Journal* No. 5, drawn by Charles Holdsworth. (Courtesy of Mrs Adèle Barclay)

16. Front cover of *The Jungle Journal* No. 6, drawn by Charles Holdsworth. (Courtesy of Mrs Adèle Barclay)

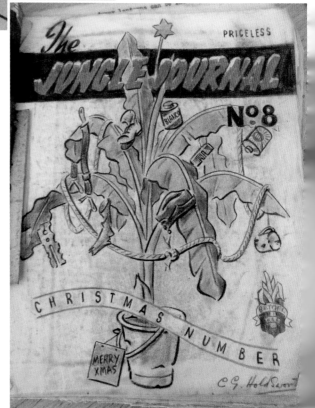

17. Christmas edition of *The Jungle Journal*, drawn by Charles Holdsworth. (Courtesy of Mrs Adèle Barclay)

18. '*Betoel*' is Malay for 'The Goods' and this was the winning competition entry for an emblem to be adopted by the 77th in POW camps. The artist was Charles Holdsworth. (Courtesy of Mrs Adèle Barclay)

19. 'Rag and bone man'. Cartoon in *The Jungle Journal* by George Ball. (Courtesy of Mrs Adèle Barclay)

20. 'Ye Gods! Gas capes?' Cartoon in *The Jungle Journal* by Charles Holdsworth. (Courtesy of Mrs Adèle Barclay)

21. 'The things you are'. Cartoon by George Ball in *The Jungle Journal*. (Courtesy of Mrs Adèle Barclay)

22. 'A batman's duties?' Cartoon by George Ball in *The Jungle Journal*. (Courtesy of Mrs Adèle Barclay)

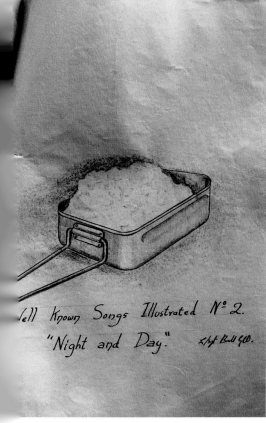

23. 'Rice, night and day!' Cartoon by George Ball in *The Jungle Journal*. (Courtesy of Mrs Adèle Barclay)

24. 'Still air activity over Java'. Cartoon by George Ball in *The Jungle Journal*. (Courtesy of Mrs Adèle Barclay)

25. Cartoon by George Ball in the Christmas issue of *The Jungle Journal*. (Courtesy of Mrs Adèle Barclay)

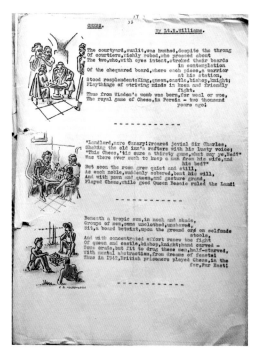

26. Illustrated poem, 'Chess', from *The Jungle Journal*. The poem is by Ronald Williams with illustrations by Charles Holdsworth. (Courtesy of Mrs Adèle Barclay)

27. 'Garden Party' 1939 and 1942 in *The Jungle Journal* by Charles Holdsworth. (Courtesy of Adèle Barclay)

28. Javanese dancer in ceremonial dress by Mike O'Mahony.

29. A Bolinese nobleman drawn by Noel James in Priok camp.

30. A copy of *The Nippon Times* demonstrating the absurd claims made in the headline. In fact, no Allied aircraft carriers were sunk in the first Battle of Bougonville. (Courtesy of the Imperial War Museum)

31. 'Silly Symphony', a satirical contribution from Gunner Edward Graham in *The Jungle Journal*. (Courtesy of Mrs Adèle Barclay)

32. Hobbies section in *The Jungle Journal*. Brian Norman writing about model ship making. (Courtesy of Mrs Adèle Barclay)

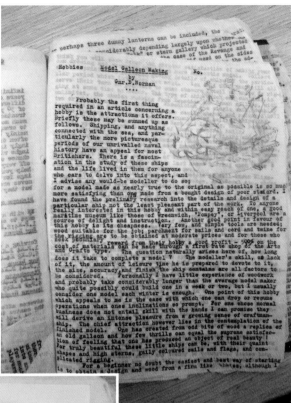

33. Other cartoons by George Ball. (Courtesy of Mrs Adèle Barclay)

34. 'A Londoner's Dream' by L/Sgt George Ball.

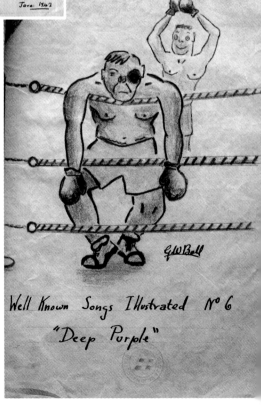

35. 'Deep Purple' by L/Sgt George Ball.

loaf of bread into the hospital for a sick pal on your way back from work? THIS MEANS YOU.

Throughout the time at our disposal for the preparation of this issue our Editor, Lt R. Williams, has been indisposed [*in hospital with malaria*], and any lapses in this issue are accepted as the responsibility of the current editorial staff.

Notices:

Evening prayers – A short informal service will be held on the Green at 2045 hrs. Come and end the day with us.

Toc H – A Toc H group has been formed in the camp and is meeting on the Green every Wednesday at 1945 hrs. We shall welcome anyone who cares to come. We are known as the 'Human Zoo' so you won't feel out of place if you do come.

Concert – Another concert is being prepared and talent is still required. If you can do a turn, give your name to CSM Sweeny.

The editorial team for this issue was likely to have been Lt C. Noel James, who also drew the cover picture, and Bdr Frank Fryett.

The next issue (No. 3, June 1942) was produced in Tandjong Priok camp, with a larger number of contributors. The editorial:

As a result of a series of strange happenings each of the three issues of this publication has been produced in a different place. Remember the first issue? [*This would indicate that* The Jungle Journal No. 1 *was probably produced 'on the road' between the time of surrender and imprisonment.*] Remember the second in the Jail? What do you think of this the third? Improving isn't it? We think that *The Jungle Journal* can be made quite presentable. With a little more thought and efficiency this journal could be made into something worth taking home … Look out for the sixth issue as we are saving up a special story for that issue. Order your copy now so as not to be disappointed.

Many complaints have been made regarding the distribution of the first two issues. Some decided not to pass it on after reading it. Others decided to use it for an unspecified purpose … Think of your comrades; they want to read the journal too. If you see any attempt to stuff a copy of the journal into a kitbag report it to your section officer. Please pass it on and on …

The fourth edition of *The Jungle Journal* was produced at the end of June 1942 in Tandjong Priok camp and, exceptionally, was printed on both sides of the paper with the following editorial comments:

Well, here we are with the fourth edition of *The Jungle Journal*, much bigger and we hope you will think <u>better!</u> You will note quite a number of new contributors, although we can always accommodate more … We never expected to publish a *The Jungle Journal* without a Fryett, but, believe it or not, here it is.

We know, however, that Bombardier Fryett has been fully occupied with concert work and, not to mention, them workin' parties. We guarantee that he will be represented in the next issue … Paper shortages will, shortly, become a serious matter … We thought we were in 'a spot of bother' when cover artist, Gunner C. Holdsworth was, unfortunately, removed to hospital in Batavia in the middle of the job. We were agreeably surprised when appealing to the 'Branch Office', that an alternative design was produced with amazing alacrity [*by Bdr Norman Saunders*].

In conclusion, we solicit criticism, ideas, suggestions, and particularly contributions which will enable us to pursue a policy of making this journal better and better.

The following is a verse from Gnr Charles Hatfield, who was part of the editorial team early on, encouraging contributions from fellow POWs to *The Jungle Journal*:

What about it?
Come get your paper, sit and think
And write down something with your ink.
You like to read these Jungle books,
So contribute unto their looks.
They could be better, brighter far,
And bigger than they really are
If only you would condescend
To use your brains a bit, and send
To us your writings, works of art,
Or any thing you have to part
With, drawings, sketches, poems, prose.
Those odds and ends; one never knows
What one can do till one does try,
So send us your works and don't be shy!

The Jungle Journal No. 5 (July 1942) contained a much longer editorial than usual, and is abbreviated here:

It may be the sunshine, it may be the growing spirit of optimism pervading, but *The Jungle Journal* (JJ) comes to you bigger, better and brighter than ever to prove, once again, that barbed wire doesn't make this a cage.

Good stories, poetry, sketches and articles are to be found in these pages covering adventure, humour, hobbies and sport. We welcome new contributors … Most of you have a hobby and don't need to be a poet to write an article. Whatever the hobby the JJ wants the low down! Then, what about a Welshman, or North countryman, defending his corner of Britain, along the lines of our 'Surreynian'? Maybe your favourite corner is in the pub; let's hear about it as we would like to be there with you!

To judge by impatient enquiries to the editorial team, JJ readers are looking forward to each issue with pleasurable anticipation and, although our mighty machine is always working at high-pressure, we want you to help entertain the rest of us.

We cannot go to press without expressing our gratitude and pride at the boys of this regiment who have so splendidly represented us in the Football Championship … two of our teams are at the top … we are grateful to the players from all camps for the excellent sport and entertainment provided on many evenings.

The Jungle Journal No. 6 was introduced as follows:

The Jungle Journal must be the only magazine in the world, at the moment, which cannot be purchased; it is priceless in spite of our new affluence. We may not be in a land overflowing with milk and honey but we can still overflow with laughter and an abundance of ideas. We can even rise to poetry of no mean standard … This issue presents several new contributors, all of high calibre and, naturally, we ponder over the considerable depths of talent that remain untapped … One cell alone has produced seven authors and only one or two of these thought they could write. Now, we haven't heard from Wales, Scotland and Ireland in defence of their corner of Britain. We recollect distinctly hearing accents from each of these countries very recently. Have they no worthy followers of Owain Glyndwr, Robert Burns and W.B. Yeats? Are these countries without champions or has their genius gone into their football boots?

To assist the shy to come forward, we offer now untold wealth in the shape of a ONE GUILDEN NOTE for the best article received in the next three weeks … To touch on a more serious note; we remain dangerously short of paper. If you value JJ remember us on your next work party – there may need to be some begging. We will bless you, bless your children, bless your children's children, etc …

PS Gunner Puddleberry approached the Editor in tears on learning of the demise of 'Jacko' (one of the camp monkeys) and he requested that his epic poem (included in this JJ) should not be published for 'E wer kwite a nize litul chap aterall'. Too late, the mighty machinery of the JJ Press has rolled and posterity will judge whether we have erred in judgement!

The Jungle Journal No. 7 is presumably lost and the final *Jungle Journal*, as far as one can ascertain, was the Christmas issue, No. 8. This contains a number of serious admonishments about the behaviour of certain POWs. Fractiousness amongst POWs was clearly rearing its head. The following is part of the Christmas issue editorial:

The question that has been exercising the minds of many, for some weeks, is what are we going to get for Christmas? The answer from the cookhouse is, we understand, almost forgotten luxuries, such as bread and jam. The camp entertainers will put on a special show. The JJ's response is a question 'What are you going to GIVE at Christmas?'… This publication has made a

'Garoet'. Scene from muster point before imprisonment drawn by Lt Noel James for *The Jungle Journal*. (Courtesy of Mrs Adèle Barclay)

real effort to help you to enjoy the festive season and our contributors have risen to the occasion … inside will be found Christmas greetings from the Commanding Officer, a Christmas message from the Padre, and Lt W. Wooller presenting the various interests of the regiment. Our artists have striven to picture Christmas humorously, and otherwise; our school of poets have put their thoughts into verse.

Now what are <u>YOU</u> going to contribute? We see little sign of a depression at this time, but we could do with a lot more give and take all round. In fact, we need a hell-of-a lot more GIVE. Just for Christmas, let us see the belly-achers stop belly-aching and the critics stop their perennial criticism, without giving thought to what they are about to pull to pieces. Let those who give everybody the lowest possible motive for virtually every action, try the other extreme or 'shut-up'. What about the unshaven and untidy gentry giving us all a treat by borrowing a razor and wearing clothes, as though they are British and proud of the fact, instead of looking like hoboes?

The Jungle Journal adds gladly its best Christmas wishes and hopes you will take pleasure in its contribution to the festive season, as much as the writers, poets, and artists have enjoyed giving of their time and thoughts to you.

The following sections will provide a flavour of the contents of *The Jungle Journal*, in a chronological order, from arrival on Java, surrender, capture, and life in POW camps as depicted by contributors.

The Java Campaign

The Short Battle of Java

It was a drab and sultry afternoon as our troopship steamed into Tandjong Priok Docks. There was an atmosphere of tense expectation among all the troops on board. Here was, at last, our destination. During our eight weeks on the water our ultimate destination had always been a mystery. But here, on that late Tuesday afternoon, we were brought face to face with the truth.

A new world was opening up before us and a new chapter in our lives was about to begin. As we gazed in wonder at the strange configuration of this new land of Java, we stopped for a moment to think in quiet. Here we were on the verge of a new venture. The future loomed dark in the distance, just like the woods on the far off hills.

That same evening, we stepped off the old ship and set foot on this new land. This was to be our new home for some time to come. This was a strange country, different to anything we had previously encountered.

As we walked along the road, we were amused to see the native vendors in their gaudy attire as they squatted by the roadside plying their various trades. The quiet of the evening air was broken by a wild jingling of bells, as rickshaws, *betjaks*, rushed passed in a wild medley.

Yes, we thought it was a grand world we had stepped into, a sort of Eldorado which our fancy had painted for us during many a leisure hour. This late evening looked charming to the naked eye, as the dying sun tinted everything with a reddish hue.

The following day, we were taken to our billets, a part of Tandjong Priok Station which had been set apart for us as and, clearly, had previously housed troops, because orders of the day still hung on the walls. Wires criss-crossed each other above our heads, which bore testament to the fact that, once, mosquito nets were suspended from them. But between the previous incumbent's departure and our arrival the place had become dirty. Cobwebs hung from the ceilings and queer creatures, such as lizards and bats, made their home in every nook and cranny. However, we got down to it and cleaned the whole place and, in a few days, it looked quite clean and pleasant.

Our first fortnight there was spent settling in to this, our new home. Our gun site was situated about 400 yards from the station. We had to bring our heavy guns from the Docks and put them ready for action at the site. This necessitated hard work and long hours but we remained quite happy. The food was good and the open air life seemed to improve our health. Any exertion, in this abnormal heat, produced profuse perspiration. However, we slowly became used to this very warm weather and our bodies were turned from white to a ruddy brown. We were becoming used to our new environment, although total strangers, and learned to converse with the local natives. We could purchase our simple requirements from the natives with comparative ease.

Unfortunately, this grand existence was to be short lived. The little cloud which appeared in the distance gradually grew bigger and soon began to cast its shadow over our life. In less than four weeks it would burst. On the fall of Sumatra, there was a great alteration in camp routine. The guard was doubled and all leave cancelled. During the day tightly packed squadrons of hostile aircraft would cross and re-cross the Java skies at considerable height. We engaged regularly these enemy aircraft but with limited success. For a gun battery, seasoned in the air defence of England, to meet with little success was a surprise and disappointment to everyone. Then, one day, what we had most dreaded happened. Java was invaded by the Japanese and we were given the order to move. For ten days we became a mobile gun battery in action by day and moving by night. We travelled right across west Java from Batavia to Garoet, passing through Bandoeng and Tasikmalaja.

We hardly knew what sleep was, as we had days of hard and earnest action, followed by moving the guns at night and having them ready again by dawn. From the swampy coastlands of Priok, we had made our way to the beautiful hillsides of Bandoeng. We were struck, when we had to move by day, by the Java countryside providing wonderful camouflage for our convoy. The tall trees, which lined the road for miles, formed a thick canopy through which the sun's rays could hardly penetrate. This process went on for more than a week, until we realised that this quick moving drama was about to end. The enemy was taking hold of the island and had considerable air superiority; usually the deciding factor in modern warfare.

On Monday 8 March the Dutch forces capitulated and, owing to previous commitments, there was nothing else left for us but to lay down our arms. We destroyed our big guns but handed over our small arms and ammunition. Thus, we found ourselves as prisoners in less than six weeks on the island. In a few weeks, we were taken to a prison camp in Batavia. I can still remember the day. It was a very hot day as we marched on a well trodden path to our prison home. The Japanese placed, at vantage points by the roadside, photographers to take pictures of dejected war-weary men. The natives, who had welcomed us a few weeks ago, laughed at us and scorned us as we passed by. This made my blood boil and, in spite of my weariness, the thought of revenge seethed in me. However, I suddenly remembered something which quelled my anger. Another prisoner, on a Friday afternoon, walked wearily up a hill to his death. Those who had hailed him as their King now despised and spat at him. They thought it would be the end, but they were mistaken.

Let that parallel be a comfort to you my fellow prisoners. This captivity is only for a time. Let us bear it with a good heart, for one day the iron gates will swing open and we will be free again … It is hard to believe that, in conditions such as these, this strange confinement will serve some good purpose. The Battle of Java is over or, shall we say, the first part is over. Let us wait expectantly for the second act … 'Sweet are the uses of adversity' says Shakespeare.

Take courage from the words of Keats:

> Aye on the shores of darkness there is light
> And precipices show un-trodden green.
> There is a budding morrow in Midnight,
> There is a triple light in blindness keen.

Gnr Daniel J. Evans, 239 Bty

(*The Jungle Journal*, No. 5, July 1942)

Battery Quarter Master Sgt Reginald Rowe describes, in verse, the train crash on Java which killed and maimed many 77th Regiment's men, and reflects on the aftermath of this terrible accident. (*The Jungle Journal* No. 4, June 1942):

Gratitude
(From a few British Gunners)
It was in a foreign country, many miles from home,
That we made this tedious journey, and in a train were borne,
We started off in Batavia, in the early hours of dawn,
For a place called Soerabaja – 'twas a lovely summer morn.
The train was extremely crowded with Gunners good and true.

The land through which we travelled was all so very new.
We travelled long, we travelled fast, not making many stops,
But we're not due to reach there before three o'clock.
Then just before the journey's end, there was such an awful crash,
Head on with a good's train – a devastating smash!
The train was smashed to splinters which were scattered all around,
And, in amongst the wreckage, many dead and injured found.
When the rescue work was finished, we lay,
On stretchers, waiting for an ambulance to hasten us away.
They took us to a hospital, in a place that's called Malang,
And the treatment that we got there was the finest in the land.
The nurses, they were angels, the boys were great as well.
Dr Lodder was a good man, as good as words can tell;
The nurses, they were excellent and also very game:
Masripah, Socharte, Swie and Anna were their names.
We cannot speak too highly of the treatment that we got,
There was nothing that we wanted, we simply had the lot!
The inhabitants of Java, they came from far and near;
They brought us things and wished us well, of comfort and cheer.
We had two lady friends as well, whose work was never done.
They shopped, did thankless jobs and translated our native tongue.
The hospital was marvellous and, may its renowned name,
The 'Ziekenhuis of Soeken' never lose its fame.
And here I'll try to thank them with words that are so small,
For everything they have done for us, by giving us their all.
And, when we return to England, we'll tirelessly allude
To all those wonderful people, who won our GRATITUDE.

Capt. Herbert M. Lloyd captured his early memories of the Java campaign in an item-
ised form of memories in May 1942 (*The Jungle Journal*, No. 3):

Getting back Soon
(The ill-fated Java Expedition – a thousand memories)
Memories of the beauty and strength of the convoy – the scream of tortured
metal as carriages dived to death in utter darkness – the rain – unending rice-
fields – the ever-present native – the incredible storms – the cool quiet of the
Dutch barracks – moths, thousands of feet high silvered in the sun – small black
specks in space before screaming down to blast hell into everything and everybody – the endless roar of the guns – all hell let loose – flames eating into
the very town – ships burning red-hot to the water's edge – the roar of dying
bridges – driving, driving, driving with empty bellies and red-rimmed eyes – the
mountain road endlessly twisting through the clouds – the end of the world –
breathtaking sunsets – cool pastel dawns – iron bars – grilling sun – barbed wire
– eternal rice – Java was dead – then so unexpectedly FREEDOM?

Frank Fryett, who had been a Fleet Street journalist and regular contributor to *The Jungle Journal*, wrote a short story entitled 'Eyes, Brown, Frightened Four', based on his true-life experiences of two women with brown eyes full of fear. The first part of this true story is of a depressed Irish dancer who befriended him in a Soho bar. He gave her short shrift and was mortified to learn that she committed suicide later that night. He writes, 'The memory of those eyes haunted me for weeks. I kept on thinking of the girl who wanted someone to talk to and was thrown, by a cruel fate in the depths of her misery, into contact with a half-boozed cynic …'

The second part of the story relates to events on Java in March, 1942 (*The Jungle Journal*, No. 1, March 1942):

I saw the second pair of frightened brown eyes when we were retreating out of Tjilatjap, through the Java jungle, with the enemy only twenty minutes behind. Our convoy was jammed in the road and a pretty little native lady, with two young children, one about nine months old, came to the tailboard of our lorry and pleaded, in her native tongue, for a lift to the next town. She was carrying her younger child, a large bundle of clothes, a box of rice and the inevitable teapot. Someone shone a torch and we lifted her possessions aboard, clumsy but strangely friendly hands lifted the two children. I leant over the tailboard, grabbed the little woman under her arms and lifted her aboard. She must have weighed little more than six and a half stone. Once on the lorry, she gathered her possessions and children and settled down for the ride, alternatively praying and thanking us for our help.

Five minutes later, the order came down the line, correctly given of course, that no natives were to be given lifts. Unfortunately, the bundle of clothes, box, teapot and babies were put back by the roadside, and the little lady, apologetically, lifted down. Soft and light she was, like a human doll. As the convoy moved off, I flashed a torch light in her face and recognised, again, stark fear shining from the woman's eyes. She was trying to soothe her crying children, sobbing herself the while, praying and rocking her smaller child in her arms and calling to the following lorries for a lift. As we moved off again, with the blazing docks of Tjilatjap in the background, she was silhouetted in the carnage, with no hope in her heart and fear in her large brown eyes. Half an hour later, a short sharp battle was fought at those crossroads, and many hundreds were killed. I pray that she escaped. Do you wonder that, at night, I cannot sleep thinking only of large brown eyes full of fear?

If only I could have understood. If only I could have helped.

The following are verses by Gnr Harry Hamer (241 Battery) describing the aftermath of heavy Japanese bombing on Tjilatjap:

Merciless bombing on a wide open field,
But we fought to the end and never did yield.
The town and docks are a-burning all red,

And we are further weakened by our injured and dead.
After the 'All Clear' 'neath the sweltering sun,
We looked over the damage the enemy had done.
The buildings, all round, were smashed to the ground,
Beneath the ruins a few dead comrades were found.

Not a drum beat or funeral note was heard,
With their bodies to the cemetery we hurried.
Not one soldier discharged a farewell shot,
Over the grave where our heroes were buried.
We buried them quietly during next morn;
The heavy sods our shovels were turning,
'Neath the sweltering heat of the Java sun,
While our bodies were sweating and burning.

No useless coffin enclosed their breast.
Nor in sheet or shroud did we wind them,
But they laid like warriors taking their rest,
With only a thin blanket placed round them.
Few and short were the prayers we said.
We spoke not a word of sorrow,
But we steadfastly gazed on the faces of the dead,
As we thought bitterly of the morrow.

We thought, as we hollowed their narrow beds,
And smoothed down their lowly pillow,
That our foe or a stranger may tread o'er their heads,
While we are far away on the billow.
But slowly and sadly we laid them down,
From the field of their fame, with flesh most gory.
We carved not a line, we raised not a stone,
Just left them alone in their glory.

[*Subsequently, efforts were made to re-bury military personnel, killed in action, in formal military cemeteries in Java.*]

Sergeant John G. Howell described in his piece, 'Comparison', the dash to the sea in England and similarly in Java in March 1942. The words in parenthesis describe the England 1938 experience:

> I remember the sudden dash of motor vehicles-the loud tooting of horns-people madly rushing to and fro – A wild (*happy*) confusion everywhere – People shout-ing and children screaming (*laughing*) – Everything forgotten except the desire to get away- the endless stream of cars carrying the 'remnants of homes' (*gay*

parties) dashing along the roads, regardless of anything in their way. Everything in a state of chaos (*happiness*), a state of sheer disorder everywhere– Nobody (*everybody*) laughed – Every face was 'grim and serious' (*happy and smiling*) – Business premises along the roads were 'a sea of flame and rubble' (*closed*). Everything was forgotten, except the mad dash for the sea. This was the capitulation of Java in 1942.

(*The Jungle Journal*, No. 4, June 1942)

The Jungle Journal Part 2: The Camp Life of the POW

Wilf Wooller wrote under the pseudonym 'Turkeyneck'. 'This is the Life!' summed up how POWs could perceive and analyse the prison life they endured; tongue-in-cheek of course!

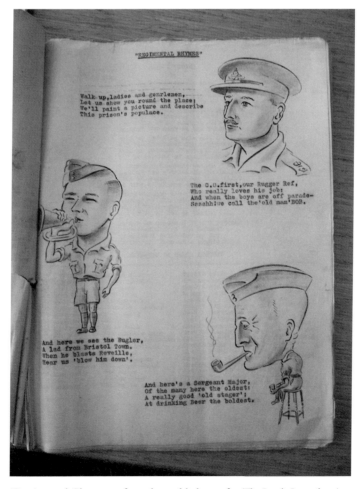

'Regimental Characters from the 77th', drawn for *The Jungle Journal*, artist unknown. (Courtesy of Mrs Adèle Barclay)

This is the Life!

Glad in a snappy sarong, I lay on my spacious couch, pleasantly reflective. To think that this luxurious sleeping lay-out, superbly sprung feather mattresses, enclosed in finely meshed mosquito-netting was to be mine indefinitely. Hey-Ho for prison life! Dressing room, and shower, too! – hot and cold taps – even the lavatory, vulgarly termed a latrine, with automatic flushing, and soft Sanitas loo paper. One would wish the low minded would desist from calling it 'bum-fodder'. Me-oh-my, how I enjoy my morning sittings.

To avoid the horrors of our existence some had deemed it wise to brave the shark-infested waters heading, north, south, east and west to escape. After all, it only takes a troop-diviner, with a couple of crissed-crossed rifles, and a balloon to find out where the Allies are. Bloggins openly stated that it was a stupid idea, far easier to enclose yourself in a net with a few man-eating mosquitos and arranging with a pal, to put you in a box and mail you home. Bloggins, admitted later, that agitated relations would find reconstruction a tedious and difficult task. Witty fellow that Bloggins, he comes from excellent stock as his father sold patent manure!

Breakfast today was tops, mind you, I don't altogether hold with having it in bed every morning. I do not think the good old English breakfast of grapefruit or porridge, bacon, sausage and eggs, followed by toast and marmalade should be eaten in the tropics, at least, not every morning, but one cannot hurt their feelings when they have gone to so much trouble to discover what we really like to eat. As Bloggins was saying to his guard the other day, 'You chaps don't need to spend all your money on us, just four-fifths would do. I am sure you would wish to go to the pictures occasionally? They may be all American films, but Hedy Lamar is the goods in any language.' Bloggins gets rather coarse and to the point at times. His mother worked, by night, in Piccadilly so she ought to know all the wrinkles.

Ah me, the happy ease of this reflecting; war, after all, is a brutal thing calling on the callous side of man's nature, enabling the bad to prosper, causing dastardly deeds to be done in the name of glory. Far, far better to recline at ease and meditate on plump rump steak, braised onions and neatly turned mushrooms that we had for dinner yesterday.

Though, some people are never satisfied with this.

Bloggins wanted cream on his fruit salad. We could not get him to understand that goats are not easy milking for these chaps, although they are halfway there. After all, they have mastered the three bubble principle of Turkish coffee already. 'Even-so', snarled Bloggins, 'One udder is as good as anudder!' I think he was trying to be facetious as he has some strange girlfriends in his cell at night. Still, one should not try to be judgemental and squash a bit of clean fun - as they always leave at dawn!

There is one thing that should be pushed a little further by the Committee of Representatives, as they are so gracious over these small points, and that is the question of seven days leave. Not that I think we should be allowed to leave the island, but the present system is so fatiguing and never gives us time to get anywhere locally. In the words of Bloggins, 'On my last 24 hours leave, I had time only to spend drinking one mild and bitter. I don't agree with too much topping though, you must admit, the prison beer is not as good as the standards of Mitchells and Butler. My idea is to get away to the hills for a rest, do a little shooting and so on.'

Reflecting thus, the mind, not tied by the fetters which bind our bodies, drifted on to the wonderful standard of the chorus girls at the last concert, the cricket games, and deck tennis, to pass the time amicably while, far away, others direct or misdirect chunks of metal at each other, according to their respective beliefs and ability. 'Only the stuttering rifle's rapid rattle can patter out their hasty orisons … and all that.' One cannot do a Java Act on them every time. It takes ability to organise these affairs. So dull of Bloggins to murmur something about, 'Enough practice and creating a precedent for change.' Gradually, and somewhat strangely, I think, the mind turned to good, in general, and, in particular, to deliberate on the respective merits of the Knickerbocker Glory and Banana Split, when its ruminations were rudely interrupted by a vigorous shaking. Slowly, through deep strata of sub-consciousness, these words, in the voice of the estimable Bloggins made them understood, 'If you don't get up you'll miss your blinkin' rice!'

(*The Jungle Journal*, No. 2, April 1942)

Both 'Turkeyneck' and Col Humphries, as 'Gnr Marhen', wrote articles about 'the Orient' in *The Jungle Journal*. Wilf Wooller's article is partly in verse:

The Gods, by 'Turkeyneck'
'The Orient, the buzzing flies', so we hear them criticise;
The heat, the all pervading smells, of countless groans we can tell,
Smouldering slowly in the tropics,
but raising hell in all their topics.
The everlasting rice and rice, and more rice and rice and rice;
The stew and stew, without a bone, 'it's muddy water', so they groan.
Such fare is hardly food for rats, dogs, natives, or jungle cats.
To fight with consummate skill, and kill, and kill, and kill,
So earthly mortals strangely reason,
Glibly wording, heavenly treason;
Think they not the food they scorn feeds more mouths than whites yet born.
By what strange guiding light do they assume the noble right
To span the earth with bands of steel and strange races bring to heel?
To be complacent in defeat and yet aspiring to the choicest meat.
Now below they savagely mutter
Words about the lack of butter!
We are tired of fever and the 'itch'; tired by dysentery's frightening pitch.

Malaria, Dengue, festering sores irritate us more and more.

So through the darkened skies the seated Gods heard their cries!

These poor mortals scarce recall what might have happened to them all,

Thus spoke the God of Mercy, surnamed Adolphus Percy.

Some might have lain in paddy-fields, stomachs gutted with burning steel,

Others slashed about the head, joining the myriads of their dead;

Yet some dying with anguished howls, while

dragging out bespattered bowels;

Others limbless in terror tremble, in this strange infested jungle.

But lo – behold in partial safety,

They groan about the issue pastry!

We should have not come out here, away from wives, cigs and beer;

In England we should have stayed, fought and loved and quietly played.

What have we done towards the cause save violate the laws,

Like some egg-bound turtles being led in egg-bound circles?

Thus arose plaintive rumination, raised in utter condemnation.

The God of Future raised his eyes, 'The human is far from wise;

Will they never rest at ease contented with the salty breeze?'

Contented with the life we gave without the comforts which they crave,

It will not be for long, even by the human gong,

Before they go their various ways, back to careless, carefree days.

But grumbling we will hear – the cost of living is far too dear.

The food is not quite right, the baby howled in the night;

The Boss is a perfect swine – an endless, constant human whine;

So on through the human life, we shall hear their toil and strife,

Until they come to rest on high in the blue and boundless sky,

Where all things they will set at nought, though as small children they were taught,

Once one on earth sought to guide, but all mortals chose to gibe!

(A Sage once said, 'Tell me of your joys; of troubles I have enough of my own.')

(*The Jungle Journal*, No. 5, July 1942)

The Orient, by 'Marhen'

'The call of the East', how often, in song and story, did one, in one's youth, thrill to the thought at what this experience meant?

The glamour under a tropical sky, the pale blue of the Indian Ocean, the languorous eyes of the Eastern maiden, the scents and perfumes of the East; one could go on and on, *ad nauseam*.

Well, I've tried it! Now please restore me, at the earliest opportunity to the fogs of London, the rains of Manchester, or the gales and sleet of the Welsh mountains.

One must have health and vigour to appreciate beauty, even a beautiful woman is a nauseating sight to a man in the throes of stomach-ache and diarrhoea!

SEEN IN JAVA — Nᵒ I

— The Prison, Boei Glodok —

'Boei Glodok prison camp', drawn by Lt Noel James for *The Jungle Journal*. (Courtesy of Mrs Adèle Barclay)

This disillusionment commenced, as far as I am concerned, at the edge of the tropics on the journey out. What the devil is the good of excellent food, if one has to perspire profusely in consequence of the slight muscular activity occasioned by mastication? Personally, I cannot enjoy food with rivulets of salty sweat pouring down my chest and back and, thence, into my stockings and shoes. Also, I prefer not to have to fight with buzzing flies for that first stab at a dainty morsel!

I like to sleep in cosiness and comfort and fail, entirely, to understand what advantages there are in a lack of air, bad smells and a bed soaking in gallons of sweat.

Originally, I thought this was merely the inconvenience with which one must put-up prior to sampling all the glories and delights of the glorious Orient. No, be patient old boy! You will soon have your reward.

I've got it! I, who could have remained at home, I, who was placed on the reserved occupation's list, I, who was too old for overseas missions, I, who was only of a fictitious A1 medical category anyhow, and was advised by many not to say. But the insidious and subtle propaganda, over the years, had created a fertile ground and I answered the call to the East. So, here am I enjoying all the beneficence, culture, glories and blessings of the most glorious Orient, as extolled by Clive, Walpole, Raffles and others, and by many generations of self-sacrificing Britishers who, believe it or not, actually spend their whole lives in this damned place!

The scenery is most beautiful, the vegetation something to marvel at, the natives interesting to observe, apart from this, as far as I am concerned, enough said! An afternoon's motor-coach tour could have adequately demonstrated these things to me but, oh no, I have to stay here for months, if not years to have further glories thrust on me! These glories I have absorbed in such fashion as will conduce to my remembering them to my dying day.

These may be summarised as follows:

Bad food, dirty infected water, bad smells, millions of bugs, fleas, moths, beetles, mosquitoes, snakes, lizards, ants, and frogs – all impressively glamorous!

Then come the really impressive Oriental attractions of:

Malaria, dysentery, Singapore feet and ears, septic sores, Dobey's itch, beri-beri, prickly heat, sweat rash, ringworm and anaemia. The superlative spectacles of typhoid, cholera, plague and sun-stroke are still to be witnessed, but it is nice to know that they can be found in the glorious Orient!

Then, of course, there are the 'Seasons'. There are two of them: 'Wet' and 'Dry'. They are very similar although it rains harder and slightly less frequently in the 'Dry' season. The lightning which, often, accompanies these rain storms is magnificent and, the thunder being so loud, you can appreciate the sight, being totally unable to sleep.

Another blessing in the East is the presence of volcanoes, the propensities of which are so well known that I will not, here, enlarge upon them. However, consider Krakatoa! What a spectacular event that was with 35,000 people taken out of circulation. Easy and pleasant isn't it?

The next advantage is the absence of coal as a fuel. If you want to cook, it can be done by burning tons of trees instead of a bucket full of coal. But, of course, you have the exercise in cutting up the trees, which is most beneficial in this climate by developing such a refreshing sweat. It is so easy taking a delightful cooling bath when one is sweating profusely. One can stand in a nice draught; an excellent way to catch a cold or a dose of pneumonia, and pour contaminated water over one's head. The water is not particularly beneficial as one can contract whiteheads and septic sores from it. However, standing on the bare concrete floors has great possibilities. Consider the delights of Singapore Foot, a charming and delightful malady, which is not too painful, spreads like 'velveata' [*sic*] and avoids one wearing stupid European footwear.

The need to protect food and utensils from flies, the necessity to sleep under a net, the importance of covering the head and neck in the sun, and keeping one's tummy warm and cosy, are all enjoyable experiences.

So, one could go on and on, enumerating on the virtues, attractions and glamour of the East. However, sufficient has been stated to illuminate my point without enlarging upon the merits of the great Eastern diet. Consider the magic word 'Rice'. Here you have a great utility food with no fuss and bother. Just a couple of trees to light and, hey presto, a meal is ready. You can boil it, steam it, fry it, roast it, eat it raw or throw it away. It does not matter at all as it tastes the same, smells the same, and does about the same amount of no good for all Europeans. There is no danger of a shortage of this valuable food commodity – oh dear, No! – This damned stuff is grown by the millions of tons. Red rice, white rice, brown rice, chicken-rice, coolie-rice, wet rice, dry rice, hard rice, soft rice, granulated rice, coagulated rice, what a boon, what a blessing to mankind they all are!

I've had the pleasure of trying it in all its forms, with each worse than the other. This is the East, the glorious, glamorous, delightful, magnificent, seductive, stupendous and superlative East. Millions and millions of Orientals of all colours, creeds and castes, cannot be wrong. So, rice it has to be and is, and shall forever be, even if I die in the attempt to live up to the motto, 'When in the Orient, do as the Orientals do'.

You must realise, from these heartfelt outpourings, that the East has made its mark on me. You are quite right, it has. You may think that I should not again return to the Orient on the occasion I succeed in leaving it. If I do leave brother, you are emphatically and indubitably right! In short brother, 'Too bloody true, I won't return!'

(*The Jungle Journal*, No. 4, June 1942)

Gnr Marhen is clearly not enjoying his sojourn in the Orient! This seems a gloomy article for the regiment's commanding officer to write. Roderick Suddaby questions why this 'remarkably downbeat' article would have been written, under a pseudonym, by Col H.R. Humphries. I cannot answer this question but the article was attributed to the colonel in *The Jungle Journal*'s contributor's key. Another article, 'Service Traditions and Practices', attributed to the colonel, was also written under the pseudonym Gnr Marhen.

The Christmas issue of *The Jungle Journal* contained an article entitled 'Flotsam and Jetsam' by 'Beachcomber'. I have not been able to establish the true identity of this author. This article was written approximately nine months into captivity, and this extract raises some interesting observations about prison life conversation:

This is the Christmas number of *The Jungle Journal*. Christmas editions of magazines, at home, are usually topical with snow, mistletoe, holly and Christmas puddings that one, at least, longs for a tale of midsummer tropical sun. Which prompts the question here is – what season is it? And when does the rainy season start in Priok? Talking of rainy seasons, did you know that it has already started in Java with a vengeance? 14,000 people in central Java have already been rendered homeless since it commenced – so says 'Asia Haya'. One day, how grand it will be to read an English newspaper.

One of the things, I most long for, is to be able to go into a room, shut the door, and really be alone … with nobody to disturb me, and regain that

Cartoon for the Christmas edition of *The Jungle Journal*, artist unknown. (Courtesy of Mrs Adèle Barclay)

delicious sense of freedom. Please, a room to breathe in, a room to move in, with no overcrowding and no press of men. Having to endure the endless babble of conversation, but wanting just the peace and quiet of it all, is rarely possible. And yet, conversation probably constitutes the greatest single amusement and recreation in the camp. Not only conversation in the camps but on working parties too. On my last working party, I brought up a subject which has been intriguing me ever since I arrived. Do we see men as they really are in the camps or do we see men behaving in an abnormal manner because they are living under a strain? This topic has always aroused a lively discussion and this occasion was no exception. It was suggested that no one saw a man as he truly is. A man has several personalities, one for his wife and family, one for his business and so on, and that your personality can change from day to day. Finally, an Australian contributed the following penetrating observation that most people were acting most of the time, so you cannot see them as they really are. An interesting thought! How much time do you spend acting?

Having decided, ask your friend's opinion – you may be surprised!

When you look back on the experience of this camp, you realise how much your mind has been broadened by contact and conversation, Singapore, Hong Kong, Sumatra and Timor, although thousands of miles apart, seem as familiar to us now, as our local parishes at home. Where did we develop this outlook? From small talk! We are constantly laying up a treasure trove of anecdotes to thrill, amaze or horrify our friends when we return home. The odd man is laying this up as an inducement for free beer and, after hearing some of the tales, I should say they are worth it. Without doubt, one's stories at home will entirely depend on one's audience. The following tale takes some beating. I was boasting how far out I had swum, after POWs were allowed a swim in the sea, when a sailor said, in no uncertain terms, that I was a fool as the sea was full of man-eating sharks. This rather shook me but Tom, who was alongside me waiting for the bathing parade to be fallen in by the Nippon sentry, capped it with a true bloodthirsty shark attack story from Singapore …

(*The Jungle Journal*, No. 8, December 1942)

Writing poetry proved to be a good way to pass the interminable amount of time in confinement. Topics varied but three subject areas were popular: camp food, the boredom of camp life and missing loved ones.

Feelings of squalor, abject hunger and fearful uncertainty were largely avoided in poetry. The following three poems reflect the popular topics:

'Foodish Dreams'
What are we having for breakfast today?
Two rashers of bacon with eggs, did you say?
May be sausage and mash with hot buttered scones?
I guarantee, then, there'll be no moans!

I'm wrong, did you say? We are not having this?
At least, what we've not had, we will never miss!
It's rice did you say? Why we've had this before!
We seem to be now getting this more and more!

Well, what have we got for our meal at midday?
Hot soup, roast beef with potatoes, did you say?
Must have puddings, for 'afters', and custard as well?
My goodness, I'm thinking this lunch will be swell!

It's not to be this! It's too much to expect?
It's rice once again! Is that correct?
I suppose you think we should not get meat,
As prisoners of war, only rice shall we eat?

At least for our tea you will surely forsake
The usual routine, and give us some cake,
With brown bread and butter, and plum jam,
Perhaps, a small omelette and a slice of cold ham?

You won't give us this? Well, then surely we may
Have dried bread and water for one meal a day?
We cannot have this! It's rice once again!
Well, really, I think it a terrible shame!

For supper I'm wondering what we shall eat?
Welsh rarebit and cocoa, or coffee I'll bet;
Perhaps, fish and chips and a ham sandwich or two?
I'm thinking with these, we can surely make do.

It's not to be this? And it's not to be rice?
Let's hope it will be something especially nice.
It's nothing at all? What a change I must say:
At least we won't have rice for one whole day!

Gnr Charles Hatfield (*The Jungle Journal*, No. 4, June 1942)

Little Lady Waiting

One day I shall return to you,
Away from this cell, to freedom again.
To freedom, to rest, to peace anew;
Away from hunger, sorrow and pain.

For months I have lain in a prison cell
Thinking and dreaming each night of you,
And although my life has been a hell,
I know that you are true.

As hours flee by I know I am near,
Near to you beyond the sea,
Hoping and praying that those I hold dear,
Will be waiting at home to welcome me?

Such are my thoughts throughout the day;
And I know my comrades think the same,
Patiently I wait and hope and pray
For the day I will return home again.

Sgt John G. Howell (*The Jungle Journal*, No. 2, April 1942)

'AD 1942'

Some years ago, before the war,
I was not bound by martial law.

I strolled around completely free
And even had my own latch key.
No budget boomed the price of beer,
And tobacco wasn't really dear.
I talked of golf and pedigrees,
And how to ripen Stilton cheese,
Indeed, Noel Coward's latest play.
Then, my one and only care,
Was how the men at Lord's would fare?

Today, behind the barbed wire,
Sitting in an old cow byre,
I curse and swat the genus fly
And hope that it will quickly die.
I scan the sky at night in vain
For all I see are signs of rain.
Then, I lie and cogitate
Upon a really likely date,
For the anticipated deal
When, I shall get a perfect meal.
For now my one and only care
Is how much rice will be to spare?

Sergeant John Forge (*The Jungle Journal*, No. 3, June 1942)

Frank Fryett, a regular contributor to *The Jungle Journal* and part of the 'Staff', produced an apposite ledger of POW's debits and credits from being confined in prison. This was preceded by a poem called 'Life's Ledger', part of which is included here:

I became a constant hedger
Against red entries in the ledger
Life, it seemed, was one long fight
To keep the balance on the right.

Money worship was the fashion
Pursued by all with avid passion
Ruling out from human ken,
The gifts of God to living men.

So now in prison, I keep a journal
Secret, even from the Colonel,
In which I enter every day,
The profit and loss, in a simple way.

Prisoners of War Accounts

DEBIT – CREDIT

Dining on water and rice – Curing a drunkard's vice

Having no money to spend – Having a book to lend

Seeing no cinema shows – Seeing glorious sunset glows

Having no girl to love – Enjoying bird songs above

Sweat in the burning sun – Delight in wit and the silly pun

Getting no letter from mother – I'm here, not my brother

Having no fags to smoke – Hearing a subtle joke

Working hard as hell – Getting a sick man well

Poetry's tax on my head – Tomorrow is the day for bread

The queue at the Gunner's Mess – Pleasure at playing chess

Yearning for a fish sandwich – Learning another language

Sores septic and swollen – Memories cannot be stolen

Prison gates that slam – A taste of somebody's jam

Insomnia's sleepless hours – The privilege of showers

The lizards which crawl about – The flies they cancel out

The water in the soup – The gifts of cantaloupe

The loss of freedom rare – A snap of a lady fair

Waiting for that day to arrive – The joy of being alive

'St George's Chapel, Tandjong Priok' drawn by Bombardier Mike O'Mahony. (Courtesy of Mrs Adèle Barclay)

Health and Disease

Disease became a major problem in POW camps throughout the Far East. There were constant efforts by the camp medical officers to improve hygiene, food and living conditions. This was often to no avail. In the first issue of *The Jungle Journal* there was reference to improving personal hygiene and food preparation. A series of regular articles entitled 'Your Health in the Tropics' featured in most of the journals. The articles were written by 'M.O. Ack' (aka Ron Williams), with help from the medical officers, no doubt:

> In a hot country, such as this, it is necessary to revise ideas of health and hygiene and to adopt a new set of habits. The Dutch, who originally settled in the East Indies some 400 years ago, have adopted many non-European habits which we should be wise to follow.
>
> The East Indian Dutchman seldom drinks water. His usual beverage, when beer is unobtainable, is tea or coffee which ensures the boiling of water. Very few sources of water can be considered reliable, as the majority are contaminated through the native's pollution. Unfortunately, rivers and streams are used as latrines, which is their form of sanitation. Therefore, the Golden Rule, is NEVER drink untreated water, NEVER even think of drinking water unless it has been boiled or treated by chemicals. Of course, if you are too carefree to concur with this rule, you must be prepared for the consequences of dysentery and typhoid. Dysentery is acute diarrhoea, resulting in the weakening of the whole body and the passing of blood. If unchecked it is usually fatal! Typhoid has a high fever which can also end in death.
>
> Discussing water raises the topic of bathing. In order to keep your skin in good condition and the body generally clean, it is important to bath at least once a day. This is not so very difficult to accomplish, particularly, during the rainy season, when it is possible to strip down and have a good wash in the rain. Footwear of some form must be worn on these occasions as disease can be contracted when walking around with naked feet. This aspect will be discussed in a later article.

(The Jungle Journal, No. 1, April 1942)

Dysentry (M.O. Ack)

Do You Strain Every Night To Evade Risking Your (Life)?

Deaths Yesterday Should Explain Noble and Tremendous Efforts Regarding Yonder (Latrine)!

(The Jungle Journal, No. 3, June 1942)

Your Health in the Tropics (M.O. Ack)
Resemble not the slimy snail
Which, with its filth, records its trail?
Let it be said wherever you've been,
'By Gad!' this man, he is damn clean.

Keep clean those plates, your cups as well,
Remember comrades, sure as hell,
The day will come to you, to me;
Once more, like birds, we shall be free.

And from this island homeward bound,
With glorious health and freedom found!
But until then, it's plain to see
That, our great enemy, is dysentery.

The moral, friends, is simply this,
Our health depends on cleanliness.
Clean in body, clean in mind,
In only this real health you'll find.

(*The Jungle Journal*, No. 3, June 1942)

Dysentery was to become the big killer in POW and civilian camps in the Far East. Another serious, and potentially fatal, disease was malaria. When anti-malarial drugs such as quinine were available, men's chances of survival were reasonably good. Norman Saunders describes his experiences in a Malaria Ward:

Thoughts in a Malaria Ward (Bdr Norman E. Saunders)
What a place a sick-bed is for thinking! I do not mean the first few days of illness, when you 'toss and turn' and grunt and groan, and curse; when you hope always for a comfortable posture on the bed, knowing full well there isn't such a thing. Still you place a pathetic trust in every movement, only to find the ache in your back or the pain in the stomach and head, much worse than before. Then you thank your lucky stars, you can, at least, lie flat on your back, only to find your mind racing with stupid and confused thoughts, which prevent rest. Why the hell did those natives leave those great nails protruding from the roof instead of hammering them in? Hope there is a nice pasty for tomorrow's tea; could do with a nice fry-up now but I won't taste it as that raw quinine destroys any taste, a witches' brew, that's what it is! I wonder if I will get a repetition of this at home? Don't worry old man; I'm used to it by now as I contracted it in the Far East – and so on … into the dark watches.

Then, at last, the blessed relief comes, when you can lie on your back and thank heaven for the sun, the green trees and, above all, your sanity. At first, the

'Senon Suka'. Scene from a POW camp drawn by Lt Noel James for *The Jungle Journal*. (Courtesy of Mrs Adèle Barclay)

tendency is one of introspection and self-pity as you ponder over your fallibility in that a little insect can inoculate you with such a powerful germ, knocking your health to kingdom come!

You felt previously so fit and strong and this little mite put you down and out. What chances have you to survive on this earth? Then this unhealthy soliloquizing gives way under a growing appetite and, may be, by the sight of some poor fellow brought in the state you were in a few days ago. A sense of superiority arises as you fetch him a cup of tea, proud that you can stand on your own two feet, although unsurely. You can now stick the briar [*pipe*] between your teeth, without the native tobacco making your hair stand on end!

Thus, you come to a stage of straight thinking helped, maybe, by the quinine deafness which cuts one off from the world of sound, beyond a few feet away. There remains considerable self analysis, but it tends to be more constructive and good resolutions are made for the future. One can see all the meanness of people, both high and low, in the camp, clearly and without prejudice; and the decency and great kindness of others; the friends who never let you down and tend to your wants and needs most faithfully.

So a bout of malaria is not all a waste. We humans live by contrasts, as we can only appreciate the quality of our fellows through the meanness of others, and what good health is as opposed to sickness. Normally, we live far too near each other for a positive focus; distances in the sickbay correct this distortion. Not that malaria is to be recommended for this purpose; the taste of quinine is sufficient to drive out the self importance from any man!

(*The Jungle Journal*, Christmas No. 8, 1942)

The Jungle Journal Part 3: Humour and Recreation

Humour proved to be an essential ingredient in *The Jungle Journal*, to offset the often inhuman and degrading circumstances the POWs found themselves. Here follows some examples of humour, either as complete works or extracts.

Just a JOKE®

A SNAPpy article for the Editor, by L/Bdr W. WHI(S)Tman

I, no doubt like many others, have been pestered a great deal during the past few weeks by the 'Staff' at The Jungle Journal, to write an article for this outstanding journalistic achievement of all time! Having, at last, agreed to their request, I was then stuck for a subject or topic about which to write. I do know a certain amount about card games and a certain amount about the inside workings of the Journal, but these subjects did not seem that interesting. Then an idea came to me. Why not try and combine the two subjects in the hope that something entertaining will result? I have received several rebuttals at the hands of the 'Staff' and threatened with almost everything, including corporal punishment. Perhaps, I can get my own back, to a certain extent, by telling you about some of the happenings inside The Jungle Journal office, and the events which lead up to this masterpiece!

I had occasion to CALL at the Journal office, on a frequent basis, in an effort to secure the typewriter for much more KINGly work, and on several occasions needed to MAKE A RUN for it on being threatened with a POKER!

I am not sure that the dress of the 'Staff' is in keeping with the title of the journal, or sweat rash is the source of their scanty attire? It seems a case of either STRIP POKER or STRIP JACK NAKED. My appearance is always greeted with some MIZAREable looks and if, perchance, I interfere with their afternoon NAP, their PATIENCE becomes exhausted! I believe, I have heard that phrase before somewhere? I fully expect to get my head SNAPped off soon.

The Editor, who is usually all at sixes and SEVENS, is, I understand, in charge of the censoring and is quite fond of CUTTING bits out here and there. The articles are then dealt with by his worthy assistants, all of Norman extraction [*This is probably a reference to Norman Saunders, Norman Sage, and Brian Norman who all worked on the journal*] who, in turn, do a bit of SHUFFLING and

RESHUFFLING. By the time the articles are produced, the contributors are sure that someone has REVOKED or there has been a MISDEAL somewhere.

The 'Staff' BRAG to me that all of the articles are up-to-date but, I must confess, I have yet to discover to which date this applies! I was informed, the other day, that one of their carrier pigeons had returned with the news that KING Harold mistook an arrow for a garden SPADE at Hastings, and, although his HANDS were full and despite his CLUB foot, he, with his usual stout HEART, had managed to deposit his DIAMONDS with his QUEEN, before William's FAT BANKER, riding SOLO, managed to ACE him with said arrow!

I cannot, in all sincerity, THROW AWAY all the TRICKS of the trade as professional etiquette would not allow me to CRIB too much. I am often TRUMPED when on the verge of further discoveries. The signature tune of the Journal appears to be 'WHISTle while you work' and believe you me, the WHISTling goes on all day. In fact, the whole affair seems a RUMMY business to me.

Do not think that I am trying to belittle the efforts of these gallant men, far from it. They have no doubt, by now, heard of the excellent entertainment provided by the camp band and are trying to follow SUIT by doing their utmost to make the camp one HAPPY FAMILY. May their efforts reap all the HONOURS and, indeed, they may have further CARDS UP THEIR SLEEVES.

<u>STOP PRESS</u> According to *The Jungle Journal* Ed's pigeon, it is now confirmed that, in the Wars of the Roses, the Roundheads have crossed the PONTOON BRIDGE and are heading for NEWMARKET in the hope of making a GRAND SLAM from the rear!

(The Jungle Journal, No. 6, August 1942)

Guner [*sic*] Herbert Puddleberry (aka Ron Williams) made a regular contribution to *The Jungle Journal* with a letter home to his mother. Clearly, this was fiction as it was not possible to send letters home during captivity; only censored postcards could be sent. The unfortunate Puddleberry had problems with English grammar, syntax and spelling. The following are extracts from a letter home:

No. 131313 Gnr Erb Puddelberry

Dere Muvver,

Wen I got up thus mornin the burds wus singin swetly which riminded me of ome, like it ust to be in spring witch wer boutiful. Robbin Smiff brort a teeny chic fom wurkin party he thort it wood grow up and give egs, but after chirpin for its muvver all nite it dyed … I wish I kud cell my boots then I wood ave sum sents to bye nesessitis like egs, baccy, cofey and suchlik … For bein the goodest camp we was alowd to go swinin teday. It wer luvely. The water was hot like a bathe on saterday nite I had a swimin koschtume. It wer a good thinge two bekaus I shal not ave to barf for a weak, ther was jeli fishes in the water wat sting

'The Fighting Captain'. Cartoon drawn by Bdr Mike O'Mahony for *The Jungle Journal*. (Courtesy of Mrs Adèle Barclay)

… In the evening our regement played the sixf regement which we one for goals to too. Til arf time ther game wer a ded loss an then it were very exsitin and we one we shud ave skord lots more gaols but our kaptin wer orf thorm peraps a jeli fish ad stung im or a krab ad im? … Slept like a log at nite bekaus of swimin an only erd n mosketo divebomin … Ope to ear from yu soun, yore luvin sun, Erb.

(The Jungle Journal, No. 3, June 1942)

Two other regular features in *The Jungle Journal* were, 'Old Nore's Corner', a star gazers column by Gnr Brian Norman, and 'Silly Symphony', a story about the mythical fairyland of Duffonia by Gnr Edward Graham.

The following are extracts from two of Old Nore's columns:

In response to popular demand and regardless of expense and considerable loss of life, we have been successful in obtaining the exclusive services of that great sage 'Old Nore', who will provide a star gazer's column into the future.

Old Nore's Corner
We are running this feature in competition with local Sages, Berrapa Lyndo and Stari Gazumi, of the Nichi Nichi Shimbum. Contrary to the practices of these two amateur Astrology dabblers, Old Nore has never failed his fans. Who tipped off young Noah about the floods? Who shook Egypt to the core with the low down on Ant' and Cleo? Who was the only one to predict the presence of meat in last Tuesday's soup? If it wasn't Old Nore, then who was it? Now, to get down to that all pervading topic 'The Future': A puzzle for all you earth bound and rice readers but, to this Seer of Seers, the future is as clear as a beer glass at closing time.

The eclipse of Jupiter's moons at the identical time to the conjunction of Venus and Mars is of great significance. To the trained visionary, it is clear that tremendous events are at hand, or near. Certain islands in the South West Pacific are due to change hands in four days but, which islands and which four days, is not possible to state at this stage!

Do not be misled by false prophets. Make a point of securing the next copy of this all-seeing, all-hearing, and all-knowing column.

September 31: The wisest and most venereal [*sic*] of sages assures his readers that on, or after, that date, if not before, those patient gaol birds of Priok will be on their way to a perfectly rice-less land.

You can, soon, expect the usual meaningless statements from the usual brainless spokesman and wheelwright regarding our current position. The next issue will contain a column of exclusive and unbelievable prognostications regarding the end of hostilities, the end of complaints, and the end of the World! Don't be an ignorant bystander.

(The Jungle Journal, No. 3, June 1942)

The abject failure, during this month, of a foolish imitator of this Sage to make good any of his wild and over-optimistic claims should convince laymen of the futility of putting their faith in presumptuous upstarts. Why choose that side of the camp, for your prognostications, when they are readily available in *The Jungle Journal*? Why place any credence in a twerp who walks around in a 'pork-pie' hat? I ask you, have you ever seen a genuine astrologer without his conical hat and hieroglyphically bespattered robe? Beware, therefore, and refute imitations!

Among the events of the coming month will be a grand dinner in a room at Whitehall of a body of aging Army officers wearing their redundant uniforms of the last century, and still discussing the Crimean War. These old boys will be immediately placed on the Army Council, and will bring ideas forward about changing tactics, in the current war, by breeding a race-horse with a rhinoceros to produce anti-tank cavalry. For this great service they will be promoted, of course, to the rank of Field Marshall …

The discovery of water buffalo secreted beneath a Gunner's bed will bring about a ban on cattle raiding and goat snatching. This will cause much heartache in rugger and peg-selling circles!

(*The Jungle Journal*, No. 4, June 1942)

Old Nore's column had a section blacked out, thus indicating that the journals were subjected to Japanese censorship. Roderick Suddaby believes that part of the purpose of Old Nore's humorous commentary was to highlight the excessive and misleading rumours which circulated in POW camps regarding the likely period of captivity. These claims were often over-optimistic and not based on any evidence.

For Sale: Hand built, thatched roofed, second hand officer's latrine, with comfortable seating, and accommodation for two; in a prominent position and in good condition. A snip at the price! Suitable as a billet for twelve gunners or would act admirably as cover for banana plants. Price: 25 davros or one large tin of milk.

News item: It has been officially confirmed that the three bread rolls, found under the Quartermaster's bed, were for the sick.

(*The Jungle Journal*, No. 5, July 1942)

Silly Symphony: The Duff Town Review by Gnr Ed Graham

The Royal Theatre of Duffonia, that fairyland of fantastic confection, was a scene of joyous activity. 'The Duff Town Follies' were putting on a show and the merry people of this make-believe isle were worked up to considerable excitement. They are a jolly, happy race the people of Duffonia, devoid of cares and worries, living in their world dreams as they make their way to the huge 'Pudding Palace'

… The gay throng passed into the stately building to fill the rows of luxurious seats; everyone was happy waiting for the curtain to rise for the 'Duff Town Review' to commence. The 'Pudding Orchestra' members file into their places in front of the stage, each with a musical instrument manufactured from rare bamboo bark. The show is ready; the lights, produced by a myriad of fireflies, die slowly to fade-out. A brilliant light suddenly pierces the darkness to illuminate the stage as the frog-skin curtain slowly rises. Then the theatre echoed with music as the girls of the 'Duff Town Follies' dance gaily onto the stage. They are all dressed like giant pasties and, as they dance, their voices are lifted in lovely song which lilts through the auditorium in rhythmic waves;

> 'Don't be disillusioned with your present state,
> Stop your silly grumblings and your woeful hate,
> Throw aside your sorrows and all gaily sing,
> The Duff-Town Follies good news to bring!

> There will be pasties in the morning,
> For the Duff Town boys and girls,
> Lovely little pasties, dainty little pasties
> With meat a-poking out in golden curls.

> Go to bed early tonight boys,
> And rise up with the lark,
> For there'll be pasties in the morning,
> Noah will bring them in his ark!'

The audience of happy Duffs cheered loudly at the merry 'Follies', who bowed gracefully to the applause. Suddenly, in walks onto the stage an evil, ominous, figure clothed in raiment of burnt rice. 'Bah!' he croaks, 'How dare you infect the spirit of the Rice people with your insidious promise of pasties. How dare you seek to destroy their staunch constitution for rice? This is the food of the mighty that, I, the Great King 'Paddy-Plant', have decreed to be the staple food of the Duffs. Be gone with you, corrupt wenches.'

This was followed by a typical 'Punch and Judy' spectacle of attrition between the Rice King 'Paddy-Plant' and the King of Duffonia. As expected, after further songs, the King of Duffonia sees off King 'Paddy-Plant' by threatening to turn all rice into stew! The revue ends with the final song:

Oh, great and glorious King of Duffonia,
We welcome you with open arms.
Your might is right, and your 'Duff' is filled with charms.
We are tired of rice, insidious lice, and bodies racked with disease.
You come at a time, in this awful clime, when our stomachs are down to our knees!

Praise to you and your Duffs, Oh King,
As we lift up our hearts and gaily sing,
Our thanks will reach the Java skies,
If you'll supplement Duff with lovely pork-pies!

(*The Jungle Journal*, No. 6, August 1942)

One can only speculate that the Rice King was the Japanese camp commandant and the Duffs were the POWs.

The 'Rice King', who was almost certainly a caricature of the Japanese camp commandant in Tandjong Priok in 1942 by Gnr E. Graham

Sport and Leisure

In the early days of captivity, the POWs entertained themselves and, no doubt, their captors by organising sporting events, theatre and concerts. The inter-camp (these were sub-camps within the main POW camps) football competition was taken very seriously. In fact, some of the teams had players who had played at a professional level and represented their countries; players included Ernie Curtis, Cardiff City and Wales, Billy James, Cardiff City and Wales, and Jackie Pritchard, the Cardiff City goalkeeper.

The soccer final, the 'Camp Shield Final', took place between sub-camps No. 2 and No. 9 on 2 September 1942 at Tandjong Priok. A report from Sgt Douglas S. Magnus appeared in *The Jungle Journal*, No. 6, end of August 1942.

On 2 September, 1942, the representative soccer teams from Camps 2 and 9 lined up to battle for the honour and distinction of being winners of the first POW Camp Shield. Camp 9 required only a draw, while Camp 2 required an outright win to secure the trophy.

Before a very large crowd, Allan (Camp 2) won the toss and elected to play from the Church end, leaving Camp 9 to face the glare of the strong sun. Straight from the kick-off Camp 2 adopted an offensive approach. In the first ten minutes, Camp 2 had several chances, but they lacked punch, and Pritchard (in goal for Camp 9) was not unduly disturbed … Until now, the Camp 9 team, particularly the forwards, had played in a disjointed manner, but they pulled around and Allerton, at inside left, taking up a good pass thirty yards out, sent in a brilliant ground drive which Bell (in goal for Camp 2), with marvellous anticipation just managed to save, diving full length with outstretched hands.

Half time: – Camp 2 – 0, Camp 9 – 0

In the second half, Camp 9 played a vastly improved game. Liaison between the backs and forwards was excellent and James, Allerton and McWhirter were a continual source of worry to the Camp 2 defence … The game continued at a hectic pace and both sides gave their all, but the defences of both teams remained solid and impenetrable.

The final whistle came with scores remaining at Camp 2 – 0, Camp 9 – 0.

For Camp 2, Bell, Hall, Allan, and Adamson played brilliantly and Gregson, at left back, was as solid as a rock.

For Camp 9, James, Allerton, McWhirter and Evident were outstanding.

The game was one of the very best seen at Tandjong Priok, with a draw a fair result. Camp 9 are worthy winners of the Camp Shield.

That was the serious side of camp sport but on 6 September a more contentious and chaotic game of soccer took place between the Officers and Sergeants of Camp 5, as reported by 'Hot Stuff', the camp sports reporter.

An Epic Game

On Sunday, September 6, 1942, took place the most magnificent, awe-inspiring, spectacular, and skillful exhibition of Association Football ever witnessed at Tandjong Priok, or in the Netherlands East Indies for that matter! The participants, by their dazzling brilliance, made the Football Final of Camps 2 and 9 appear tame and uninteresting by comparison.

TEAMS:

OFFICERS
In Gaol (mostly): Lt Stuart D. 'Keep 'em out' Mitchell
Full Stops: Lt Ken 'Shops' Taylor and 2/Lt Reg W.J. 'Macbeth' Mitchell.
Half Bakes: Capt. Herbert 'Trilby' Lloyd, 2/Lt Frederick S. 'Stolid' Fawcett, and Lt Ron 'Fall-down' Williams.
Frowards: Lt Robin 'Speedy' Charles, Lt Henry M. 'Stores' Clatworthy, Lt Henry M. 'Bull' Bullard, Lt Ken 'Shoot Straight' Vick and 2/Lt Johnny 'Pedlar' Probert.

SERGEANTS
In Gaol: R.S.M., W. Arthur 'Rice' Evans.
Full Stops: Sgt Walter 'Plants' Pritchard and Sgt Edwin 'GTV' Kirby
Half Bakes: Sgt Tom O. 'Rations' Jones, Sgt William G. 'Lats' David, and Sgt John J. 'Hefty' Glover
Frowards: Sgt Douglas S. 'Legs' Magnus, Sgt John W 'Chess' Baker, Sgt John 'Fists' Phillips, Sgt Gwyn T. 'Crib' James, and Sgt Mike J.P. 'Dev' O'Mahony.

It was a beautiful day, with the temperature above 100 degrees in the shade, as the teams took to the field. For some reason, the Regimental Band failed to make an appearance. It was later learned that their instruments had become too hot and melted. The bandsmen, all two of them, reported to the sickbay with severe burns.

There were four teams on the field as, apparently, two matches had been arranged! Fortunately for Camp 5, a referee was produced in the person of Lt W. 'Woolly' Wooller (did you see his hat?). He strode majestically onto the pitch and with a long blast on his whistle dispelled the parasites that had been congregating at the east end goal.

Just as the match was about to get underway, there was great consternation in the Officers' team, for the selected centre half had failed to appear, none other than Lt Col H. Robert 'Blanco' Humphries. At the crucial moment, a messenger, 'Don', sauntered onto the pitch with a note for Capt. 'Trilby' Lloyd, in which the Colonel begged to be excused as he had spent most of the day trying to find a push-bike. 2/Lt 'Stolid' Fawcett was dragged from his sickbed to fill the breach.

From the centre kick-off, 'Bull' Bullard flashed (Yes – literally!) the ball to 'Speedy' Charles, the right-cum-left supporting winger, who sped up the touch-line with a huge roar of encouragement from the large crowd; Robin's name was on every spectator's lips. Meanwhile, for the Sergeants, 'Hefty' Glover passed the match ball to 'Cribs' James who, sidling around 'Shops' Taylor, passed to 'Fists' Phillips who tested 'Keep 'em out' Mitchell with a gentle side footed shot which was most brilliantly saved … Half Time Officers – 0: Sergeants – 0. What a game! What a spectacle! What a shower!

When the players had recovered they implored the referee to shorten the second half to three minutes. 'Woolly' Wooller, mercilessly, refused to comply with this request. The game continued and immediately the crowds were treated to a new and fascinating form of attack, known as gyroscopic penetration. 'Dev' O'Mahony placed a very clever pass but completely missed the ball in the process. The ball trickled into the path of 'Trilby' Lloyd who, jamming his hat firmly onto his head proceeded to dribble in circles in an effort to make the Sergeants dizzy and ineffective. 'Hefty' Glover would have none of this and spoilt this manoeuvre by taking the ball off 'Trilby' Lloyd. 'Trilby' Lloyd was enraged by this wanton interference and hurled himself at 'Hefty' Glover in a bull-like charge. 'Hefty' Glover managed to get out of the way and 'Trilby' Lloyd hit the dirt!

… From a throw in (definitely a foul), the Sergeants 'Rations' Jones delivered the goods in a masterly fashion. He raced down the field in mass formation with his forwards, passed to 'Legs' Magnus, who tapped it to 'Chess' Baker, who made a pawn of 'Macbeth' Mitchell, the ball was then propelled between 'Crib' James and 'Dev' O'Mahony. 'Dev' avoided a vicious tackle from 'Shops' Taylor and gave a scoring pass to 'Crib' James, who neatly tapped the ball into the net despite 'Keep 'em out' Mitchell's valiant and strong appeal for off-side.

Where was the defence? Where were the half-backs? Up the field telling the forwards how to score a goal! After this setback the Officers rallied and stormed their opponent's goal. Fine shots were sent in by 'Speedy' Charles, 'Stores' Clatworthy, and 'Bull' Bullard. However, 'Rice' Evans (in gaol) was quite unperturbed, although spectators near the corner flag had a few uncomfortable moments!

… 'Chess' Baker scored a second goal for the Sergeants as 'Keep 'em out' Mitchell just failed to reach the ball. Of course, the Sergeants were clearly offside again. The sun had so affected the referee that he allowed the goal …

Although faced with this dire defeat the Officers fought back gallantly and twice 'Stolid' Fawcett passed the ball accurately to the referee, shouting, 'Shoot, Wilf, shoot', but 'Woolly' would have none of it and let the Officers' team down badly as, on one occasion, 'Woolly' faced an open goal. It was at this stage that the referee was no longer controlling a football match but a melee of reeling men, staggering and falling about, through sheer exhaustion. 'Woolly' humanely blew his whistle for time. The huge crowd cheered their approval for the excellent entertainment that had been provided.

(*The Jungle Journal*, No. 6, August 1942)

The score appeared to be Officers – 0: Sergeants – 2, but there was no mention of the final result in the match report.

On Saturday October 3, 1942, another Tandjong Priok Camp Soccer Final took place involving Camp 9. This event would have been reported in the missing *Jungle Journal*, No 7. Gnr Henry 'Harry' Hamer composed some verses to celebrate Camp 9 winning both soccer competitions.

The Team

In a place called Tandjong Priok,
Far from England's coral strand,
Lie fourteen camps all packed in one
With prisoners who do not envy this land.

In the middle of this camp lies a football pitch,
Where many a match has been lost or won.
The best of these camps is number nine
Who won two finals, before the season was done.

Now, I'll tell you a tale of this football team
Who won both finals' indeed, 'twas a very good feat,
They were English, Scots and Welsh in one,
And still they have yet to meet defeat.

We have a star named Billy James,
He's our captain hail and hearty.
All he thought of, when we won the shield,
Was to supper or to party.

We had a supper thanks to Smith
Two eggs and beef and cigarettes to go with
When we bid goodnight to each other,
We had thoughts, in our minds, of having another.

We have two goalkeepers Betts and Pritch
Who to pick? We don't know which,
As each of them give of their very best
If they do their worst we would still lick the rest.

Our fullbacks are Evident and Barrie
Occasionally the team they have to carry
Some referee's decisions have met with a boo
But the team have always managed to pull through.

Our right half Quirke is a young Welsh dan
Nicknamed by the crowd the 'Monkey Man'
On the field of play he gets stuck in
If he doesn't get the ball, he will elbow your chin!

Our left half position is a puzzle I say
We have Dugay, Hart and Jones T.J.
They have all worked hard to play with the rest
And with flying colours they have stood the test.

Our centre half James I've told you he's a star
When he runs down the middle he could catch a car
He's always on form, he plays clean and fine
And opposing forwards have a very lean time.

We have Harry Hamer on the extreme right
When he runs down the wing the crowd get a fright
When he cuts towards goal the crowd with a roar
Shout 'If he wasn't offside I'm sure he would score'.

Jordy McWhirter is our inside right
Who plays the game with all his might.
He's not very clever but that doesn't matter
When he opens out, defences they scatter.

At inside left we have a Scot named Mickey
And, blimey, isn't he blooming tricky.
When he gets the ball he's a wee bit hot
But he's too tired and lazy to have a shot.

To play wing with Mickey you've got to be sure
This position is filled by Ron Bradshaw.
The only trouble is, with our Ron,
He seems to hang on to the ball far too long.

To say this about Ron is a little bit tame
Because, in the Final, he played a grand game.
He's a good tricky player and carries a good shot
And on a good few occasions has found the pot.

At centre forward we have been weak in the past
But we've settled with Davidson now at last
As a utility man he's been fairly grand
And at centre forward we hope he will stand.

Our reserve back, Welsh is his name,
On many occasions he has played a sound game.
Then there's Evans and Millward, I'm sorry to say
Malaria and Dengue stepped in their way.

Those last two players I had to mention,
As the committee paid them special attention.
They both deserved to be in the side
But tropical diseases kept them outside.

Our Officer of Sport is Major Rutter.
In the selection room no word he must utter
Against the word of Dutton and James,
Who have selected the team for all the games.

Gnr Harry Hamer, 241 Bty, 77th HAA. Tandjong Priok Camp, 1942

Team players from Camp 9 who played in the finals:

Pritchard, Evident, Barrie, Quirke, James,
Milward, Hufton, McWhirter, Davidson, Allerton,
Bradshaw, Hamer, Cullerton, Dugay, Hart Jones.

Shakespeare featured strongly in POW camp entertainment. *The Merchant of Venice* appeared to be the first main production. The following extract from *The Jungle Journal* also contains a plea for further participants:

The Merchant of Venice was a memorable event. In the words of our Commanding Officer, history was probably made.

The agonies of Shylock (Lt R. Beresford-Smith) went straight to the heart, and the graciousness and cool presence of Portia (Gnr E. Tarleton) delighted many. It would, however, have been a sorry spectacle without support. Those thankless parts of Bassanio (Lt A. Dent) and Antonio (Squadron Quartermaster Sergeant (SQMS) Harry Lambert), made excellent foils and gave greater shine to the Lady and the Jew. The story becomes a disjointed snatch without the timely utterances of Solaino (Sgt Patterson) and Solarino (BSM E. Neale) Do you remember too, how dignity and presence was brought to a few odd stools by the Doge of Venice (Lt Col Ernest J. Hazel)? How we laughed at the discomfiture and re-establishment of the boisterous lover Gratiano (Lt Arthur J. Steeds). Suppose Shylock's knife had not been on the table and suppose the fatal caskets failed to arrive? Try to imagine what would happen if no one knew which scene came next! Therein lays the man who counts, and the power behind the control of the scenes, with his staff, which are mundane necessities. In the last performance, he combined also three speaking parts of various servants and courtiers. For all this he appeared once in the programme as a 'servant'. His name is Lt Reginald W.J. Mitchell.

You can see our difficulties and you know your capabilities. Are you interested?

E.P.F.

Are you interested? If so, please contact Lt E.P. Fitt RA, who will furnish you with the necessary information. Ed.

(*The Jungle Journal*, No. 4, June 1942)

On July 30, the St. George's Players presented 'Macbeth'. This is a bald statement of fact, but a great tribute to the sheer energy, ingenuity and perseverance of those responsible … I have heard, on occasions, Dramatic Societies glibly declaring that they are falling back on Shakespeare. This appalling attitude is probably adopted for two main reasons; a perceived immunity from intellectual criticism, and the resources available to the stage manager. A production launched with these aims is doomed to failure. Shakespeare is not some weedy last resort when other dramatists are found to be unsuitable. He is the master craftsman and, rather than a last resort, should remain an ultimate ambition …

The factor which lifts a production, from a mediocre rendering to something inspirational, is interpretation … I mean an extra effort, on the part of the players, to give the audience more than a mere recital of beautiful words. In attempting this, Lt Dent and his company succeeded extremely well. Lt Mitchell took his heavy part in his stride and aided by a delightful speaking voice gave a very polished performance. Lt Fitt dealt with the hardest part in the play and performed with great competence and stagecraft. Lt Wooller was regally aloof, contrasting magnificently with the foul harpies, who appeared to have flown non-stop from Hellespont. Finally, the atmosphere of the play was clinched by a dash of Celtic mysticism in the music.

Sgt John Forge

(*The Jungle Journal*, No. 5, July 1942)

I have attempted to portray the essence of *The Jungle Journal*, covering some of the key areas, by providing whole articles and extracts. It seems incredible that, if all eleven of the journals had come to fruition, over 200 separate items would have been published in a little over ten months.

There appeared two interesting admonitions in *The Jungle Journal,* one of which relates to POWs swearing and, the other, POWs' behaviour at camp football matches:

Admonition

You are a separate band alone,
A long way from your native home,

With enemies on every hand;
You're underneath the Nip command.
And yet like fools you can't agree:
You argue more than when you are free.
You grouse, you grumble, and complain
Pointlessly, for no fathomable gain.
Your language foul pollutes the air;
Your one enjoyment is to swear,
And if those words we do deplore,
You seem to do it more and more.
There are many words that you can use
So why our English do you abuse?
Be plain, be simple, and please try
To keep those bad words, from slipping by.

(*The Jungle Journal*, No. 6, August 1942)

The author of this submission is listed as Gnr Hoarfield, who does not exist in the COFEPOW database as having served in the Far East. Also, no initials were included, which is a feature of pseudonyms used by the Editor of *The Jungle Journal*. I postulate that the author was my father because he detested any form of bad language, which I discovered once to my cost! Also, the style of verse is similar to my father's other material. Ronald knew the Horfield area of Bristol well, which could be the origin of the pseudonym.

However, Kathleen Booth pointed out that there was a Gnr Hoare in 239 Bty, who lived in Kingfield. This is a plausible alternative explanation, although Gnr Hoarfield does not appear elsewhere in any extant *Jungle Journal*.

The following is an extract from an article entitled 'Sportsmanship', by Norman Saunders:

The recent warning to the spectators at our football matches was really no surprise to anyone who has the least understanding of the meaning of sportsmanship. It was not just a question of fruity language aimed at the referee and players alike, but a failure by some spectators to comprehend the functions of players and referee on the field! Naturally, we all want our respective camps to win, but not at all costs. Not all doubtful decisions can go in your team's favour. And, do we want our team to win irrespective of the safety concerns of our opponents?

I hope I can answer this question by stating 'No, and a hundred times, no!' Yet, listen to some of the comments and exclamations from the pitch side and see what you make of them?

'Play the game Ref!'

Loud cheers when a decision goes in your side's favour.

Loud 'boos' when the reverse is true.

Applause when your player pulls off a 'smart piece' of work, but cries of 'dirty' when an opponent puts in an apparently over-zealous tackle.

I am sure some of you are feeling indignant at what I have written and refute what I am stating? This doesn't apply to you, of course, but you must agree that this happens at nearly every camp football match. Don't you? Do not forget that we are supposed to show the greatest sportsmanship in the world!

What conclusions can you draw, chums??

(*The Jungle Journal*, No. 5, July 1942)

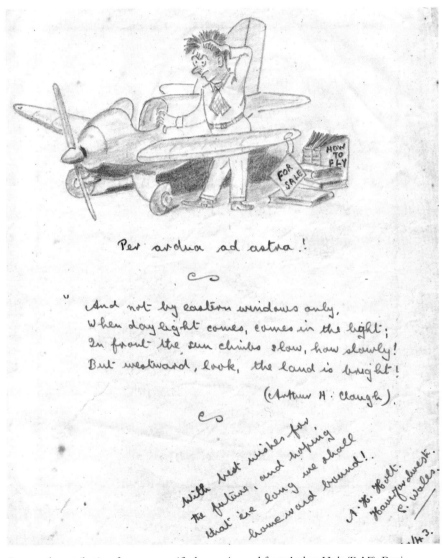

A penned contribution for an unspecified camp journal from Arthur Holt (RAF), Boei Glodok camp, 1943.

'No Insects in This House'. Cartoon drawn for *The Yasume Times*. Reference to 'insects' was a synonym for the Japanese guards. Other cartoons displayed 'gallows humour' with reference to keeping a cork handy for diarrhoea and a tennis racquet for swatting flies.

Ronald documented that a number of his journal contributors died at various times in the Far East, including most of his editorial team:

Harold Davey, Reginald Rowe, Norman Sage, Norman E. Saunders, Charles W. Tinsley and William J. Whitman died on board a Japanese prison ship *Suez Maru*, which was torpedoed by the submarine USS *Bonefish*, on 29 November 1943. The story of the sinking of this hell-ship is well documented in the book *The Suez Maru: Atrocity-Justice Denied!* by Allan Jones, which states that nearly a hundred members of the 77th Artillery Regiment died in this incident.

Thomas A. Griffiths died on 20 December 1943 and was buried in Batavia.

John G. Howell died 29 June 1943 and Clifford Herbert died 20 August 1943, both in the Hintok Road camp and were buried at Kanchanaburi.

Brian Norman died 23 May 1943 and Edward Graham died 1 June 1943, both on Amboina

D.J. Evans died on Moena in September 1944.

George W. Ball died on Java, on 3 June 1944, and was buried in Batavia.

Charles Holdsworth went with 'H' Force to work on the Burma–Thailand railway and survived the war.

Mike O'Mahony was drafted to Japan, worked in the Ohama mine, and survived the war.

Charles Hatfield and Douglas Magnus were sent to the Inasuki camp in Japan and survived the war.

Noel James went on a labour-draft and survived the war.

4: Alleged Japanese Atrocities Committed on Java and on the Java Sea in 1942

By Frank Williams

Kertosono

A small detachment of Dutch marines made a counter-attack against a Japanese force holding a bridgehead at Kertosono, Java, on 5 March 1942. The Dutch marines became scattered during the attack and one contingent, under Lt den Hartog, was captured by Japanese infantry. All nine Dutchmen in the small contingent were summarily executed by bayonet and beheading.

Tjiater

On 6 March 1942, the 5th Battalion of the Dutch KNIL put up fierce resistance against the advancing Japanese Army at Bandoeng, West Java, being well dug-in in foxholes. The Dutch were eventually overwhelmed by a larger force and from constant air attacks from Japanese Zero fighters. Seventy-two Dutch soldiers were taken prisoner, tied up, and taken to a nearby hill. They were machine gunned. Three feigned death and managed to survive.

One, Pieter de Lizer, avoided Japanese capture until 12 March at Bandoeng, and survived to tell the tale. The murdered servicemen were eventually buried at Bandoeng cemetery.

Maos

Following the bombing of Allied shipping at Tjilatjap in early March 1942, a large number of British and Australian Air Force men failed to escape from Java. They moved west by rail to Tasikmalaya. Two trains carrying about 600 airmen were ambushed by an advanced guard of the Japanese Army. A number of Allied airmen were killed in this action.

Groups of survivors from the wrecked trains made their way by foot to Maos. The more seriously wounded men were put into huts by the side of the railway line and told to wait for help. A few medical orderlies stayed with them and the rest of the able-bodied airmen made their way over the railway bridge at Kesogihan, towards Bandoeng. Unfortunately, Dutch engineers blew the bridge later that evening, effectively trapping the wounded airmen and medical orderlies. During the night, the advanced Japanese guard (from the 56th Infantry Regiment) came across the wounded men in the huts and proceeded to bayonet them all to death.

Two men managed to survive the massacre and made their way to Bandoeng, having to swim a river in the process. RAF Cpl Bob Finning, (84th RAF squadron) was one of two survivors to document this atrocity.

Kalidjati airfield

There was fierce fighting at Kalidjati on 1 March during which many RAF personnel, fighting as infantry, were killed in action. The Japanese were later full of praise for the determination of untrained Allied personnel attempting to protect the airfield.

A number of RAF ground staff were butchered by Japanese soldiers after surrender. Staff and patients at nearby Soebang Hospital were also put to death by Japanese infantrymen. Although the incidents were investigated by Australian war crimes teams after the war, there was insufficient direct evidence against individual Japanese to effect a prosecution.

Augustina massacre

The tanker *Augustina* left Batavia docks late in February 1942, en route to Australia. She was intercepted by a Japanese destroyer on 1 March. The captain, A.J. Moerman, had orders to scuttle the ship in the event of capture. The scuttling process was put underway and the men abandoned ship. The Japanese destroyer came alongside the lifeboats and ordered the men back to the tanker and were told to follow the destroyer.

The *Augustina* men returned to their ship, but the scuttling process was too advanced to make the boat seaworthy again. On returning to their lifeboats they were fired on by the Japanese destroyer. The *Augustina*'s men were then systematically machine gunned.

The 3rd engineer, L. Meyer, managed to swim underwater for some distance and when he broke the surface he found no other survivors and the Japanese destroyer steaming away. Meyer managed to get back to the slowly sinking tanker and found an undamaged life raft and headed out into the open sea. He was eventually picked up by another Japanese destroyer and taken to Makassar on 7 March. Meyer spent most of his POW years in Fukuoka No. 2 camp in Japan.

Following liberation in September 1945 he made a statement about the *Augustina* massacre to the war crimes investigators at Manila. Identification of the Japanese destroyer involved in the massacre proved impossible. Nine officers and thirty Chinese crew had been murdered by the Japanese. Two other seamen, both Chinese, who also survived, ratified these events.

The Cheribon Atrocity

In late July 1942, a Japanese submarine departed from Cheribon, north Java, with over ninety Dutch and other European women and children standing on deck. After riding for an hour on the surface the submarine, without warning, dived under the sea.

Most on deck either drowned or were eaten by sharks. One Dutch woman, although injured from a shark attack, managed to stay alive long enough to relate this story to Javanese fishermen who plucked her from the water.

At the end of the war this story was conveyed to the war crimes investigators but, as was often the case, all records of Japanese naval movements had been destroyed and, consequently, the Japanese submarine could not be identified.

The 'pig basket' atrocity

A group of Allied soldiers had escaped into the Java Mountains, near Malang, but they were soon captured by hostile natives and handed over to the Japanese. A short while later, the captured Allied servicemen were seen being driven to beaches tied up in pig-shaped basket containers which were then dropped into the shark-infested waters from the boats.

These are a small number of recorded atrocities committed by the Japanese army and navy during fighting on Java in March 1942. Numerous stories circulated POW camps about Japanese atrocities, but many could not be verified. Many of these accounts came from Dutch female residents who continued to have a certain amount of freedom during the early months of Japanese occupation. NESA (National Ex-Services' Association) research concluded that nearly 10,000 civilians were murdered by the Japanese on Java during the period of occupation, 1942–45.

Account of the sinking of a Japanese transporter ship taking Allied POWs to mainland Japan

The following is an account from Dutchman Lt T.C.W. van Oortmerssen of the Inf. KNIL. It demonstrates the perils of being a passenger on Japanese transporter ships taking POWs to mainland Japan, Thailand, Burma and islands of the Dutch East Indies:

> On 10 May 1944, a draft of prisoners was assembled in the Batavia area of Java for transportation to Japan. Many Allied POWs had already been drafted to Japan, Formosa, Siam and Burma previously. The whole party comprised 772 men and was under the command of a young Australian officer, Maj. J.D. Morris.
>
> The party was subdivided into groups of 150 men in the charge of two English and two Australian lieutenants and me. The party included thirty doctors and sixty medical orderlies. The men were well equipped by Japanese standards, being fitted with leather shoes released from the Red Cross store. The strength of the various nationalities was as follows: 197 British, 42 Americans, 247 Australians and 276 Dutch. I was the only troop officer in the Dutch party. I found Maj. Morris to be a most agreeable and co-operative officer.
>
> On 19 May, we embarked on the *Kisla Maru*, a 2,500-ton boat, which transported us to Singapore without incident by the afternoon of 22 May. We were packed into the boat like sardines and sleep proved very difficult, if not impossible. We were housed in Singapore in a camp on the River Valley road previously inhabited by British Indians. Food was poor with no added vegetables. The doctors feared an outbreak of beri-beri.
>
> On 2 June we were herded aboard a large cargo ship, which sailed the following day in a convoy of ten other merchantmen and four corvettes. In the China

Sea, we were aware of danger from Allied submarines and on the night of 6 June, west of Borneo, one of the corvettes was torpedoed and sunk.

There were life jackets on board, but these had only been issued to the Japanese. We were all confined to the hold following the sinking of the corvette. Depth charges were exploding fairly close to our boat and, with expectation of further torpedo attacks, the situation was very unnerving. The Japanese sergeant eventually issued us with life jackets some two days later, and on the 11th we arrived at Manila, where we camped by the side of the road for two days.

During the passage from Manila to Formosa, we encountered a fearful storm which tossed and turned the ship incredibly. We, eventually, arrived at Takao, a southern Formosan port, and transferred to another cargo ship, placed in the top hold forward of the bridge. Two stairwells led to the deck and it was just about possible for all the men to find somewhere to lie down. One of the holds was full of Formosan sugar but the rest were empty.

From Takoa we passed the Riukiu Islands for Moji, one of the harbours of Kyushu, southern Japan. Overnight it became a lot cooler, and the men were wishing the long journey would end.

On the evening before we were due to arrive in Moji, on 24 June, we were quite excited that the arduous journey was almost over. We had absolutely no idea what awaited us in Japan. The Japs were also in a good mood and permitted music to be played. I was now confident that we would at least survive the journey as Japanese land was nearly in sight and the coastal waters were heavily patrolled.

I was sleeping near the masthead hold with the other troop officers, which was very stuffy and unpleasant. At about midnight a loud explosion awakened us and the ship shuddered very heavily. Clouds of dust and debris descended on our heads. All the lights went out and I could hear Maj. Morris shouting 'Don't panic!' In fact, these were the very last words I heard from the Major. The ship next to us had taken a direct hit.

There were two exits from the hold up the two stairways. Many men were trying to force their way up the stairs. I barged my way to the base of one of the stairways to try to introduce some order, when we were hit on the starboard side by a torpedo. All I can remember is a glaring flash of light and I must then have been knocked unconscious. Next, I felt myself being held upright in rapidly rising water, I do not know by what but my instinct was to swim and swim hard to safety. The boat was clearly sinking fast. Incredibly, my passage out of the hold and over the side of the boat was largely unhindered.

I found myself alone in the cold waters with little obvious activity around me. This was a very frightening experience, swimming at night with no companion-ship and in enemy, probably shark-infested, waters. Eventually I found a piece of floating timber from one of the wrecks and later a sizeable plank I could paddle with. I was uncertain about rescue knowing the Japanese respect for our lives.

The first group I encountered in the water were Japanese sailors who were singing and took little notice of me. Then I met up with some of our own men and we drifted towards a gathering of small rafts containing friend and foe alike.

The remainder of the convoy had disappeared towards their predetermined destination. A Jap destroyer was making depth-charge runs in the distance, although we were very conscious of the vibrations from the underwater explosions.

The water seemed to get colder and we were all shivering. Early the following morning spotter planes flew over and eventually rowing boats from a Japanese whaler started picking up the survivors. I was one of the last to be pulled out, and I must have been in the water for at least ten hours by this time.

It was an unforgettable moment climbing up the webbing onto the whaler to find groups of survivors. We compared notes to who was alive and who had perished. Some men had a much better idea than I did about what had happened. Apparently, the upper deck of the boat had taken a direct hit and most men on the deck fell through to the bottom hold and drowned. Those men who were near the middle and bottom of the stairways faired best and were swept out by the rising water. Some sleeping in the upper hold not hit by debris also survived, but many succumbed to the water undertow.

A selection of Japanese war criminals drawn by Karen Williams (Ronald Williams' granddaughter) from various sources, including photographs in Ronald Williams' collection.

560 men perished in about two minutes. Of the 772 POWs on board only 212 survived (forty-two British, eighty-five Dutch, seventy-two Australians and thirteen Americans). The ship had been sunk about 40 miles west of Nagasaki.

We arrived at Nagasaki and were then transported to a Dutch POW camp, Fukuoka 14, which was later destroyed by the atom bomb. As we had lost all our possessions, we were given some basic clothing by the Japanese. After six weeks in isolation, we were allowed in to a larger camp. Conditions were poor and sickness and malnutrition took their toll.

However, this would be another story to write. Conditions did improve after a visit from a Japanese staff officer who came to investigate the sinking of the ship. Of the eighty-five Dutch, who survived the sinking, a further ten died, mainly from tuberculosis. These deaths were hard because I had come to know some of the survivors very well.

Lt van Oortmerssen was freed from Mukden POW camp, Manchuria, in August 1945. This is one tale of many Allied submarine attacks on Japanese transporters containing prisoners of war, because the Japanese consistently refused to place suitable recognition marks on their ships. The Japanese deliberately murdered some prisoners of war who survived the sinking, usually by machine gun fire while they were still floating or swimming in the water. The incident described by Lt Oortmerssen was the sinking of the *Tamahoko Maru*, by the submarine USS *Tang*, in Nagasaki Bay, Shimodo, Japan.

Captured and handcuffed Japanese – the tormentors of Java POWs. Lt Colonel Anami (left), Pte Kasayama 'Slimey' (centre) who tried to escape disguised as a civilian, and S/M 'Bamboo' Mori. They are flanked by S/L Pitts and W/C Alexander. Anami and Mori were both hanged in Singapore.

Lt Colonel Anami (1), alias 'Knitty Whiskers', the commanding officer of POW camps on Flores, Ambon. Ceram, Java and Haruku (Japan); alongside Captain Shimada (2), Anami's medical officer. Both were executed following a war crimes trial at Spè in July 1946. (Courtesy Richard Reardon-Smith)

Japanese war criminal suspects. 1–4 are unidentified. 5 is S/M 'Gunso' Mori, alias 'Bamboo' and 'Blood', who was sentenced to death by hanging. 6 is S/M Kawai of 'hell-ship' *Maros Maru* infamy (Liang, Ambon) who was sentenced to death by hanging. 7 is S/M Yamamoto (Liang) who received ten years' detention. 8 is KG (Korean Guard) Kasayama, alias 'Slimey' who was sentenced to life imprisonment. 9 is KG Toyada (Haruku Island), who received ten years. 10 is KG Kanakada (Haruku Island), who received ten years. 11 is KG Kuyumoto (Liang, Ambon), who was sentenced to life imprisonment. 12 is Kimoupang (Liang, Ambon), alias 'Four-Eyes', who received seven years. 13 is Captain Kurashimi (O/C, Haruku Island camp), who was sentenced to death by hanging. (Courtesy Richard Reardon-Smith)

Japanese War Crimes Trial, for Ambon cases, held at Spè in July 1946. Judges from left to right are Lt Col Monod de Froidville, Lt Col Smith (President) and Captain Hassan (Indian Army). The trial lasted fourteen days. (Courtesy Richard Reardon-Smith)

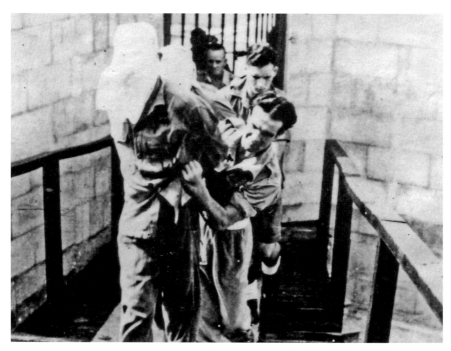

Hooded convicted Japanese war criminals being led to and awaiting execution. (Courtesy Richard Reardon-Smith)

5: *One Came Back Home*

The following is an extract from a play, written by my father, called *One Came Back Home*. (This was a reference to the Dutch light battle cruiser *Tromp,* which was the only Dutch surface warship to survive the Battle of Java Sea and return to anchor off Tandjong Priok, Java, following the Japanese surrender in 1945.)

The play was written in the early 1950s and intended for BBC radio. It was met with a BBC complimentary response, but ultimate rejection. This was not the sort of topic the BBC was interested in at that time. This play, approximately forty minutes in duration, gives a flavour of Ronald's experiences on Madoera Island before the Allied surrender and also conveys some of the undoubted friction between British and Dutch officers in the defence of Java.

The action takes place on Madoera Island, a hilly island off the north-east coast of Java, in mid-February 1942. The characters are Lt Jon Gwilliam (perhaps a pseudonym for my father?) a British artillery officer, Sgt Evans, a British artillery NCO and a signaller, Pte Jones, Capt. K. Muller, a Dutch KNIL officer, marine man First Class Simin, and his sister Waginah, along with various Dutch Observer Corps members.

SCENE ONE:
The scene is set in a large room in a camouflaged native hut; an installation containing wall charts, maps and sophisticated radio equipment. Simin, dressed in smart white drill, is seated at the radio and his sister, Waginah, dressed in a kain [*sarong*] and kebaya [*a long-sleeved blouse*], is tending to the three newly arrived British soldiers, whom she has brought to the radio station. They are waiting for Capt. Muller, the local Dutch army commander.

LT GWILLIAM: [to Simin] Your sister, Waginah, speaks good English and is a safe guide.

SIMIN: Yes, I know. Take off your gear and sit down, you look tired and thirsty. Waginah, fetch the men some beer and *makan* [*food*]. Please excuse, messages coming through on the radio…

The three British soldiers relax with their beers and cooked meat on skewers, watching Simin intently. Eventually Simin turns back, after placing the receiver down.

LT GWILLIAM: [to Simin] What is the news on Singapore?

SIMIN: Sir, bad news. It looks as though the Japs are breaking through Malaya most quickly.

SGT EVANS: Singapore is supposed to be impregnable and Malaya difficult to get through. What's going wrong?

SIMIN: The Japs are most determined and seem to overcome any obstacle in their way.

LT GWILLIAM: You have some impressive equipment here, Simin.

SIMIN: Yes sir, we must be able to stay in contact with *Darwin* and *Colombo*.

SGT EVANS: Sir, what exactly are we doing here? We were yanked away from our gun battery without so much as an explanation!

LT GWILLIAM: Sergeant, I am sure everything will be explained to us once Capt. Muller arrives.

SIMIN: Capt. Muller should arrive soon. He will tell you all. We are a secret radio station and we don't think the Japanese know of our existence. We have concealed observers all around the island coast too.

SGT EVANS: You speak very good English, Simin, as does your sister.

SIMIN: I went to high school in Soerabaja. We are both children of the Maduran *kepala* [*headman*], so I had a good education and have taught my sister to speak Dutch, Malay, as well as English, of course.

SGT EVANS: Why didn't Waginah go to school?

SIMIN: Local girls do not go to school in Java.

Enter Capt. Muller (KNIL officer), dressed in a meticulous green tunic and breeches, high black riding boots and a gleaming Sam Browne. Waginah disappears promptly.

CAPT. MULLER: *Guden Morgen*, I am Capt. Muller.

LT GWILLIAM: [salutes Muller] Pleased to meet you, sir. I am Lt Gwilliam of the Royal Artillery and these are my men, Sgt Evans and Signaller Jones. Have you any updated information on the situation in Singapore?

CAPT. MULLER: Very bad news, Gwilliam – the Japanese earlier crossed into the Jahore Strait and they appear to be attacking in great strength from the north. I feel sure Gen. Yamashita is close to taking Singapore Island. The Japs have also landed on Banka Island.

LT GWILLIAM: I don't like the look of things, but we must try and stop the Japanese completely over-running the Dutch East Indies. The airfields and rich supplies of oil will be very important to them and they will gain great advantage if they capture these.

CAPT. MULLER: Yes, I agree with you. We are still in radio contact with much of the Dutch East Indies. We should remain reasonably secure on Java and we are expecting reinforcements to halt this Japanese advance.

LT GWILLIAM: What exactly is our role here, sir?

CAPT. MULLER: This is a forward defensive observation post and radio station, which you can see is well camouflaged by trees. We will be relied upon to coordinate defensive manoeuvres for East Java, providing there is no radio silence. We have also lookouts scattered around the island to inform us of plane and shipping movements. This will almost certainly be the final radio station in action if the Japanese knock out those on the mainland. This will be important if we need to guide in reinforcements.

Muller walks to one of the wall charts.

CAPT. MULLER: Gwilliam, look [*he points*], here is Kamel on Madeora Island close to Soerabaja, which, as you know, is our General HQ and Naval base. Here is Malacca, or Malaya, as you English choose to call it. The Japs landed here at Kota Bharu and came down through the jungle with some ease. I guess that the Singapore defences were not expecting this direction of attack, as all the heavy guns are built facing out to sea! I am very surprised at this lack of defensive foresight, as the water supply to Singapore would surely be a key target for the Japanese, but your English generals did not anticipate this. Singapore is likely to go 'kaput' soon. No Dutch to help you! Huh!

Muller scowls, over his shoulder, at Gwilliam. Muller then turns to Gwilliam with a wry smile, lights up a large cigar and continues…

On 10 December, the British battleship *Prince of Wales* and battle cruiser *Repulse* sailed out from Singapore to try and stop the Japanese landings off Kuantan. But, with no air cover, the Japs had a, what do you English say? A 'turkey shoot' with torpedoes. Boom! No more British battleships! Then Guam is overrun, Rangoon is bombed, Wake Island lost and, worst of all, Hong Kong surrenders on Christmas Day! My concern is that Java will become vulnerable if we lose our air cover.

LT GWILLIAM: Well, it is not the first time a naval fleet has had no air protection, and probably not the last. I am sure reinforcements will be coming – aircraft in particular.

CAPT. MULLER: *Ja, ja, ja.* Perhaps you British have run out of planes. Our planes are old and no match for the Japanese 'Zeroes'. Also, you English have come here in desert gear and with heavy artillery, but few planes and tanks; this does not bode well if Java is invaded, does it?

LT GWILLIAM: Sir, that is a bit rich. We were diverted here, having been originally heading for North Africa and the Middle East to fight the Germans. I agree our gear is not suitable for jungle warfare, but it will have to do. We can put up a jolly good fight, I am sure of that.

CAPT. MULLER: Huh! To continue, in January whilst you were enjoying a cruise in the Indian Ocean, the Japs made their first landings in the Oost Indies. Look here, [*he points*] in British North Borneo, they also attacked the Dutch Island of Tarakan, rich in oil, and the east coast of Borneo. The next day they went on to Celebes, the Minhassa, and soon afterwards on to the mainland of Dutch North Borneo. This has occurred with alarming speed, particularly the laying down of coral airstrips. They are now bombing Java on a daily basis.

LT GWILLIAM: I know, we had a nice welcoming party when we docked in Tandjong Priok, some twelve days ago.

CAPT. MULLER: I have to say, Gwilliam, you English officers enjoy your cocktail parties, bridge clubs and life's comforts, but react in a panic when it is too late and then blame others for your mistakes. I admit there are some brave British officers who have been badly let down by their superiors. This is why we, Dutch, welcomed the news of Pearl Harbor and America's entry into the war. Do not get me wrong Gwilliam; I was as concerned as anyone about the loss of American ships and men, but the entry of the Americans into the war has given us new hope. Just one example, Gwilliam: on the 20th of January, four old style American destroyers wreaked havoc on a Japanese troop convoy off the coast of Celebes and withdrew without so much as a scratch!

LT GWILLIAM: [looking distinctly annoyed] Sorry – enough of this Capt. Muller! I could say a thing or two about you Dutch, such as – some of you seem to enjoy your food [looking at Muller's impressive paunch] more than soldiering – but I will not waste my breath on such matters any further. Let us get down to looking at convoy movements and do we know what is happening at Palembang (Sumatra)?

SIMMIN: [interrupts] Capitan, Capitan, message from Fort Canning, Gen. Percival[5] is about to surrender Singapore to the Japanese...
Resigned silence follows.

The play continues with coverage of the battles of Badoeng Strait and Java Sea, which have been described in Appendix 2.

The scene had been set by Air Chief Marshal Brooke-Popham, GoC of Land and Air Forces Malaya, stating that the Allies' Air Force (described as 'museum exhibits' by some observers) and army was far superior to the Japanese. Numerically this may have been true, but in all other respects it was a fatally flawed and an ill-advised statement. He prevaricated over taking on the expected Japanese invasion of southern Siam and northern Malaya, giving the Japanese great advantage. The poor northern defences of Singapore Island are another story, well documented in British military history.

Recent declassified War Office documents have revealed that Col William Forbes Sempill, later Lord Sempill, and First World War fighter ace Sqn Ldr Frederick Rutland, both experts in naval aviation, had furnished the Japanese with considerable naval and aviation intelligence between 1925-41, which proved decisive in Japanese attacks on Pearl Harbor and Singapore. Rutland committed suicide when he was exposed but Sempill managed to escape charges of treason because of his influential connections (his father was at one time aide-de-camp to King George V). To have exposed him might also have tipped off the Japanese that their codes had been broken.

In 1937, Malaya-based MI5 intelligence officer Joe Vinden accurately predicted that any premeditated attack by the Japanese on British interests in Singapore would not come directly from the sea, but from the east coast of Malaya somewhere in the region of Kota Bharu. He advised against the further strengthening of already powerful south shoreline gun batteries at Singapore but strongly advocated improving the defences of the airfields and also expanding the numbers of military aircraft in south Malaya. The British military hierarchy said that this was 'poppycock', as the Japanese would not attack through such remote jungle-bound terrain. Also, the monsoon season was variable and it would not be worth the risk of attempting amphibious landings. How wrong they were!

Joe Vinden was soon replaced as the Malayan MI5 operative. This is yet another example of prudent and accurate military intelligence gathering being ignored or disregarded by military leaders, which ultimately proved costly to the frontline soldier and the Allies' war efforts.

---

5 Percival was very reluctant to surrender, but Gens Heath (Indian Corps) and Gordon Bennett (Australian International Forces) stated that he (Percival) had no option but to surrender due to the fragmentation of defending forces, although still three times the strength of the Japanese, a rapidly deteriorating water supply and mounting civilian casualties. Churchill described the surrender as 'the greatest military catastrophe of World War 2'.

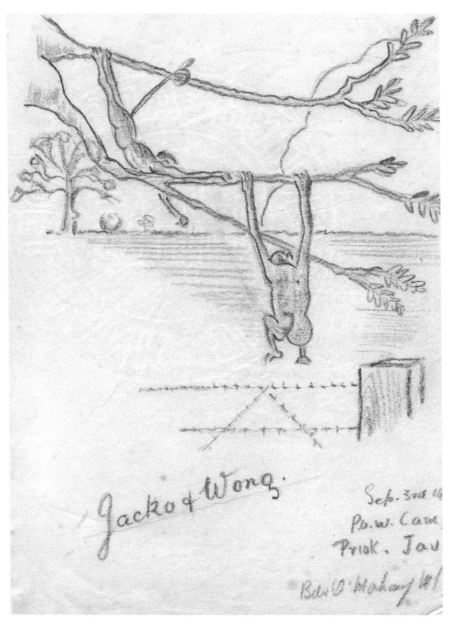

'Camp monkeys in Priok camp'. Illustration by Bombardier Mike O'Mahony.

6: *Christmas Day and the Monkey* (1943)

I wrote this short story in the late 1950s. The events I am about to relate are based on true POW camp events, although a number of them have been amalgamated for effect. The names of certain individuals have also been changed.

Sebastian awoke to the clatter of tin utensils and high-pitched jabbering from some of the camp guards in the nearby guardroom, who were about to fall on their first meal of the day, with dirty hands and a chorus of loud belches. The tropical sun had barely risen and Sebastian felt a cold chill, which sent a shudder through his almost naked body. A sudden sharp pain jerked him back as he attempted to sit up and swiftly, as full consciousness returned, he felt torment in all his limbs and he gradually realized the predicament in which he found himself.

Thoughts tumbled back as warily he fingered his thickened, bloodied lips and the closed left eye with a gaping wound above it. Then that sharp stab in the back again – that is what those dirty little yellow bastards did to you. They beat you unmercifully and gleefully and threw you into this loathsome cramped cell, built by the Dutch for Javanese murderers, with hardly any food or water.

What had he had yesterday? Twice a tin of tepid dirty water and mangy boiled rice a rat would turn its nose up at and beatings from the guards who brought the filthy swill. The first guard had struck him in the back with his rifle butt and the second had knocked him down with his clenched fist and then kicked him repeatedly about the head and chest as he lay squirming on the hard stone floor. What could you expect from them? They were brutes with no concept of civilized behaviour.

They were animals just like the monkey they kept as a 'pet' in the guardroom and teased unmercifully. Sebastian had seen them throw the poor monkey on to the steep guardroom roof and laugh uncontrollably at its attempts to avoid a rapid descent back to earth. The poor little monkey was often observed shivering with fear and pain after it had received another beating for escaping, after managing to bite through the rope tie. The monkey had the habit of pinching small objects during these periods of freedom. These usually belonged to the prisoners.

Good God! He had almost forgotten that it was Christmas Day. It was enough to make a cat laugh! Christmas Day is supposed to be about peace and good will to all men. What bunkum! Soon Sebastian would be hearing the iron clad boots approaching again and the inevitable beating. How much more could he take? Not very much more, he feared. His strength had been sapped by months of starvation, tropical disease and general neglect.

Christmas Day! Would he ever see another Christmas Day? Peace and good-will to all men kept going through his mind. What a mockery! Christ was born on Christmas Day to save all men. Sebastian thought that he could hear distant carollers, but he knew this was just a mental aberration. Sebastian believed that Good Friday was a more appropriate day for his present predicament. Christ was beaten and tortured on this day. Christmas Day is supposed to be a nice and happy day. Sebastian felt great affinity with Christ but hoped that the Japanese would not resort to crucifying him. He had heard rumours of such happenings taking place.

What was that? The clatter of boots again – coming ever nearer. Sebastian was bracing himself for another round of punishment but felt difficulty in breathing owing to the tension. Nearer the boots came, until the sound was immediately outside. Nothing happened and then the boots started walking away. 'Thank God!' whispered Sebastian to himself. What a relief! It was probably a camp guard, on his rounds, just checking things were in order.

Back came his thoughts of the events which took place two evenings before. He could see vividly the evening parade, which had so rudely interrupted his evening meal. The men had been about half way through their meal when a call came to *tenko* (parade). This meant trouble – sudden requests to parade usually did.

The men speculated about the reason for this. Was there to be another search of their quarters for books and study notes the guards would eagerly remove and destroy? Some men had lost considerable works of art they had spent many a week working on. Alternatively, had they discovered the secret camp radio? The loss of the radio would be a big blow, as to be totally cut-off from the out-side world, with no knowledge of the Allies progress, would be very dispiriting. Heads could roll, maybe literally, if the radio had been discovered.

Perhaps someone had tried to escape, though one would have to be deranged to attempt this on Java. It was the duty of all POWs to attempt to escape but the Japanese did not play by the rulebook. If caught, you would be a certain goner and your pals punished for not informing on you. Trying to escape in Java was nigh on impossible anyway, because the locals would prob-ably turn you in. There were no white men free in the community, so that blending in with the locals would be ludicrous. Should you develop a cloak of invisibility and reach the coast, the nearest friends were two thousand miles away across a merciless, sun-scorched and shark-infested sea.

When the men arrived grumbling and moaning on the parade ground, guards turned out with fixed bayonets, with machine gunners positioned on the wings, and confronted them. A shrill '*Ke—otsuki*' ('attention') had brought them shuf-fling together in line as Captain Zammo, the prison commander, strode into the compound. He snarled an order to his interpreter who echoed this in English. 'Bring all sick to parade ground-*lekas* (quickly)!'

The Australian John Standish, the senior doctor in the camp, stood forward and protested vehemently against this move. For his pains, Standish was set upon by two of the camp guards, and knocked to the ground. Some stretcher cases were brought first and placed at the end of the line. Then a wraithlike group, pale and very thin, arrived, staggering on uncertain legs, victims of malaria, beri-beri, dysentery, malnutrition and jungle sores. They were pushed into the line by the ruthless guards.

Kanamori, the Japanese interpreter, shouted out in a wild animal-like shrieking voice, 'Unless the one of you who stole Captain Zammo's watch from office make full confession, all men stay on parade ground. I repeat you stay very long time.' No one moved, apart from a machine gunner pulling back the breech lever on his machine gun. The air was electric. The whole situation was highly volatile. A dull fear gripped the hearts of the prisoners. Literally anything could happen.

A sea of faces swung to the left as one of the sick men collapsed limply to the ground, groaned and stayed still. A medical orderly stepped forward and went to help his fallen comrade, but a guard knocked him back with his rifle butt. Another and then another man collapsed in the heat. Sebastian could stand this situation no longer and pushed his way from the second line. 'I took the watch,' he said, almost inaudibly, to Kanamori, his pulse racing and sweat pouring down his brow. He was quickly seized by two guards and dragged before Captain Zamo.

'You took watch?' demanded Zammo, who had learned some English whilst on business trips to the United States.

'Yes,' agreed Sebastian.
'Where is it? Go fetch now.'
'I haven't got it any more.'
Zammo, angrily asked, 'Where is most valuable watch?'
'I sold it.'
With a yell of bestial rage, Zammo rushed at Sebastian and rained blow after blow on him, before the questioning resumed.
'Where you sell it?'
'When I was out on a working party, I sold it to a native on a river boat.'
'Where is money?'
'The native took the watch without paying me. He cheated me.'

Zammo, satisfied that he had discovered the culprit, ordered the guards to throw Sebastian into the solitary cell. The men trooped back soberly to their compounds and the sick were assisted back to their beds.

Fatigue was overcoming Sebastian in the dim, cramped cell as he tried to sleep, but his respite was short lived. The clatter of approaching iron-studded boots again jerked him back to a hopeless reality and, on this occasion, the guard stopped and undid the outer lock. Then the inner lock was opened and finally the door was flung wide open, flooding the room with bright light.

Like a gorilla, the large guard lurched into the cell, grunting and spitting. Sebastian tensed himself, expecting a kicking and verbal abuse … but it did not come. Instead, the big, moustached guard squatted down on his haunches and placed a large mess tin on the hard floor next to Sebastian. '*Makan* (food), good *makan, kopi* in tin.' The guard tossed a packet on to the lap of Sebastian as he was getting back up, followed by a box of matches.

'Cigaretto,' exclaimed the guard.
'War over?' asked Sebastian.

'No, it Clistmas Day, me Clistian man, samma-samma you? Eat *lekas* (quickly). No tell Zammo or me…' the guard drew an imaginary knife stroke across his throat. 'Melly Clistmas,' he said and then disappeared out of the cell, leaving an astonished Sebastian.

In the guardroom, the little monkey climbed deftly into the rafters at the end of its rope tie, though it was now much shorter since his recent escape bid, including several hours of freedom. The monkey grabbed the bright ticking bracelet from on top of the rafter and held it to his ear. A guard, looking up, shouted angrily at the monkey, who promptly dropped the object onto the bamboo floor, whereupon it burst open revealing small flywheels, springs and fragments of broken glass. The guard looked in horror at the bits at his feet, gleaming in the sun …

Sebastian did make the following Christmas Day …

7: *The Nippon Times*

The following news reports from *The Nippon Times* are typical of the propaganda that the Japanese published for their own people's consumption. *The Nippon Times* was also published as an English-language newspaper in Tokyo and so the Allied officer POWs may well have read them. This four page 'newspaper' was fairly widely distributed and named *The Nippon Times*.

INTREPID NIPPON PILOT DISPLAYS DEATH-DEFYING COURAGE

Somewhere in Burma: It has been reported that Lt 'Jonnie' Yamha, flying an unsurpassable '*Mikimuki*'[6] fighter, while on patrol X,000 feet over Burma, suddenly detected with his eagle eye a squadron of Spitfires approaching several thousand feet below. Bowing his head to the East, his lips parted with a fervid prayer to his God Emperor, while his heart filled with gratitude for this opportunity to display his love and devotion to his God Emperor by destroying these wicked enemies of world peace.

Skillfully manoeuvring his plane for position, he reached the ideal height in the firmament and screamed down in a death-defying dive upon his unsuspecting enemies, spitting relentless death and destruction.

The Spitfires immediately turned tail and attempted to flee back to their base. One of them, displaying the usual British cowardice, disappeared into a bank of cloud and thus escaped the vengeance it richly deserved. Robbed of his rightful prey, Lt Yamha turned on the other Spitfire, which had now become a distant speck, with fury and absolute determination.

Opening the throttle of his superb fighter to maximum power, he hurtled after the beleaguered and retreating enemy and overhauled it with ease. The enemy Spitfire was now caught in a trap like a rat and the Britisher was forced into combat. With cool ferocity, our Japanese pilot raked the enemy aircraft with bursts of machine gun fire which the Spitfire attempted to dodge.

Unfortunately, Lt Yamha had run out of ammunition and although the Spitfire was trailing smoke, it was still flying. Lt Yamha had to think quickly and remembered a rucksack containing hard rice balls in his cockpit, left from a previous mission. In a flash, he pulled back the cockpit canopy and hurled the bag at the Spitfire. The Spitfire veered erratically and crashed into the mountainside in flames. Good work Lt 'Jonnie' Yamha.

6   '*Mikimuki*' was the artilleyman's name for Mitsubishi Japanese aircraft.

A Nippon Red Cross plane bristling with guns. Illustration by Charles Holdsworth.

DASTARDLY ATTACK BY ALLIED FIGHTERS ON UNARMED NIPPON RED CROSS PLANE

Our domestic correspondent reports that two British fighters, in complete disregard of International Convention, perpetrated a cowardly attack on an unarmed Nippon Red Cross plane undertaking a sacred mission, taking wounded soldiers out of New Guinea. Fortunately, our air force had the foresight to arm this plane in anticipation of this sort of dastardly act by the British. The enemy were successfully shot down by our plane and the brave crew and wounded were successfully transported to their destination. The bad British deserved their fate.

BRAVE NIPPON PILOT SEEKS TO CAPTURE TOP SECRET ENEMY PLANE

On the Burma front: On a recent mission over the Burma jungle, fighter pilot, Sgt 'Uglymoto' describes his combat with a 'hush-hush' new British Mosquito fighter and resolved to capture it. He guessed that the plane would contain many new gadgets to be analysed by Nippon's brilliant scientists.

'I spotted the new British plane and immediately closed in and placed a careful burst of machine gun fire to disable the plane but not to destroy it! This achieved clearly its purpose because the British pilot raised a white flag and waved it to surrender. I circled him and indicated that he should follow me and we both turned towards my base.

We were doing well until I noticed that the Britisher was losing power. I circled behind him and he indicated that he had lost a lot of fuel and wished to land. I reluctantly obliged to comply, and found a clearing for him to land in the dense jungle.

However, the British pilot went in to land much too fast and the secret plane exploded on hitting a tree. I pin-pointed the area, but this is dense jungle and very difficult to get through.'

The scheme of this most noble of pilots may have come to negation, but it will undoubtedly help the war effort. The Mosquito is built of wood, which is not a new technique to us Japanese, as we have successfully built wooden planes over many years.

Sergeant 'Uglymoto' says he did not feel that the performance of the Mosquito merited all the claims made for it by the British. He stated that his plane is the best and is constructed by the best in the world, dedicated to absolute victory and freedom for the peoples of Greater East Asia.

HEROIC BOMBER PILOT DESCRIBES VIVIDLY A NIGHT BOMBING MISSION

Our death-dealing, superlative and unconquerable bombers were lined up in perfect and symmetrical formation on the runway of bomber base ZX1, from which our faithful bombers soared daily like birds of prey to wreak vengeance on our miserable enemy by inflicting destruction on troops, railways, factories, military bases and communications.

The bomber engines were palpitating with eagerness in anticipation of leaping away into the darkness to wreak destruction on our enemy. Into our glorious mission we commenced after our unbeatable leader completed the final instructions for this Imperial mission.

Following our esteemed leader, we sped in unbroken alignment from the lit runway into the eye of the setting sun, whose rays pervaded a benediction on our Imperial mission. Climbing at great speed, we approached rapidly our cruising height, levelled off, and flew through the heavenly orbs.

With the utmost of velocity and unstoppability we shot true like arrows towards our target. Our target was well lit in the utter blackness of the sky. Fearlessly we circled the target as enemy searchlights tried, in vain, to locate us and anti-aircraft shells burst randomly in our vicinity.

Below us lay a vast ammunition dump to which we knew every detail through our death-defying reconnaissance aircraft, which had flown at 300 feet to obtain the photographs. The buildings were all in neat lines and typically, the Allies had painted red crosses on the roofs as a wicked pretence! We assembled in formation for our bombing run and delivered with breathtaking accuracy the 'coup de grace' to these caverns of evil intent.

Our assignment completed with 100% efficiency, we rapidly climbed to our pre-determined height to return to our base, when we encountered control problems with our aircraft. A lucky enemy shell must have hit the controls. We soldiered on for a while but realized that our aircraft was losing control and height. When Sgt Tasamoto, with blood streaming down his face, came to tell me that two of the crew had joined their noble ancestors, I decided to do the most honourable thing and return to the target to destroy the guns that had inflicted such a grievous blow on us.

With the utmost of resolve and cool handling of the crippled plane, I turned the aircraft around and we headed back to our target. The buildings were now well lit because of our earlier bombing and we could see many people running around, many being carried on stretchers. One of the gun batteries was still firing, so we headed straight for it and crashed into the guns killing all before. We die as true sons of Nippon.

The Nippon Times was always keen to portray the Americans as having highly inflated opinions of their own ability and we British as Anglo-Saxon barbarians.

8: Life in a Women's Internment Camp on Java

The following is an account by Jean Teerink, a Scotswoman Ronald met whilst returning from Java. She had been married to a Dutch engineer and was held prisoner as a civilian internee under Japanese rule on Java:

I arrived in Bandoeng, by car, on the night of the Dutch capitulation on 8 March 1942, but was only interned towards the end of the following November in Tjiapit camp, where some 13,000 Dutch women and children were housed. Initially, we had to register and obtain an identity card from the local town hall. Malay became the official language of communication. We could only obtain Nippon radio so knew little of outside events.

In the beginning, things were not too bad and were straightforward. We had native servants for a short time and a food market, although the native traders had increased the prices whilst dealing in Japanese currency. At first, uniformed Indonesians – 'heihos' – controlled us. This was not pleasant, because they enjoyed having the 'whites' under their control. They behaved a bit like immature boy scouts, until the Japanese gave them full authority to punish us. We were rude to them most of the time, although full powers for the Indonesians gradually cramped our style!

Later, the camps were taken over by the Japanese and things changed for the worse. Most of our possessions were confiscated; electrical apparatus, nice furniture and useful utensils, were all taken. We had increasing numbers of people moving into the houses with us. We were officially allocated about three square yards per adult, although it proved to be far less than this.

Increasingly, every available space was taken up and we could no longer eat communally, but only in our sleeping areas. Every room was allocated for sleeping accommodation. To begin with we could cook in our own houses but, eventually, cooking could only take place in the community kitchen. Meals consisted of bread and tea in the morning, rice and soup midday and bread and tea, again, in the evening. The sugar ration was meagre and, of course, we did not have meat or fish.

The camp needed tremendous organisation as can well be imagined. Housing, lighting, the community kitchen, bakery, medical and dental care had to be catered for and organised. My camp was known as the 'Rebel camp', because we did everything in our power to annoy and defy our Japanese oppressors. When we were ordered to hand over all our torches, we soaked the batteries in water and flicked the bulbs until the filaments broke. They took our bicycles, but we messed with them so much that they would have needed a good deal of repair work to be of use.

The children proved to be great wreckers. This did not endear us to our Japanese captors, who sent in progressively more evil camp commandants. Then a reign of terror began under Capt. Sonei in April 1944.

Food became shocking and daily beatings became the norm. The Japanese were past masters in sadism. You have probably heard all about their behaviour, so I will not elaborate further. It is sufficient to state that all the terrible stories you have heard regarding the treatment of women in Japanese camps are true, with no sense of exaggeration. I have also witnessed the behaviour of the dreaded *Kempeitai*. Men and women, as old as seventy, would be beaten, usually for some trivial reason, such as failing to bow quickly enough and being slow to undertake tasks. Boys who looked older than ten years were carted off to the men's camp. Those who survived, we learned, were often orphaned by the end of internment.

Gas appliances were removed from our houses, but we managed to rig up our own gas burners using bicycle inner tubes and metal rods we punctured with holes. This was, of course, a dangerous thing to do, but effective. One day, a house was caught, by a Japanese guard, making breakfast with gas. They were all punished with a beating, and then tied up and marched, like cattle, to a lock-up. Twenty-five people were left in this lock-up for twenty-one days with little food and water, unable to wash, and only a few people could lie on the stone floor at any one time.

When they were released, they looked very thin and had their heads completely shaved. This did not deter them from cooking with gas, although they arranged a much better lookout system, following their experience.

Many things in the camp were contraband, and we had to use all our ingenuity to outfox the Japanese. The camp was periodically raided for illegal items, particularly wireless sets. These short-wave radios were never found, although there were a few very close shaves. The penalty for having a radio was torture, followed by death. When we moved from camp to camp we managed to take the radios with us, despite searches by the guards. The radios were dismantled to do this. One radio would be distributed amongst twenty women for carriage.

The black market was in evidence, of course. We tried to barter with the locals through the wire fence. Contact with the outside world went on in this fashion most of the time. These were quite hair-raising experiences, particularly when conducted at night. If caught, the natives would come in for a fearful beating, sometimes ending in death. The prices for food and goods crossing the wire fence reflected this possible deadly outcome. We sold most of our clothes and bedding. It was quite common to sell a bed sheet for a slab of bacon or a few eggs. It was a case of buying anything nutritious to augment our meagre diet. Unfortunately, Japanese money could buy very little.

Before leaving the Bandoeng camp, I became very ill, collapsing with anaemia. I was in hospital for six weeks, after which I had to be discharged for an even sicker patient to fill my bed. The work of the doctors and nurses was incredible, with the general lack of medicines and surgical equipment – I owe them my life. I was ill quite frequently in camp, usually due to over-work. I worked in the kitchen cleaning vegetables during the day, and spent evenings caring for some of the sick.

One time we were moved from our large camp to an adjacent smaller camp, while the larger camp was searched. We had to move everything, and had all our belongings searched, which was a most unpleasant experience. On our return, we were denied our mattresses for over a month. Sleeping on hard floors was a very painful experience, so we lay on our clothes and towels.

Then we were transported to Batavia, on overcrowded trains. There were some seats in the carriages. We left our camp at about 2 p.m., but were kept locked up in the carriages until the train left at midnight. Some of the guards sent with us were notorious fiends who made sure our journey was most unpleasant.

We arrived in Batavia at 8 a.m. and reached our new camp after a cramped ride on a motor bus. Again, we were thoroughly searched and had no help in moving our belongings, which were dumped by the Japanese as far from our accommodation as possible.

The new camp was Spartan, with no beds or furniture. A family of six Chinese had previously occupied the house in which I was accommodated, before the Japanese invasion. The house and grounds now accommodated 165 people! I shared the kitchen with four other people. The ceiling had disintegrated and the house was heavily infested with cockroaches, scorpions and mosquitoes, so rainwater entered freely – fortunately, it was the dry season.

This was a very strict camp and we 'rebels' from Bandoeng were picked on regularly for not bowing correctly. We had to wear our prisoner number on our chests. Woe betides anyone who forgot. The principal punishments in this camp were no food for three days, beatings and standing for hours in the blazing sun.

Outside news was very scarce and I believe that this was the only camp not to have a secret radio. Rumours were rife and often false, so were a source of huge discontent in the camp, particularly when the message came through that we were about to be freed, and then nothing happened. We were made aware that there were a number of camp informants, especially when we had been in Kramat camp, Batavia, where we had to be very careful who we spoke to, and look around to make sure no one was eavesdropping.

We were not allowed to write in Dutch or English but in Malay, and then only one letter consisting of twenty-five words. From our husbands we heard very little and later did not know if they were dead or alive – the Japanese, even if they knew about the fate of a woman's husband, would take months or years to tell them.

The Japanese took perverse delight in telling a woman that her husband was dead. This is an example: a woman internee would be called to the camp officer's room, and asked by the Japanese, 'Have you a husband?' The reply would be 'Yes!' 'No you haven't!' the Japanese would retort, 'He's dead. Get out.' No woman was allowed to go to the office alone because of the callous attitude of the Japanese.

Towards the end of June 1945, rumours were hectic that the Allies were coming, and Priok was bombed. The Japanese suddenly increased our rations and better quality food and sleeping accommodation materialised. We started to form our own conclusions and when Allied planes dropped leaflets we went deliriously mad.

By this time we had managed to find an old Japanese propaganda radio, and listened to the Japanese surrender on board the USS *Missouri*. We knew our terrible ordeal had ended, although many of the civilian internees had many months of uncertainty ahead. The arrival of my brother on the cruiser, HMS *Cumberland,* came as a wonderful surprise to me, as I had just learned that my husband had died in Japanese hands.

After release, I worked as a nurse in the children's hospital until I was flown to Singapore, where I embarked for England.

Although I am Scottish, I was classified as Dutch and spent my time in Dutch internment camps. I must state that during this time, the spirit of the Dutch women was wonderful. They never gave up, and retained their humour, even in the most difficult of times. A sense of humour was essential in these insane circumstances, watching people suffering greatly and dying. The ingenuity of the internees, particularly the doctors and nurses, will live with me for ever.

My father added a note to Jean Teerink's account: Jean Teerink had both her kneecaps broken by the Japanese during captivity. She came back to Britain and eventually remarried to an American and settled later on the west coast of the United States. Capt. Sonei was tried and sentenced to death by the Far East War Crimes Tribunal. He was shot by a Dutch firing squad in December 1946.

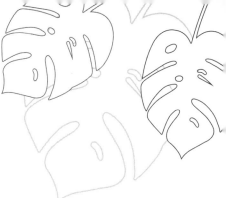

9: The Island of Java

A number of *The Jungle Journal* magazines contained articles, called 'Java Notes', about the history and geography of Java written by Capt. Harold Davey and Lt Ronald Williams. These articles were expanded on substantially by Ron Williams for this chapter. This exercise was completed, on Java, following the Japanese surrender in 1945. Much of the information was gleaned from Dutch reference books, which Ron Williams translated, and by talking to Dutch civilian and military POWs who had spent considerable time on the island prior to the Japanese invasion.

The descriptions are entirely apt in accurately describing the island before the Japanese invasion in 1942. Many prisoners of war appreciated the beauty of the island, its people and ancient culture sufficiently to write, even in the most dire of human experiences, about their impressions of Java.

JAVA, the most important island of the Netherlands East Indies, is one of the most beautiful and romantic places on earth. Almost eighty years ago, the famous British naturalist, Alfred Russell Wallace, described it as 'the very garden of the East, and perhaps, upon the whole, the richest, the best cultivated, and the best governed island in the world.'

The island is long and narrow, with a length of 622 miles and a width, which varies between 121 and 45 miles. It runs from west to east, with a steep rocky coast to the Indian Ocean on the south and low, flat shores to the Java Sea on the north, and lies on a great volcanic girdle.

It maintains a vast population of 45 million, which is mostly rural, as the Javanese have a great love for the land. The figures concerning population growth are interesting… When Marshall Daendals ruled the island from 1807 to 1811, Java's population was a mere 3.75 million, but by 1865, when Wallace visited, it had increased to 14 million. Fifty-five years later, in 1920, this figure had more than doubled to 35 million, while by 1936 it had rapidly grown to 45 million.

Volcanoes

Throughout the length of Java, volcanoes lift their majestic heads above the enchanting scenery. Many of them are beautifully shaped in the form of a cone, particularly the Tjareme, the Merapi and the Semeroe. Some of these volcanoes have a vast crater or caldera caused by the top having been blown off through eruption or due to a collapse. The Tengger, for example, has a caldera nearly 7 miles across, while the Idjen has one even greater, at 10 miles. Often, points of eruption are again formed in the caldera, as in the Tengger, where one, the Bromo, is very active. On the southern edge of the Idjen, twenty new miniature volcanoes have formed. Sometimes the craters contain a lake.

The most terrific and terrible volcanic eruption in recent times occurred in 1883, when a volcanic island, Krakatoa, in the Soenda Strait between Java and Sumatra, blew up and scattered ash over a wide area to a distance of 1,500 miles. The finer dust rose to the upper stratosphere and reddened the sunsets of the world for over a year. Sounds of the explosion were heard as far away as 3,000 miles and the resultant tidal wave, besides playing havoc with shipping in the area, caused the deaths of an estimated 36,000 people.

Despite the fact that some of these volcanoes are undoubtedly a menace to human life and habitation, they nevertheless serve useful purposes. The ash is rich in salts, which increase the fertility of the soil. Their height forces the rain clouds to release their burdens to the benefit of the surrounding countryside, and those volcanoes which conserve water in their craters act as reservoirs for the plains below and ensure a valuable water supply during the dry season.

Earthquake shocks are frequent in the East Indies and are caused by sinking and displacement in the earth's crust or through volcanic activity. Most of these, however, emanate from the seabed and are seldom felt on land.

Rivers and Coasts

The rivers of Java carry a tremendous amount of silt, which, when deposited, is continually raising land above the level of the sea. Merely a few centuries ago, for instance, Mount Moerjo was an island on the north coast, which has, by this action, become part of the mainland. This natural reclamation of land is a rapid process because the Java Sea is calm and shallow. Not one of the rivers is navigable, with the exception of the lower reaches of a few, but they are of great importance for irrigation.

The low-lying northern coast of this island, on the shallow Java Sea, is not suitable for navigation and those vessels, which call at such ports as Semerang and Cheribon are obliged to stand off in the roadsteads, while a fleet of small steamboats and *praws* (small sailing boats) convey passengers and merchandise between ship and quay.

Splendid harbours have been constructed at Tandjong Priok, near Batavia, and at Soerabaja. The only harbour on the south coast, Tjilatjap, is a natural one.

Climate

The climate of Java is tropical, but there is rarely extreme heat, although the temperature averages between 78°F and 80°F, and high humidity is general. Sea breezes cool the coastal plains and as the mountain ranges, which rise up almost everywhere from the plains, are ascended, there is naturally a drop in temperature.

During the west monsoon, from October to April, Java has its wet season. Between April and October, the east monsoon season, rain is a great rarity. The rainfall varies across the island, with the heaviest being in the mountain ranges, such as those in Middle Java. The highest rainfall is at Krangga, on the southern slope of the Slamet – 327 inches annually, while at Batavia the rainfall averages 71.31 inches.

A VIEW OF THE HARBOUR AT MERAK, JAVA.

Merak harbour, Java, which proved to be a major Japanese invasion point. Drawn by Lt H.
Clatworthy in Tandjong Priok camp, 1942.

The Inhabitants

The native population of Java is of the Malay stock, made up of Javanese, Soedenese
and Madoerese, each having their own language. The men have little body hair and
beard growth. Their eyes are not slanted, with the exception of the Soendenese. They
are largely agriculturalists, with rice being the main crop.

Of the two types of cultivation, wet and dry, the former is their preferred method.
The rice is grown in terraces, which are in narrow strips high up in the mountains
and gradually widen descending into the valleys. This greatly aids irrigation as water
gradually descends through the terraces. These rice fields, or *sawahs*, are an amazing
sight, with their great variety of colours and earthen retaining walls.

The natives dwell in little houses clustered together in kampongs or *desas*, usually marked by adjacent clumps of tall feathery bamboos and palm trees. There is a
complete absence of galvanised steel roofs, and the roofs are made from bamboo shin-
gle, grass thatch or weathered tiles. The walls and floors are made from split bamboo
woven into firm structures. The houses are separated by bamboo fencing.

The people profess to follow Mohammed, which in the fifteenth century supplanted
the ancient Hindu faith. As in Europe, every village has a church, called a *langgar,* while
in the larger towns there is usually a mosque. Ramadan is strictly adhered to and the
final day of Ramadan, Leberan, is celebrated with a festival of forgiveness. It is the
ambition of most natives to make the pilgrimage to Mecca and gain the title of 'Hadji'.
This entitles the holder to wear a pure white turban and be held in high esteem by his
less well-travelled contemporaries.

Most of the population is animistic and revere animals and plants, believing that they have mysterious powers and that all possess a soul. They believe also that different parts of the human body have special powers: for instance, a native would burn the parings after cutting his or her nails in case an enemy used the powers of the nails against them.

The casting of evil spells could consume the spirit of a native. Rice is believed to have a great number of powers, including great healing powers, and is very prominent in local folklore and legend. Odd-shaped stones and bits of wood are treasured as lucky charms, especially if they had belonged to an ancestor. The *kris,* a ceremonial knife, and special pieces of clothing are held in high reverence.

Offerings are frequently brought to control the powers of these objects. It is considered that the soul of a sleeping man moves outside the body and dreams are the soul's experiences. If the soul fails to return to the body because the body is too sick to receive it, then the body dies!

A definite distinction is made between the soul of the living and that of the dead. Although believing in an afterlife, the animist does not look forward to it with any relish, because he considers it to be by no means as pleasant as life on earth. Consequently, the souls of the dead are jealous of the living and make them greatly feared.

This fear displays itself in many ways, such as elaborate burials to appease the dead and the reluctance to kill dangerous wild animals, such as the man-eating crocodile, for fear it may contain the spirit of an ancestor. Spirits are recognised in connection with natural phenomena, inhabiting trees, streams, waterfalls, high mountains, the steep rocks of the coast to name a few.

The dress of the peoples of Java consists mainly of the following:

The *sarong* is a strip of cloth, from nine to fourteen feet in length, worn in various ways about the body according to taste. There are two types, one for normal wear and the other, much more elaborate, for celebrations.

The *slendang* is a piece of material about nine feet long and narrow in width; this may be worn twisted about the head or, more often, slung from one shoulder, and may be used by the women for carrying a baby or other burden on their hip.

The *kemban* is a narrow girdle, worn only occasionally by the women, twisted tightly around their breasts or waists.

The *sarong kapala* is a square piece of material similar to a very large handkerchief and is worn by the men, twisted around the head in the manner of a turban. From the way in which this is done it is possible to determine both the locality from which the wearer comes and his social standing.

Many of these garments are richly designed or coloured, the batik-work of Java being famous. 'Batik' in Javanese means 'wax-painting' and the method is to apply a wax resist to the material being processed. It is then placed in a bath of dye, which readily acts on the material, with the exception of those parts in design that have been waxed, resulting in a pattern. By elaborating this process and utilising various dyes on the same piece of material, most pleasing and beautiful effects result.

'Javanese Dancer', drawn by Bdr Mike O'Mahony for *The Jungle Journal*. (Courtesy of Mrs Adèle Barclay)

— JAVANESE DANCER —

Javanese is the richest of the three languages, followed closely by Soendanese. Madoerese, however, is not so well developed, but the lingua franca of Java, and the whole of the Indies and Malaya for that matter, is Malay, which is so simple that anyone can learn a smattering of it.

The natives are skilled in metalwork and boat building, but the Hindu tradition in architecture seems to have been lost long ago. The indigenous music, or *gamelan*, is much cultivated, as is dancing and drama, particularly the *wayang*, shadow plays performed with puppets.

Of the 250,000 Europeans who live in Java more than half dwell in the seven largest towns, where the Chinese and Arabs are also numerous and control most of the trading. Most of the Arabs originate from Hadramaut, in Southern Arabia, while the Chinese are from the south of China and comprise several groups:

The Hokkians first came to Java a long time ago and married native women. They retain the religion and customs of their race, especially the house-altars, temples, graves and burial ceremonies. Most of them are traders, but others readily undertake such work as bridge building and road construction.

The Hakkas are mainly artisans – boot-makers, tailors, wicker-workers and so forth, while the Kwangfo, sometimes called Cantonese, are usually furniture-makers or carpenters and the Haklo, or Tio-tsio, make excellent coolies.

The Chinese are to be admired for their sober way of living, their healthy family life and their industry, which has been instrumental in bringing much wealth to Java. Moreover, they are cultured and often well educated and it is a fact that at least half of the children over nine years can read and write.

Many British Indians have also settled in Java. Most of these come from the coast of Coromandel and Malabar in the province of Bombay and so are known as Bombayers, while their shops are 'Tokos Bombay'.

In and around Batavia live a million Malay-speaking Batavians and later reference will be made to two curious peoples, the Badoejs and the Tenggerese.

Javanese man and son at Merak market. (Courtesy of Nikki Sullivan)

Horsedrawn taxi at Merak market. (Courtesy of Nikki Sullivan)

West Java

This part of Java has 12 million inhabitants. The mountains of South Bantam and those of the Preanger occupy the southern part. The region of the former is not fertile and is covered with virgin forest. To the south of Rangkasbitoeng a certain amount of rubber is cultivated. In the west rise the mountains of the Goenoeng Karang-Poelasari and north of these mountains runs the railway, from Batavia to the port of Merak, from where a steamboat ferry service connects Java with Oosthaven, in Sumatra. At the foot of the Karang is the town of Serang, situated in the midst of a fertile region with splendid rice fields.

The history of Bantam is characterised by numerous uprisings, the last of which occurred in 1926. The Bantammer is known for his rebellious nature and is difficult to handle, but the area is thinly populated.

The mountainous country of the north Preanger has a large number of volcanoes, including the Salek, the Gede and the Tangkoebanpraoe, to the south of which are the four plateaux of Soekaboemi, Tjiandjoer, Bandoeng and Soemedang with *sawahs*. On the slopes are tea, rubber and quinine plantations.

At one time the plateau of Bandoeng was a lake, but as the bed of the river Tjitaroen became deeper, the level of the lake dropped, until eventually it was totally drained. On the slopes of the Tangkoebanpraoe, the white cupola of the Bosscha astronomical observatory is prominent.

Bandoeng, with a population of 175,000, enjoys a pleasant climate and has grown greatly in recent years. It is the seat of the War Department and of the department concerned with traffic, buildings and roads. The scientific institutions are the Technical High School and the Pasteur Institute. Bandoeng also possesses several industries: artillery construction, a quinine factory and tapioca meal factories.

Drawing by a Dutch civilian, C. Berk, interned in Tandjong Priok camp, 1942.

South of Bandoeng rises the Malabar, with large quinine and tea plantations, while in a gap in this volcano stands the radio station which is responsible for broadcasting communications from the East Indies.

The plateau of Garoet is also a dried lake through which flows the Tjimanoek River. It is renowned for its magnificent panoramas. To the left of the river rises the active volcano, Goentoer, with its twenty small craters and the Papandajan (the Smithy), so called because of the continual noise made by volcanic vapours forcing a passage through the vents. To the right of the river are the Tjikoeraj and the Galoenggoeng mountains, while, standing completely apart in the north-west, the giant Tjareme dominates the scene.

The broad northern plains of West Java were formed by silt, which the rivers have deposited for thousands of years from the Java Sea. The coastal strip is mostly swampy and the matter of drainage has been a problem. However, the Government have already provided two systems of irrigation in Bantam and Krawang, with dams in the Tjisedana, Tjioedjoeng and Tjitaroem. The chief product of these plains is rice, but they also produce a large quantity of copra. Rubber and *sereh* are grown in the south and around Kadipaten and Cheribon, in the east there are sugar plantations.

Batavia, the capital of the Netherlands East Indies, is situated in this province. It has a population of about 600,000 and is the seat of the six State Departments. The great banks and offices of the trading companies are to be found in the lower town. There are law, medical and high schools, a museum, the Library of the Batavian Association and the Meteorological Observatory. One can find the palace of the Governor General and the world famous Botanical Gardens at Buitenzorg.

The majority of the people of West Java, some 9 million, are the hospitable Soendanese, who are not as dark as the Javanese and are usually of smaller stature, not so slender, and having more oblique eyes. They are scrupulously clean and of a peaceable disposition, patient, polite, gentle, with a great aversion to quarrelling, and inclined to be introspective; though, surprisingly, divorce is not uncommon. They readily live in a world of fantasy and illusion, but fortunately easily overcome difficulties, so their disenchantment with reality does not cause as much problem as it might.

The Soendanese faithfully follow the precepts of Islam and almost every village has a mosque or *langgar*; there is also a large number of religious schools throughout West Java.

The clothing is very similar to that of the Javanese, but the women's garments are very beautiful and colourful. The principal food is rice, usually flavoured with salted fish, while tea and coffee are in great demand.

The houses are raised on piles or stone supports and at the front have a verandah, which sometimes stretches the whole length of the house. That of the village headman has a *bale desa*, which consists of a long front verandah and two rooms, one to the left and the other to the right. The village scribe usually sits in one while the other is often used as an office for the village bank or for informal meetings.

Social distinctions are not as pronounced as in the rest of Java, although the nobles and higher officials receive the respect of the common people.

The Soendanese did not experience the Hindu influence to the same extent as the Javanese and, consequently, are not so conventional; nevertheless, they have absorbed

Javanese *praw* and fishermen. (Courtesy of Nikki Sullivan)

much of the Javanese culture, such as batik, the *gamelan* and the *wajang*. Weaving is prac-tised in many places, particularly in Garoet, Tasikmalaja and Tjiamis, while Tangerang and Singaparna are well known for their wickerwork, the copper beaters, and the gold and silversmiths of Buitenzorg provide excellent articles for the internal market.

The *wajang*, with round wooden puppets, is performed during festivals to the great delight of the people. The *ogel* is also very popular, and comprises a number of men playing on drums and other musical instruments, while one or more clowns amuse the audience with dancing and short dramas.

Another entertainment is the strolling bard, where a singer and poet perform in the evenings to the accompaniment of a zither. In Garoet and other villages, ram fighting is a favourite sport.

The Soedanese language is soft, sweet-flowing and possesses three different vocabularies.

Middle Java
This part of Java has 12 million inhabitants, excluding the Vorstenlanden.

The mountains of Middle Java form a chain through the centre of the province and are crowned by the majestic cone of the Slamet. In the east, the chain terminates with the Dieng Mountains, in which, on a crater plateau, are to be seen five beautiful temples from the Hindu period. These are the remnants of a temple city devoted to the worship of Siva the Destroyer, reached by hewn-out steps to the plateau.

To the east of the Dieng Mountains lies the thickly populated plateau of Magelang or Kedoe, on the west side of which rise the Prahoe and the twin peaks of Soendoro-Soembing, while on the eastern side are located the Oengaran, Meraboe and Merapi. Rice and native tobacco are cultivated on the plateau and the town contains a noteworthy establishment founded by Pa van der Steur, which accommodates 900 young boys and girls, teaching them a trade or profession.

On the south side, not far from Moentilan, are the famous Hindu monuments of Boroboedoer and Mendoet, which are considered among the architectural wonders of the world. Borboedoer was constructed, about AD 750, and consists of a mound, surrounded by terraces of stone, in which thousands of figures have been cut in relief, illustrating the Buddhist religion.

It is estimated that these reliefs, placed side by side, would form a line three miles long. As the pilgrim ascends from the lower terraces, where scenes of ordinary life are displayed, he sees in the reliefs the principles of Buddhism unfolding before him, until finally; at the summit, he meets an image of Buddha, face to face. The base is in the form of a square, each side being approximately 122 yards in length and the walls being almost 100 feet high. For centuries this monument was hidden beneath a mass of earth and vegetation and was discovered by the enthusiast, Sir Stamford Raffles.

Bordering on the plateau of Magelang is the basin of Ambarawa, where there is another garrison town, that of Salatiga.

The southern plains of Middle Java are very swampy along the Tjitandoej in the west. The Sarajoe, which springs from the Prahoe, streams through Wonosobo, a region of tobacco culture, and Banjoemas, an area of sugar plantation, and then flows southwards through the South Srajoe Mountains to the coast. The port of Tjilatjap serves the whole of the southern region and is situated in a portion of the coast which is protected from the sea by the island of Noesa Kambangan, which produces rubber, and eastward by a line of dunes.

The swamps in the eastern part of Banjoemas and in the south of Kedoe have been drained and support a large population engaged in the cultivation of rice and coconuts.

The northern plains of Middle Java are entirely devoted to the culture of sugar, rice and kapok. Sugar is grown principally around the towns of Cheribon, Tegal, Pekalongan and Semarang, all of which have harbours to handle exports. The northern plain extends eastwards to the borders of the Residency of Djapara-Rembang and is watered by several rivers.

Demak, Java's foremost place of pilgrimage, is situated here – seven journeys to the mosque on prescribed special days are considered the equivalent of one visit to Mecca. Other towns are Koedoes, with sugar factories and manufacturing of *strootjes*, the native cigarettes; the ruinous Djapara, with beautiful woodcarvings, and the principal town, Pati.

The extinct volcano, Moerjo, stands completely isolated, having been, but a few centuries ago, completely surrounded by sea.

The principal harbour of Middle Java and the Vorstenlanden is Semarang, with a population of 220,000, and it exports sugar, tobacco, copra, kapok and cocoa. During the west monsoon, it is not always safe for shipping and as a result, the Government have planned the construction of a more suitable harbour.

Javanese restaurant thought to be the old guard house for Bandoeng POW camp. (Courtesy of Nikki Sullivan)

The Vorstenlanden

The Vorstenlanden comprises Soerakarta with a population of 2.5 million and Jogjakarta with 1.5 million and consists of four Javanese kingdoms

The plain of Jogjakarta is a continuation of the southern plain of Middle Java and is watered by the Progo and the Opak, while the plain of Soerakarta accommodates Java's greatest river, the Solo. On both these plains are extensive European-owned plantations of tobacco and sugar, but the southern part is less cultivated, being composed quite literally of thousands of lime-hillocks – *duizendgebergte*. However, there is some tobacco grown in the basins between the hillocks, and despite its infertility, the region is thickly populated.

The heavy seas, which batter the rocky southern coast, have formed innumerable grottoes, where sea swallows make the nests that are collected to make the bird's nest soup, so dearly loved by the Chinese.

The economic position in these lands has been greatly improved in recent years because of various important reforms to the feudal system. The income from the land ceased to be considered as belonging to the princes and was instead managed by an exchequer for public expenditure; the princes were provided with a fixed allowance and the budget became the responsibility of the governor.

The *apanage* system was abolished. An *apanage* was a piece of land given to relatives, state officials and favourites as a reward, which meant the holders could obtain high rents or forced labour from the tenants. The land might also be hired to Europeans.

In Solo, the inhabitants now have more say in their affairs, since the establishment of the 'bale agoeng' a small people's council.

The foremost prince is the Soesoehoenan, who is in direct descent from the ancient ruling house. He lives in the capital, Solo, where the European governor and the Mangkoe Negore also live; the population is 180,000. Jogia is a little smaller, with a population of 130,000; the governor, the sultan and Prince Poeko Alam live here.

Although making some regulations, the Soenan and Sultan are relieved of the ordinary business of state by regents, who receive a salary, both from the government and the princes. The translation offices are indispensable in order to aid communication between the governor and the princes, translating from Dutch to Javanese and vice versa and providing a link between the Kraton (palace) and the European administration.

The Kraton is a world apart; it covers an area, which would take almost an hour to walk around, and houses some 10,000 Javanese. The high outer walls hide an extensive conglomeration of buildings, dwellings, squares, lanes and gardens, in the midst of which stands the palace of the prince.

The palace has a large reception *pendopo* or verandah, ornamented with splendid gilded carvings and a marble floor. At the back of the *pendopo* there are several chairs of gilt, used by the prince and his prominent guests. In front of these seats is an open space, reserved for the dancers, both male and female, the most beautiful and artistic are girls of royal blood – the *serimpi*. The area to the right and left accommodates the remainder of the guests.

In the palace are kept the golden regalia, each with a special name and attributes, such as the sacred pike-like weapons, which when borne outside in times of drought, are supposed to influence the weather favourably.

The Kraton also contains a private prison for the punishment of any malefactor related to the ruling house.

In Solo and Jokja, Javanese dancing, the musical art of the *gamelan* and the *wajang* are fostered, while at Kota Gede, where at one time the Sultan had his palace, gold- and silversmiths are still famed for their workmanship, as are workers in tortoiseshell. Batik and weaving are popular throughout the Vorstenlanden.

Most of the population are Javanese, a people much influenced by Hinduism. This is seen in their high intellect and culture; they are humorous too, as is apparent in their stories. The nearer a Javanese is related to noble blood, the lighter the colouring – this again is attributed to the Hindu and intermarriage in former times. They are slender in build, particularly the women, in whom this desirable quality is a mark of beauty.

The villager favours a calm and balanced existence, not liking excitement, hurry, or emotion. He is born polite and the *sembah,* a salutation suggestive of deep respect or homage, is one way to express this. He is educated to show respect to his parents, grandparents, teachers and prince. The politeness and humility of the Javanese is also apparent in his language. Unfortunately, he is also inconsistent and too complacent, although in recent years he is becoming more self-reliant. Although professing Mohammedanism, at heart he is still Hindu and animistic.

His blue-black or brown clothing distinguishes the Javanese. He wears a neat head covering of batik-worked cloth, a jacket and a *sarong*, under which a short pair of trousers is usually worn. On celebrations, he carries a *kris* (a ceremonial knife) in a girdle at his back.

The *desa* (village) is the centre of Javanese society. A chief or *loerah*, who is assisted by a deputy, a writer and a messenger, exercises the administration of the *desa* and is a person experienced in police affairs. There are still communal possessions, although this practice is declining. The villagers are divided into three groups: those who possess land and houses, those who possess only houses and those who have nothing. The descendants of former and present-day princes have a variety of titles.

Formerly the culture was Hindu. However, an examination of the language has proved that the *sawah,* the drama (*wajang*) and the music (*gamelan*) are pure Javanese and the Hindu temples here have typical Javanese characteristics. The language is highly developed, rich in vocabulary and expression.

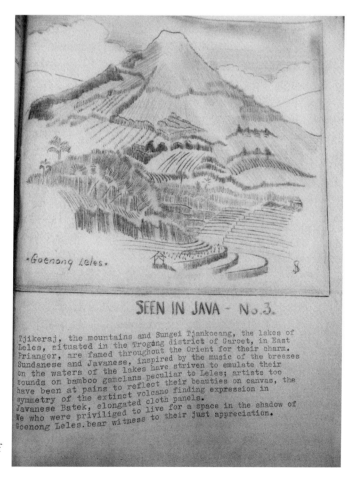

'Goenong Leles'. Scene from Java drawn by Lt Noel James for *The Jungle Journal*. (Courtesy of Mrs Adèle Barclay)

SEEN IN JAVA - No.3.

Tjikeraj, the mountains and Sungei Tjankoeang, the lakes of Leles, situated in the Trogong district of Garoet, in East Prianger, are famed throughout the Orient for their charm. Sundanese and Javanese, inspired by the music of the breezes on the waters of the lakes have striven to emulate their sounds on bamboo gamelans peculiar to Leles; artists too have been at pains to reflect their beauties on canvas, the symmetry of the extinct volcano finding expression in Javanese Batek, elongated cloth panels. We who were priviliged to live for a space in the shadow of Goenong Leles. bear witness to their just appreciation.

East Java

East Java has 16 million inhabitants, including those of Madoera.

The mountain chains of the Northern Kalkgebergte (Lime Mountains) and the Goenoeng Kendeng run through the broad part of East Java; both are thickly wooded with teak forest. On the south side of the Northern Kalksteen (Limestone) region, in the Loesi-Solo valley there are oil wells. The Solo valley is not well irrigated, although work is in hand to improve it, both by the construction of *wadoeks* (small reservoirs) and a major dam, the Patjal, which provides water in the dry season.

To the south, the Zuidergebergte (Southern Mountains) rises up steeply from the sea. Here, in the cliffs, one can again see the grottoes of the sea swallows, which provide the edible nests known locally as *rongkob*.

There are also mountains in the central plain, including Lawoe, Wilis and the group comprising the Welirang, Ardjoeno, Kawi and Keloed. This area, the plains of Madion, Kediri and Soerabaja, is devoted to the cultivation of sugar. The latter plain is watered by the Brantas, which splits into two rivers, one of which, the Kali Soerabaja, is closed by sluices, so that the water flows through the southern arm, the Kali Porong, which has been dammed to provide irrigation via two large canals that have been constructed in the delta.

The greatest coffee tracts in Java are on the mountain slopes of Malang and the Tengger in the west and the Semeroe in the east. European vegetables are also cultivated in the Tengger district to supply the needs of Soerabaja. In the south are rubber, coffee and agave plantations.

To the north of Blitar lies the volcano Keloed, notorious for many terrible eruptions. In the volcano crater is a lake, the water of which was forced through a crevice by volcanic activity. When the eruptions occur, this water mixes with ash and pours in molten streams down the mountainside. A large volcanic eruption in 1919 led to the deaths of 5,500 locals. After this disaster, a large tunnel was dug into the base of the crater and excess water piped away, in an attempt to avert future catastrophe.

The Tengger and the Semeroe provide a great contrast. The Semeroe is a perfectly shaped cone and is the highest mountain in Java at 12,061 feet. The Tengger, on the other hand, has a giant elliptical crater; it would take an hour and a half to walk its greatest length. The crater is a vast sea of sand and contains two small volcanoes; the pudding-shaped Batok and the gaping and active Bromo.

The Bromo is a wide, grey inverted cone with a large mouth measuring 765 yards across and a depth of 656 feet. The walls of the crater, described as the mucous membranes of a dragon's throat, hang down in large grey creases, with caverns at the bases of the creased hangings, and are rumoured to contain monsters. From the 'dragon's gullet' spew forth poisonous vapours containing steam and sulphur. Tengger tribesmen perform ritual self-beatings with cane rods, whilst stripped to the waist, on top of Mount Bromo. This tradition is centuries old.

The Tenggerese, who number about 16,000, live on the highest part of the Tengger. During the conquest of the country in the name of Islam, many Javanese fled to this inhospitable area and their descendants remain Hindu, which for the Tenggerese is the worship of Brahma and a household god.

Every year there is a festival of offering money, food, fruit and farm animals, by throwing these into the Bromo. It is the practice during burial to place the corpse facing the Bromo, as they believe this is where the soul goes for purification before being admitted into the Semeroe, which is the seat of Brahma. However, they are no longer as isolationist as they once were, and trade with the Madoerese and Javanese. Consequently, many are now converting to Islam and it is interesting to note, that a number of Madoerese are now living amongst the Tenggerese in their high mountain villages.

Soerabaja, with a population of 350,000, is the largest trading and industrial town of the Netherlands East Indies and owes its prosperity to a successful export trade in sugar, tobacco, coffee and rubber. To the east of the Kali Mas are the large naval dockyards with their warships and submarines; while to the west is the spacious new harbour of Tanjoeng Perak, built to accommodate ocean-going ships and flying boats. Apart from the dockyards and harbour, the town has several large factories.

Along the northern coastal plain, there is extensive cultivation, with sugar plantations being grown along the coast. While mangoes are the main crop in some places, rice, coconut and banana are grown on the plain of Banjoewangi and on others are extensive maize, tobacco, coffee and rubber plantations.

Madoera is a hilly island of lime and marly soil to the south. Along the coast are *sawahs,* fishponds and saltpans; the natives produce salt privately, but the Government has also set up production near Soemenep, and factories at Kalianget and Krampon press the salt into brickettes. Much of the area has the appearance of parkland, with dry fields and solitary groups of trees, planted by the natives to separate their fields, where cattle are put out to graze. Irrigation is not practicable, so the maize fields are laid as *sawahs* and divided by small walls to retain rainwater.

Apart from Bali, Madoera is the most thickly populated island, but it cannot support a larger population than the 2 million inhabitants, as the soil is infertile and so poorly irrigated, consequently many people cross to the mainland to work on the European plantations. The Madoerese trading *praws* (small sailing vessels) venture as far as Singapore and the Moluccas. Fishing is also of importance.

The island's towns are linked by railroad.

The Madoerese total some 4.5 million and are easily distinguished from the Javanese, being more robust and muscular, though not taller, and having broader faces and features. In character, they also differ, lacking the refined social formalities, and being more energetic, independent, out-spoken and unrestrained, although they are thrifty, lively in gesture and trustworthy. They are, however, quick to take offence and equally quick to use the *kris,* and are consequently feared by the Javanese, who nevertheless look down on them as inferior.

They are popular with the Europeans, being excellent workers and good soldiers.

Madoerese independence is manifest in the possession of land and the character of their village. They do not recognise the principle of communal possession and their houses are spread about with no attempt at uniformity. The administration similarly lacks cohesion and the customs, which play such a great part in the lives of the Javanese and Soendanese, are apt to be disregarded.

The principal foods are rice and maize, the latter being ground into a fine meal, to which is added *lombok* (a hot spice) and a piece of meat or fish. Although rice is favoured after the harvest, maize and ketella gradually supplant it - there is a theory that this maize diet explains the Madoerese's energy!

The Madoerese has a real affection for his humped cows and is an excellent cattle-breeder. He also excels as a trader, journeying from village to village with his packhorse, exchanging perhaps his maize for rice, which he then sells elsewhere at a profit. Wandering is in his blood, although he has an attachment to his birthplace, and it is on this account that the Madoerese are noted for their courage and endurance at sea, both as fishermen and sailors.

Steer racing is a favourite with these keen sportsmen. In these contests, a kind of sledge is attached between two steers in a splendid harness; the driver balances on this and, at a given signal, the teams speed like arrows towards the winning post. Cock-fighting – and bull fighting – are also popular and the consequent gambling often results in bloody quarrels. Music and dancing are far less popular!

The language is by no means as varied as Javanese or Soendanese, but is spoken widely among the Madoerese, on the mainland as well as the island communities.

The History of Java

The first definite reference to Java in European literature is probably that of Marco Polo in the thirteenth century. However, it is known that conquerors from both east and west came to Java far back in time and were met with a tired resistance, the Javanese being content to poison them with fevers and enchant them with beauties.

The Southern Indians were the first 'civilisers' in historic times and have left their influence in religion, customs and art. Their first kingdoms appear in the first centuries of our era, and one of these, the Sumatran Kingdom of Sri-Vijaya, with its capital at, or near, Palembang, is most important in Malayan history. Its ruler, or Maharajah, King of the Mountains and Lord of the Isles, is said to be the Maharajah mentioned in the voyages of Sinbad, the Arab sailor of the ninth Century, and in his dominions was found the great bird, the Roc.

Certainly, by the seventh century, Sri-Vijaya had become very powerful and is recorded as having sent a punitive expedition into Java to quell a rebellion. Ambassadors were sent to China too. The strong territorial position was held for six hundred years and records tell of the might of its fleet, the prowess of its warriors and sailors, and of the fabulous wealth extorted from all ships and traders using the Straits of Malacca.

Sri-Vijaya was not merely skilled in the arts of war, but was also a celebrated centre of Buddhist science and religion, to which Chinese monks resorted to study the holy Sanskrit language, and its Maharajah was a great supporter of the Buddhist religion.

The remarkable Buddhist monuments in Middle Java date from early in this period, when the Sailendra Dynasty was in the ascendancy. The Boroboedoer, most renowned of the Sailendra monuments, dates from about the middle of the eighth century and is one of the wonders of the world, while in the temple of Mendoet nearby, dating from the same period, are three statues of Buddha, the face of one being said to be the finest piece of work ever wrought by the chisel of a Buddhist artist.

During the ninth century, the power of Sri-Vijaya in Java was shaken by a new dynasty that arose in the centre of the island and the thirteenth century witnessed the rise to supremacy of this purely Javanese dynasty and the downfall of Sri-Vijaya.

Around 1487 the Mohammedans, whose missions had long been at work, overthrew Hinduism but it survived for some time in the eastern corner of Java and we have seen some evidence of influences persisting, however, it is only practised in Bali now.

The Portuguese were the first Europeans to establish relations with the Javanese in around 1520; they found them to be the most civilised people in that part of the world.

In 1595, the Dutch arrived and ousted the Portuguese, forming the Dutch East India Company six years later. When the first Dutch governor was appointed in 1610, permission was obtained to build a fort in the neighbourhood of the present Batavia. Subsequently there was a policy of systematic conquest, which culminated in the subjugation of Bantam in 1808.

The ablest and most notorious of the Dutch Governors was Marshal Daendals, who ruled from 1807 until 1811. His policy of extracting the last ounce of tribute reduced Java to a state of terror and exhaustion and it was undoubtedly a good thing for the island when such a skilful administrator succeeded him as Sir Thomas Stamford Raffles.

During the later Napoleonic period, France had claimed the Dutch possessions in the East, and the hoisting of the French flag at Batavia had brought in the British. In August 1811, the British expedition, accompanied by Lord Minto, and with Sir Samuel Auchmuty in command of the troops, which numbered 11,000 - half British and half Indian – occupied Batavia with no fighting.

However, on 25 August a battle was fought at Cornelis, a few miles south of Batavia, resulting in a complete British victory, and on 18 September the French commander, Gen. Janssens, capitulated. Following this, and until March 1816, Raffles, who was appointed Lieutenant Governor, ruled this large island with conspicuous success.

After the return of Java to the Dutch, an attempt was made to oust British trade from the area, but Raffles, in a masterly counter-stroke, acquired Singapore on 29 January 1819 and it remained a British Colony thereafter.

Sir Thomas Stamford Raffles was born on 5 July 1781, on board a merchantman, commanded by his father, when off Port Morant in Jamaica. He became a clerk with the British East India Company and was sent to Penang in 1805. From there he went to Malacca, which the British were about to abandon, and prevailed upon Lord Minto, the Governor General, to refrain from such a dangerous step. He also persuaded him to take Java from the French. Besides founding Singapore, he helped in the founding of the London Zoological Society and wrote a comprehensive history of Java.

Finally, Djojobojo (aka Joyoboyo), a twelfth century Javanese king of Kediri, had proclaimed that his island would be under white man's subjugation for three centuries, but be freed by yellow-skinned people ('little yellow monkeys') from the North (*tembini*)!

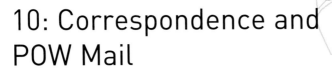

10: Correspondence and POW Mail

My mother received a letter from the War Office, dated 1 May 1943, which was over seven months late due to address errors, requesting information about my father's personal details and stating that Ronald had spoken on Tokyo Radio.

This message had been picked up in New Zealand on 23 April 1943, and was as follows (corrections are in parenthesis):

> Ronald Williams, age 32, Rank: Lieutenant. Home address: Hanlin [*Tanlan*] Farm, City: Hanbray [*Pembrey*]. Mrs Margaret Williams, Hanlin [*Tanlan*], Hanbray [*Pembrey*], Carmarthenshire. Greetings to Berry [*Barrie*] and family. Please convey love to Mother and Dad at No. 1, The Avenue, Bristol 9, and Melba Lou [*and Lew*] and children, Hugh, Babs, Ray and Bruce. I am a prisoner in Java. Fit and well. How is the little wife? Keep smiling and don't worry dear. All my love and God Bless to you all. From Lt Ronnie's camp.

The letter from the War Office contained a caveat that broadcasts from foreign sources were not the recognised official channels for communicating information and, on occasion, had been found to be unreliable.

In November 1942, both my mother and my father's parents received letters from the War Organisation of the BRS (British Red Cross) to confirm the Tokyo Radio message and that the letter from the War Office to my mother had been returned to them through the 'Dead Letter Office'. The BRS did not have any record that my father was missing and needed confirmation of my father's rank (he was still listed as a battery sergeant major), regiment, serial number and any other useful particulars.

Ronald's army papers had been sent to the Prisoner of War Department, Far East Section, at 9 Park Place, St James Street, London, SW1

My mother remembers receiving only three POW mail cards from my father during the period of March 1942 to August 1945. These are all undated with two from Java X and one from Djawa, W.N. The Java X cards were from the Batavia area of Java, which applied to cards sent between early 1943 and April 1944. These two cards had similar messages, a mixture of stock phrases and personal statements. Examples of stock phrases are:

A letter from the War Office to Margaret Williams requesting verification of information based on a Tokyo Radio broadcast. Margaret did not receive this letter for some considerable time due to address errors.

Telephone: Mayfair 9400

Any further communication on this subject should be addressed to:—
The Under-Secretary of State,
The War Office
(as opposite),
and the following number quoted.

THE WAR OFFICE,
Cas. P.W.,
Curzon Street House,
Curzon Street,
London, W.1.

1st May, 1943.

Reference SS/41/102
(Cas. P.W.)

Madam,

I am directed to inform you that information has been received from New Zealand to the effect that the following item was included in a broadcast from Tokio on the 23rd April, 1943:-

"Ronald Williams, age 32, rank Lieutenant. Home address Hanlin Farm, City Hanbray. Mrs. Margaret Williams, Hanlin Farm, Hanbray, Carmarthenshire. Greetings to Berry and family. Please convey love to Mother and Dad at No. 1, The Avenue, Bristol 9, and Melba Lou children, Hugh Babs, Ray and Bruce. I am prisoner in Java. Fit and well. How is the little wife? Keep smiling and don't worry dear. All my love and God bless you. From Lieutenant Ronnie's camp."

Will you please be good enough to verify or furnish the service particulars (e.g. Rank, Army Number and Unit) of the soldier to whom the broadcast refers, if these are known to you, quoting the above reference in your reply. An envelope label which does not require a stamp is enclosed for your use.

It is pointed out that broadcasts from foreign sources are not the recognised official channels for communicating information, and that on occasion they have been found to be unreliable.

I am,
Madam,
Your obedient Servant,

mhlubbolt

Mrs. M. Williams,
Hanlin Farm,
Hanbray,
Carmarthenshire.

A letter to Ronald Williams' parents from the BRCS (British Red Cross Society BRCS), asking for confirmation of details on Ronald's military records. It is interesting to note that the BRCS had no record of Ronald Williams posted missing.

WAR ORGANISATION
OF THE
BRITISH RED CROSS SOCIETY and ORDER OF ST. JOHN OF JERUSALEM

President:
HER MAJESTY THE QUEEN

Grand Prior:
H.R.H. The Duke of Gloucester, K.G.

WOUNDED, MISSING AND RELATIVES DEPARTMENT
Chairman: THE DOWAGER LADY AMPTHILL, C.I., G.B.E.

Telephone No.
SLOANE 9696

In replying please quote reference:

MA/MD

7 BELGRAVE SQUARE,
LONDON, S.W.1

2nd November, 1943.

Dear Mr. and Mrs. Williams,

I think you will already have heard that some weeks ago a message was broadcast over the Tokyo Radio from Lieut. Ronald Williams to his wife, Mrs. Margaret Williams. The message ran as follows:-

"Greetings to you dear, to Barry and family and greetings also to Mum and Dad, 1, The Avenue, Bristol, 9. Keep smiling and don't worry. All my love and God bless you all."

We shall be very grateful if you could give us Lieut. Williams' rank, regiment and number and any other particulars available, as we have no record that he was missing.

We have also written the same request to Mrs. Margaret Williams, but as her address is not quite clear in the broadcast, we are also getting in touch with you.

Yours sincerely,

Margaret Ampthill

Chairman.

Mr. and Mrs. Williams,
1, The Avenue,
Bristol, 9.

I am in a Japanese Prisoner of War Camp in Java.
My health is excellent.
I am waiting for your reply earnestly.
I am constantly thinking of you.
It will be wonderful when we meet again.
Goodbye. God bless you.

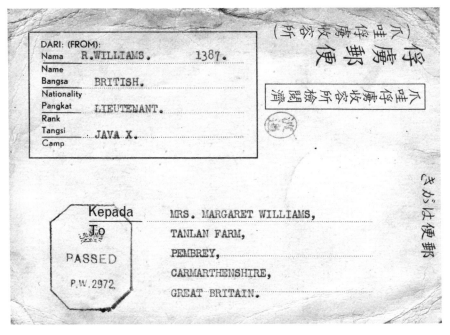

POW mail sent home often took a long time to reach its destination. Formulaic phrases had to be used, which were mostly a complete fabrication. Text was limited and had to pass the Japanese censor.

Personal statements had to comply with the Japanese censor. Examples:

> Dearest,
> All my love to you, Barrie and both the families. Remember 'blue skies are around the corner'.
> Always yours,
> Ronnie-Skins.

> Keep the home fires burning, sweetheart. Love to Barrie, Dad, the two mothers and all their children. I love you.
> Ron.

The card from Djawa, WN, would have been sent after 1 April 1944 as at this time the Japanese Imperial Army had taken over the running of all POW and civilian camps on Java. WN became the new code for the Batavia district. The stock statements were identical on this card, although the personal statements were slightly different:

> Dearest,
> Keep smiling. It can't be long now. Wonderful times ahead. Give fondest love to all, especially yourself and Barrie.
> Ron.

Although the Japanese surrendered on 15 August 1945, my father did not send a proper letter home until 14 September 1945. This was almost certainly related to the fact that Java POWs were effectively still under the control of the Japanese until the arrival of the Allies on the island in September. There are seven surviving letters that my

POW mail showing the circuitous route mail took from home via Japan's Examiner. Mail could take several years to reach the POWs.

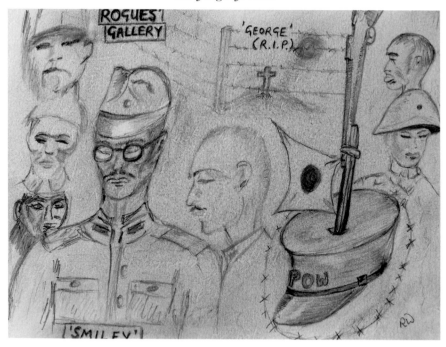

A drawing of Japanese and Korean rogues and related events by Lt Ronald Williams in 1945.

father sent to my mother between 14 September and 23 October 1945. The following substantial extracts from these letters, demonstrate my father's frustration at delays in getting home to see his wife and child, and his utter delight in being free and alive. Surprisingly, there appears to be minimal bitterness towards his captors, but he was clearly none too impressed with the disastrous Allied military campaign on Java.

Batavia, 14 September 1945
Dearest,
I can, at last, believe, with some confidence, that this letter will reach you as, believe it or not, I am a free man, although still confined to No. 1 Camp, Batavia. I can write almost what I wish. Firstly, I must apologise for being away for so long from you. It will have been four years before we are together again. This is definitely a dirty trick for a fellow to play on his wife! These could be sufficient grounds for a divorce, without a doubt? Hopefully you will not wish to divorce me? I hope not, as I am still head over heels in love with you!

It will be wonderful to come back to dear old England or Wales, to you and the lad. I have longed for a photograph of Barrie but have been disappointed not to have one. I wanted, so much, to see if he takes after you so that his future will be assured. Unfortunately, the postal service here, for the past three and a half years, has been very poor and, I suppose, we have only received a small number of those sent to us? In fact, I received your first card in May, 1944, which did me a power of good. Previously, I had received two from Dad, a year before. The last communication I received from you was in February, 1945, so I pray and hope nothing unpleasant has occurred? I have been worried about Hugh and Bruce [*brother Hugh, a flight engineer and brother-in-law, Bruce, a bomber pilot, both RAF*] owing to the nature of their duties.

We have the camp radio again and are rather worried and unhappy about you people, at home, hearing all those stories about Japanese atrocities. While these are, by no means, exaggerated, please let me reassure you, sweetheart, that I am one of the lucky ones. I am still sound in body and mind, well at least the latter. Well, I think I am, but you will be the judge of that when I return home?!!

Talking of returning home, I think that there is a good chance of me being home for Xmas. However, it is impossible to get hold of anything definite at this stage. I am not writing any more at present, as there is a chance of this getting away by air and I don't want the plane to go without it!

Look after yourself dearest. Kiss Barrie for me, Kiss Mother and Dad; oh kiss everybody!

Shall be with you very soon.

Love, Ron.

PS Order me about fifteen overcoats as I am not used to the cold! Or is it true that love will keep me warm?

Java, 16 September 1945

Dearest,

I am using every available opportunity of getting an early letter home to you. I hope this letter will be flown out to Australia tomorrow enclosed in a letter of a very good Australian friend of mine. It will then be forwarded on. I pray that you and Barrie are in the best of health and that everyone, at home, is well. I am quite fit and longing to be with you once again. Things are moving very slowly, but I am so grateful that I have come through this dreadful show alive and relatively unscathed. Nothing worries me very much now. I have already written one letter to you, which has not left the camp. There is a chance it will go tomorrow. Gee! There'll be a lot to talk about when I come home and it will be great to make Barrie's acquaintance, at last!

All my love,

Be seeing you soon. Ron.

Batavia, 17 September 1945

Dearest,

How wonderful it is to be able to write to you again, freely, and to have achieved, at last, the status of ex-POW. I have already written you a letter and a note. However, not knowing which will arrive first, this makes it difficult from the repetition point of view. The first thing I want to know is, how are you and Barrie, and I hope everything at home, is OK? I have received no information covering the last seven months and a lot can happen in that time! As for myself, Dearest, I am quite fit and just longing to take you in my arms again and kiss those lips, I have only been able to dream about over recent years. It is going to be great to make Barrie's acquaintance. I hope that he won't be too disappointed for, I am sure, I will not be quite the fellow, as a father, he expects? Never mind, I'll do my best.

I learned, yesterday, that some of our lads, including that fine fellow, Wilfred Wooller, who went away to Singapore about two years ago have already left and are on their way home. There is no indication, as yet, if we will be leaving, although things seem to be moving. The small New Zealand contingent was flown out this morning, followed by the Americans, of which not many were left. So here's hoping!

I shall have so much to tell you when we are together. It will be difficult to know where to start and finish. This affair has been an 'amazing' experience and I am most fortunate to have come out of it so well. Many of my friends will never return as they were as good as murdered. In one of your cards you mentioned that Mrs Evans was staying with you. Arthur was promoted to regimental sergeant major (RSM) in Java, and left us on February 9 1943 with Colonel Humphries and a couple of hundred officers and men of the 77th for Japan.

I am sure you are wondering how I obtained my commission. It was thus: When we arrived in Batavia, my Battery remained behind while the other two Batteries entrained to Soerabaja , situated at the other end of Java. En route the train was in a collision, head-on, with another at terrific speed. Among the twenty odd who were killed, six were officers and the remainder NCOs. In consequence, I was sent to Soerabaja to replace one of the dead officers.

The best friend I have had in the Camps was our MO, Dr John W. Goronwy of Pontypridd. Remember, it was he who packed me off to you, on sick leave, after my motorcycle accident. He was in the train smash and was the only one to survive in his compartment, and managed to crawl out although he had a broken jaw and many abrasions. He joined up with us again in February, 1943. He and I and Mr Johnny Johnson lived together until he went away on a draft last year. I wanted to go with him, but only MOs were required from our camp. Subsequently, the news came through that his ship had been torpedoed and sunk off Nagasaki. His name was not listed among the survivors. This has been a terrible blow to me, although there is always the chance that he was picked up by a submarine and is still alive. These things do happen.

It is possible that you may have contacted quite a few relatives of men of the 77th, but there is little news I can give about most of them. The Unit has been scattered all over the Far East and, I fear, has suffered heavily.

However, mentioning happier things, I received a letter, last July, which you had written two years earlier in which you mentioned that you wanted a little girl and you seemed to suggest that I would not agree! Far from it, Dearest, I am very fond of children and always have been. Our family will be controlled entirely by your wishes. After all, it is you that has to suffer the pains, not I. I shall provide for them, and I will do this even if I end up in jail! That experience would be nothing to what I have been through.

I was hoping, on my return, that we could have our honeymoon, although it will be the wrong time of year! I am sure we can fix up something. How about going to Paris, or somewhere similar? I'm dying to see you beloved. Longing to come home to all the love you have promised me. Kiss Barrie for me.
I love you,
Ron.

PS. In case there is a hitch, please tell the folks that I have already written to them.

Batavia, 19 September 1945
Dearest,
This is my fourth communication to you in this post-war series. I am longing for news of you and awaiting, impatiently, a real letter in the post. By 'real' I mean a letter that has not had to conform to Japanese regulation and censorship. There is so much I want to know and I want, particularly, reassurance that you still love me?!! For all I know you have fallen for some Colonial or a youth? A girl could hardly be blamed for such an action in the circumstances! Gee! I can't wait to see you, and I feel there will be some wonderful moments ahead. The first sight of dear old England and seeing you and Barrie again; then having you in my arms, and that first sweet kiss. Just that experience, and the nonsense of the last few years would seem worthwhile.

It is difficult to know what to write about. There are so many things to consider. I could write books about POW psychology and essays on rice, but perhaps I had better tell you a bit about myself. Perhaps, I have changed – I don't know? It is only fair to prepare you for the worst! There is something to be said in my favour, dearest, in that I have been completely faithful to you. Why! I haven't even spoken to a lady for three and a half years. From now until our reunion, as I love you so much, I am sure if I meet another woman, she would not interest me!

I have thought a great deal during my captivity as often there was not much else to do. I have come to realise that it is the simple things in life (as opposed to the most expensive) which bring the greatest happiness. Surely to be happy in making a success in life, without needing to create a fortune or attaining power by stamping down on rivals or ruining others, should be my goal. Our greatest treasure is our love, the most wonderful thing in life and yet so delicate that it must be tended thoughtfully and carefully. Neglect of tending love will, as sure as sand is sand, lead to ruin. I feel that our love will not suffer by this parting as there is a bond of mutual suffering and longing between us. We are older, wiser and more tolerant than we were and I feel that Mr and Mrs Williams will always be happy together.

Then there is the fruit of our love. We have Barrie already. Do you know that I can hardly believe that I am coming home to a son of four years old! I am sure he has been a great joy to you and I am also sure that he is going to bring great joy to me. It will be wonderful watching him grow up, helping him in all things, influencing his character in the right direction and the pleasure of his companionship. This reminds me that, in one of your letters, you said that you would be expecting some thing in the fairy story line from me. Actually, I did make a start in 1942, but then the Nips kept pinching our notes, books, pencils, pens, and just about everything else until it became impossible. The only thing I managed to retain was a collection of poems. I have still the ideas, so I promise Barrie that I will get myself together in writing them. Incidentally, I hope to do some serious writing when I return. Whether it will be successful is questionable. Over the first twelve months, in captivity, I spent most of my time writing and typing whilst running a magazine entitled the 'Jungle Journal'. It was great fun but eventually it became impossible to continue production. I'm afraid that I am getting away from my subject and there is not much space left. I can return to the 'Jungle Journal' some other time.

Please congratulate Bryn [*mor*] for me on his marriage, and the birth of the twins, and John and Maureen for the birth of Anne. I have felt for a long time that I want lots of children around me. Gee! The things I have missed!! My memory, for normal life, is returning in abundance and I feel able to appreciate life more than ever. How is your dear mother? I have still a pair of socks she knitted for me. I hope to bring them home to show her how well they have worn. How's dear Bettie? Please give her my fondest love and to the rest of the family too. Please kiss Barrie for me and ask him to kiss you for me!
All my love,
Ron.

Singapore, 30 September 1945
Dearest,
I received your letter dated August 22nd on the 23rd of this month and one from Dad on the 21st at Batavia. I was so delighted to learn that all is well and now feel on top of the world. There is so much to look forward to. It is going to be grand meeting my wife and son. I can hardly wait, but wait I must as there remains a lot of sea between us. I am aboard the ship that will take us home – the *Cilicia*, late armed cruiser, and very comfortable with good food. We are supposed to sail on Thursday next and will take about a month!?

On the 24th, about three hundred of us left Batavia in three Landing Craft, escorted by a frigate to Singapore. We arrived at midnight on 27th September. It proved quite a pleasant trip, although we struck a couple of squalls and the barges tossed and turned all over the place with the consequence that many of us were violently seasick. I didn't care, as nothing matters any more, dearest. Life is very sweet and you are going to make it sweeter! You know that you have quite a 'funny' chap coming home to you.

For instance, I have developed a keen interest in natural history and, at one time on Java, I had quite a collection of caterpillars, butterflies, of all shapes and sizes, some very wild, which I used to take for daily exercise, feeding on plants and exotic flowers and so forth. Therefore, be warned! I consulted a number of Dutch biologists and from them I have gained a lot of knowledge about the natural history of the East Indies.

Java is a most wonderful island, although the Nips have tried to ruin it. I am sure it will be again once things settle down. To me it is full of romance with jungles full of exotic animals and ancient Hindu temples, as Java has been Mohammedan for nearly a thousand years. There are three main races of people with their own language, culture, customs, legends and folklore. There is wonderful mountain scenery, many active volcanoes. I should love to bring you here, when life has returned to normal.

By the way, one of the first officers to fly out from Java was a Mr Ballinger, from the *Western Mail* newspaper. He had taken with him a few caricatures of 77th Officers drawn by Fl/Lt Audus, a lecturer from Cardiff University. I did not see them myself, but Audus told me that he had drawn me posing with a flower! I am sure my previous remarks will explain this! Watch out for the *Western Mail*!

Soon we will need to get down to planning the future, although it is impossible to be definite about anything at the moment. I am not keen about going back into Dad's business, although I am quite prepared to do so for a year or two while there is money available. I want to utilise my spare time for those things I am most interested in. I want to travel and always have and always will. I want to write as a professional, and take up photography. Of course, the three can be combined, but we will have to wait and see?

Anyway, whatever we do, it will be fun!

Please start making plans for our honeymoon, sweetheart. I suppose Barrie will be alright at being left for a couple of weeks, wouldn't he? Don't think me being unkind but I feel that you, particularly, deserve a break and a change.

We could, perhaps, go to Paris or Madrid or somewhere on the Med?

Think it over darling!

All my love, Kisses for Barrie, and love to all the families,

Yours for ever,

Ron.

My father never managed to break into professional writing circles, although he did write prolifically after the war. His main areas of interest were children's stories, plays for schools and poetry. He took up photography seriously and was credited with being the first person to create individualised photographic album records for children in care. He did manage a great deal of travelling, when he could afford to, including three weeks in a Kibbutz. Ronald did not achieve his ambition of returning to the Far East, although his sister, Nikki, spent time in Java as her husband, Bruce, was flying for Garuda Indonesian Airlines. In the early 1950s, Nikki was tasked, by my father, with trying to locate former POW camps in Djakarta and Bandung, but failed. I think this deterred Ronald from making an effort to go to Java, although the beauty of the Island must have remained a strong influence during his life. Perhaps, if he had reached retirement, he would have made the effort. The honeymoon never took place due to austerity measures after the war. My parents never went overseas together, although my father tried to make it up to my mother, by taking her on a romantic trip to an isolated cottage on the Cornish coast, when they were in their forties.

The final two letters to my mother were written at sea, on board the MV *Cilicia*. The letters are highly sentimental and personal. Therefore, I will only include extracts from them. The change in style of letter writing indicates to me that my father had previously put on a forthright and stoical front to cope with his incarceration and, at last, he felt that he could release his deep, pent-up emotions.

MV *Cilicia* (at sea)
Monday 6 October 1945
Dearest,

It is a great pity that we cannot celebrate our fifth wedding anniversary together. The ship is ploughing through the waves relentlessly westward, and every moment I am coming closer to you. In, a day or two, we shall reach Colombo, where we shall stay for a couple of days, and then on again to Suez. It shouldn't be so very long now. I have been left in charge of sick and injured troops, which has kept me very busy over the last few days. I had almost forgotten that I am coming home.

Being together again will be most wonderful, and I am so looking forward to meeting Barrie. This parting has been a rotten time for you, and I will do my utmost to compensate you for all the unhappiness you have felt during the past few years. You will still be my beautiful red-headed girl, whom I love so much … Do you remember the time in Cardiff [*Cardiff Royal Infirmary Nurses' Home*] when, sometimes, I used to climb through your window during the early hours of the morning and you would, half asleep, say so drowsily, 'Oh, Ron!' That was sweet music to my ears and one of my happiest memories. [*They were married at the time, but nurses, of any grade, could not entertain any men, even husbands, in their rooms.*] And then in the cold dark morning we would catch a tram. When Barrie was coming, you were so brave and fine about it all, particularly at the end. Everybody says that you have given me a wonderful son. Gee! I am lucky having such a sweet girl for a wife – far more than I deserve really. I hope you won't be disappointed in me, Sweetheart, for during the past few years you may have forgotten my faults? Still, I know that we will be very happy together and we still love each other. If it had not been for you, I would surely be dead now! I will tell you the story when we are together again.

When I reach England, I shall go down on bended knee and thank God for bringing me through the darkness. It is a miracle that any of us have survived.

Please tell Melba [*older sister*] that I am delighted with her news and it is awfully jolly having another nephew [*in fact, a niece named Lesley*]. There are now eleven children in the respective families. What about our Anne? Isn't it wonderful to think that, as we love each other so much, in a few years a sweet little girl will be sitting on the floor playing with her dolls? [*My parents did have a little girl, Jane, who died, aged five, of pneumonia in 1960.*]

And now beloved, I bid you adieu. This letter will, hopefully, reach you sooner than I. I am coming nearer and nearer to you, to fill your heart with love. Other things may be rationed at home, but not love.

Love to all,

Ron

MV *Cilicia* (at sea)

Tuesday 23 October 1945

Dearest,

After a couple of cold days, today the weather is beautifully warm with the sea being a real Mediterranean blue. All day we have been sailing in sight of the North African coast. We are due in Gibraltar in two days, where we call to pick up mail. Some time next week we should dock at Liverpool and tomorrow week there should be a good chance that we are together again. Won't that be wonderful! I'm scared that this is all a dream and I will suddenly wake up and find myself back in prison on Java.

Don't do anything at all, Darling. Just stand fast as I have requested to be dispatched to Pembrey; so don't go running off anywhere else!

I have been rather a silly boy. After leaving Colombo, I went down very suddenly with a high fever and only came to and out of hospital yesterday, after spending eleven days there. A silly thing to do, but I am OK now.

We happened to obtain some copies of the *Western Mail*, in which our CO, Lt Col Humphries, has been severely chastising the Japanese Army's treatment of his men. A lot of it is, of course, true, but he did lay it on pretty thick! I understand that we shall receive forty-two days leave on arrival in England. This should allay any worries and troubles, and is very nice indeed.

Darling, I am just dying to see you again … For four whole years, I have just dreamt about you and longed so much for you. Now, it is all going to come true. You said, in a letter, that we are going to have wonderful times together, and I am determined that we will.

I am seriously thinking of bringing out a book covering the experiences of the past four years. This is something I will start on straight away. You must help me and be my inspiration.

So beloved, until we meet again, I love to you. Kiss Barrie for me and love to all.

Yours,

Ron

BUCKINGHAM PALACE

The Queen and I bid you a very warm welcome home.

Through all the great trials and sufferings which you have undergone at the hands of the Japanese, you and your comrades have been constantly in our thoughts. We know from the accounts we have already received how heavy those sufferings have been. We know also that these have been endured by you with the highest courage.

We mourn with you the deaths of so many of your gallant comrades.

With all our hearts, we hope that your return from captivity will bring you and your families a full measure of happiness, which you may long enjoy together.

George R.I

September 1945.

A message from the King.

P/359162   13th March, 1946.

Sir,

    Now that the time has come for your release from active military duty, I am commanded by the Army Council to express to you their thanks for the valuable services which you have rendered in the service of your country at a time of grave national emergency.

    At the end of the emergency you will relinquish your commission, and at that time a notification will appear in the London Gazette (Supplement), granting you also the honorary rank of Lieutenant. Meanwhile, you have permission to use that rank with effect from the date of your release.

                    I am, Sir,

                        Your obedient Servant,

Lieutenant R. Williams,
    Royal Artillery.

A message from the War Office.

11: The History of the 77th Welsh HAA Regiment, Royal Artillery (TA)

2nd Glamorganshire Artillery Volunteers, 1890-1961

1 June 1890
1st Glamorganshire Artillery Volunteers HQ in Cardiff, with eleven batteries.

1 November 1891
2nd Glamorganshire Artillery Volunteers.

1 June 1924
82nd (Welsh volunteers) Field Brigade, Royal Artillery.

1 November 1938
77th (Welsh TA) Anti-Aircraft Brigade, Royal Artillery Regiment based at the Drill Hall, Dumfries Place, Cardiff.
239 (Glamorgan) Battery, Cardiff.
240 (Glamorgan) Battery, Cardiff.
241 (Glamorgan) Battery, Rhondda.
242 (Glamorgan) Battery, (Howitzer) Rhondda.

1 January 1939
77th (Welsh TA) Anti-Aircraft Regiment, Royal Artillery.

1 September 1939
Mobilised and lost distinction with Regular Army (Home Forces Coastal Defense, Wales).

1 June 1940
77th HAA Regiment, Royal Artillery (242 Howitzer Battery transferred to LAA Regiment).

1 September 1940
Part of 45 AA Brigade, 9 AA Division, UK.

3 February 1942
Part of 16 AA Brigade, Java.

9 March 1942
Unconditional British surrender, Bandoeng, Java.

15 August 1945
Unconditional Japanese surrender, USS *Missouri*.

30 October 1945
Remnants of the regiment arrive back in England from the Far East.

1 July 1946
TA unit suspended.

1 April 1947
Became the 282nd (Wales TA) HAA, RA (Cardiff).

1 May 1961
Amalgamated with other artillery regiments.

The 77th Royal Artillery Regiment had 24 x 3.7 inch heavy anti-aircraft guns by 1941, with eight guns per battery. There were three batteries, 239, 240 and 241 (the howitzer battery, 242, had been transferred by this time) each with 166 men including six officers. The Regimental HQ had eighty-eight men including nine officers. Attached to the regiment were men from the Royal Signals, Royal Electrical and Mechanical Engineers, and Royal Army Medical Corps. The total was around 1,000 men.

Twelve men manned each gun; the guns were usually operated in emplacements of four guns. The 3.7 inch guns had a firing range of 7.75 miles (32,000 feet height) and fired shells weighing twenty-eight pounds. Up to twelve shells could be fired in one minute. Each gun weighed a massive 9.17 tons. Unlike the Germans, with their famous 88mm artillery guns, the 3.7 inch guns were, surprisingly, never adapted for anti-tank or battlefield use.

A German equivalent artillery gun would have been very effective on Java.

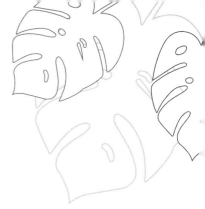

Epilogue

On return home, Ronald was promoted to Army Captain (temporary) and took on the role of welfare officer for the regiment, which he continued up to the time of his release from the army in July 1946. He found difficulty in adjusting to civilian life after the war and returned to his wife's family home in Pembrey, Carmarthenshire, to work outdoors, part-time, for the Forestry Commission.

He felt strongly that there was public and Government indifference to the plight of the FEPOWs, a view he held until his dying day. British FEPOWs felt let down by the British authorities, particularly when they learned that Commonwealth and American ex-FEPOWs were rewarded with a medal for enduring this long period of captivity and were provided with a pension and free medical treatment. British FEPOWs did receive a sum of £100 compensation, in 1951. Ronald was aware that some returning FEPOWs became very troubled spirits with divorce, alcoholism and suicide being a consequence.

He needed to re-evaluate his life and decided he did not want to return to his father's business, as a hide and skins broker (hence his nickname 'Ronnie-skins'), but would rather retrain as a schoolteacher. This he did at Nelson Hall Teacher Training College, Staffordshire, on the emergency teachers training scheme, followed by post-graduate studies at St Luke's College, Exeter.

He had a very successful career as a schoolmaster and rose rapidly to become a deputy head teacher, but declined headships when offered to him, as he much preferred teaching to administration. In 1960 he went to the Rose Bruford Drama School, London, for a year and gained a certificate in speech and drama.

During this time he took part in Noel Coward's *Cavalcade* at the Sadler's Wells Theatre, with the likes of rising young stars Nerys Hughes, Ann Cronin, Gareth Gwenlan, John Carbury and a very young Tom Baker – it was one of the highlights of his life. He could have been a great actor, but had difficulty in remembering his lines! Writing and producing school plays became a big part of his life. These plays were often based on the writings of his hero, John Bunyon.

He kept in close contact with some of his former POW colleagues from the 77th Artillery Regiment and Australian Infantry 2/40th and, also, Jean Teerink, who had been a prisoner in Dutch women's camps on Java, and was on the same boat home, the MV *Cilicia*, to Liverpool.

According to my mother, Ronald did not attend any regimental reunions of the '77th', apart from the Civic Lord Mayor's reception in Cardiff and an invitation to a luncheon held in honour of the 77th Welsh HAA Regiment by Col Sir G. Bruce on behalf of the Glamorgan TA and AF Association (December, 1945) at Dumfries Place Drill Hall.

He did not offer any explanation for this but, knowing my father, there are a number of plausible explanations. Firstly, most of his close regimental friends, including Capt. John W. Goronwy (RAMC) and Lt Ken Taylor, had died in the Far East and the reunion would probably have brought back painful memories.

Secondly, he was conscious that remaining as a prisoner on Java had been a better option, as many men from his regiment, who had been drafted to other Far East islands as slave labour, mostly had a worse time of it. Although this was not his fault, perhaps conversations would be uncomfortable with other ex-POWs in these circumstances.

Thirdly, he had mentioned that some senior Allied officers had not looked after their men in captivity as well as they might. I do not know if this was a reference to his own regiment, but if this was the case, he would not wish this subject to be discussed at a reunion, and he would want to avoid any possibility of this arising.

Fourthly, there was also a strong rumour that a large number of junior officers of the regiment boycotted the reunions because the regimental CO had wrongly accused one of the junior officers of illegally disposing of regimental funds while in Java. Wilfred Wooller has documented this episode in his memoirs, Andrew Hignell's *The Skipper.*

Brig. Sir Phillip Toosey, late Allied commander and POW at the Tamakan camp made famous by the film *Bridge on the River Kwai,* and subsequently honorary president of the FEPOW Association, noted in his memoirs that former FEPOW junior officers generally stayed away from regimental reunions. He was baffled by this occurrence and could not proffer an explanation.

Incidentally, the other 'Skipper', Winston Churchill, Ronald considered to have been subject to grossly unfair recriminations over his involvement in the Far East campaign and the fateful decisions made. My father maintained an immense lifelong admiration for the great man, and was shocked by the post-VE day election result ousting Churchill as Prime Minister. My father was not able to vote in this election as he was still a POW in the Far East!

One of his great regrets in life was his inability to foster a strong fatherly bond with his eldest son Barrie. This was not an uncommon experience for ex-POWs coming home to their children. In my brother's case, he had not known his father until he turned up, unexpectedly, when my brother was four years of age.

Barrie had been brought up on a Welsh-speaking farm, by his big, strapping uncles. Ronald, with a very English public school (Queen's School, Taunton) accent and looking sick, was no substitute for Barrie's surrogate fathers. Young Barrie told my mother, on many occasions, clearly and in his native welsh tongue, 'Send that man away'.

During his life, Ronald did an immense amount of work in raising money for charities, especially for the *Save the Children* Fund. He spent many an hour busking with his harmonica and Scandalli accordion to help raise funds. Sometimes these occasions included singers, such as myself and my brothers.

He died on 7 July 1969, at the age of fifty-eight and was thus denied the opportunity of completing and publishing his war memoirs.

Another close friend, the late Revd Wg Cdr George Kerslake, who narrowly escaped the Japanese invasion of Malaya, best summed up his post-war life in an obituary written for the local parish magazine of St Paul's Church, Weston-super-Mare:

At fifty-eight years of age, Ron Williams suffered a fatal heart attack at his home after returning from his school near Bristol, where he had taught for over twenty years. Ron was an exemplary member of the teaching profession, a faithful and regular communicant, a monthly reader of the Gospel and a writer and producer of school plays. He was also a keen sportsman, having played first class rugby for Bristol during the 1930s.

Ron never paraded his wartime experiences before the public or his friends and, consequently, very few people knew about his frightening and terrible years as a prisoner-of-war of the Japanese. He bore no hatred or enmity towards his former oppressors.

Ron possessed a great and sincere love of children, both at his school and those to whom he acted as a foster father through the county council residential scheme for disturbed children. To his widow, Margaret, and his three sons, Barrie (a medical doctor) Jan (a trainee teacher), and Frank (a medical student) we extend our deepest sympathy in theirs, and our, great loss.

Picture of Ronald and Frank Jnr walking along the Promenade at Weston-super-Mare in 1951.

Bibliography

Aldrich, Richard, *The Faraway War: Personal Diaries of the Second World War in Asia and the Pacific*, Great Britain, Corgi, 2006

Baxter, John, *Not Much of a Picnic*, Trowbridge, Wiltshire, self- published, 1995

Bayly, Chris and Tim Harper, *Forgotten Armies: Britain's Asian Empire and the War with Japan*, London, Penguin Books, 2005

Colijn, Helen, *Song of Survival*, Great Britain, Headline, 1995

Daws, Gavan, *Prisoners of the Japanese*, London, Simon and Schuster, 2007

Dunlop, Sir Edward, *The War Diaries of Weary Dunlop*, New Zealand, Penguin Books, 1990

Fletcher-Cooke, Sir John, *The Emperor's Guest,* Great Britain, Corgi, 1982

Forbes, Cameron, *Hellfire: The Story of Australia, Japan and the Prisoners of War*, Sydney, Pan MacMillan, 2005

Jones, Allan, *The Suez Maru Atrocity – Justice Denied!* Hornchurch, Essex, self-published, 2002

Kinvig, Clifford, *Death Railway,* London, Pan/Ballantine, 1973

Klemen, L., *Forgotten Campaign: The Dutch East Indies Campaign 1941-42*, Wikipedia

Lomax, Eric, *The Railwayman*, London, Vintage, 1996

MacArthur, Brian, *Surviving the Sword: Prisoners of the Japanese 1942-45*, London, Abacus, 2006

Paley, John, *The Sparrows*, Hanley Swan, Worcester, self-published, 1992

Paris, Erna, *Long Shadows: Truth, Lies and History*, London, Bloomsbury, 2000

Prisoners in Java: Accounts by Allied Prisoners of War in the Far East (1942-45) Captured in Java, Southampton, Hamwic, 2007

Rollings, Charles, *Prisoner Of War*, Great Britain, Ebury Press, 2007

Rees, Laurence, *Horror in the East*, London, BBC Worldwide, 2000

Russell, Lord Edward Frederick, *The Knights of Bushido: A Short History of Japanese War Crimes*, London Greenhill Books, 2002

Spence, Les and Greg Lewis, *From Java to Nagasaki: the Complete Secret Wartime Diaries of a Prisoner of the Japanese*, Cardiff, Magic Rat Books, 2012

Thompson, Peter, *Battle for Singapore*, London, Portrait Books, 2005

Titherington, Arthur, *One Day at a Time – Kinkaseki*, South Africa, Covos Day, 1993

Toland, John, *Rising Sun*, South Yorkshire, Pen and Sword, 2005

Urquhart, Alistair, *The Forgotten Highlander*, Great Britain, Abacus, 2010

Van der Post, Laurens, *The Night of the Moon*, London, Penguin Books, 1977

--------------, *The Seed and the Sower*, London, Penguin Books, 1966

Warner, Lavinia and Sandilands, John, *Women Beyond the Wire*, London Arrow, 1997

Index

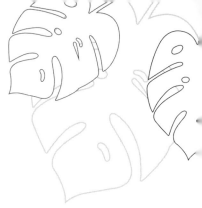